Genograms
Assessment and Intervention

Other Books by Monica McGoldrick

The Expanded Family Life Cycle: Individual, Family and Social Perspectives, 3rd Edition (Edited with Betty Carter)

Revisioning Family Therapy: Race, Culture, and Gender in Clinical Practice (Editor)

Ethnicity and Family Therapy, 2nd Edition (Edited with Joseph Giordano and John K. Pearce)

You Can Go Home Again: Reconnecting with Your Family

Living Beyond Loss: Death and the Family (Edited with Froma Walsh)

Women in Families: A Framework for Family Therapy (Edited with Carol Anderson and Froma Walsh)

A NORTON PROFESSIONAL BOOK

Genograms
Assessment and Intervention
SECOND EDITION

MONICA MCGOLDRICK, M.A., M.S.W., PH.D. (H.C.)
RANDY GERSON, PH.D.
SYLVIA SHELLENBERGER, PH.D.

W.W. Norton & Company
New York • London

Composition by Paradigm Graphics
Manufacturing by Haddon Craftsmen

Library of Congress Cataloging-in-Publication Data

McGoldrick, Monica.
Genograms: assessment and intervention / Monica McGoldrick,
Randy Gerson, and Sylvia Shellenberger. — 2nd ed.
p.   cm.
"A Norton professional book."
Prev. ed. cataloged with title: Genograms in family assessment.
Includes bibliographical references and index.
ISBN 0-393-70283-9
ISBN 0-393-70294-4 (pbk.)
1. Family psychotherapy—Technique. 2. Behavioral
assessment—Charts, diagrams, etc. I. McGoldrick, Monica. Genograms
in family assessment. II. Gerson, Randy. III. Shellenberger, Sylvia.
IV. Title.
RC488.5 .M395   1999
616.89'156—dc21   99-17993 CIP

W. W. Norton & Company, Inc., 500 Fifth Avenue, New York, N.Y. 10110
www.wwnorton.com
W. W. Norton & Company Ltd., 10 Coptic Street, London WC1A 1PU

2 3 4 5 6 7 8 9 0

To the memory of Randy Gerson, coauthor of the first edition of this book, whose creativity with genograms did so much to make them accessible to all of us, and whose ideas and spirit are still deeply represented in this work.

CONTENTS

LIST OF ILLUSTRATIONS

Chapter 5: Assessing Family Roles, Functioning, Balance, Resilience and Resources

Chapter 6: Using Genograms to Track Families through the Life Cycle

Chapter 7: Clinical Uses of the Genogram

Preface

This book evolved out of a long interest in the clinical, research, and instructional value of genograms. Over the past few decades use of the genogram as a practical tool for mapping family patterns has become more and more widespread among health care professionals. As genograms have become widely used in the fields of medicine, psychology, social work, and the other health care, human service, and even legal fields, we have felt a need to update *Genograms in Family Assessment*, to illustrate more fully the growing diversity of family forms and patterns in our society and the applications of genograms in clinical practice. The genogram is still a tool in progress. Based on feedback from readers and other developments in the field, we have expanded the book and slightly modified some of the symbols used since the first edition appeared in 1985. We hope that evolution of the genogram as a tool will continue as clinicians use genograms to track the complexity of family process.

While a genogram can provide a fascinating view into the richness of a family's dynamics for those in the know, it may remain a collection of meaningless squares and circles on a page to those who don't know the players in the drama. Our solution to this dilemma has been to illustrate our points primarily with famous families about whom we all have some knowledge, rather than clinical cases. We are family therapists, not historians, and thus the information we have been able to glean about these famous families is limited. Most of the sources have been biographies found in libraries or bookstores. In fact, certain readers may know more about some of the families than we were able to uncover from published sources. I apologize in advance for any inaccuracies in the material. Hopefully the descriptions sketched here will inspire readers to pursue further the fascinating stories of such families as the Fondas, Freuds, Kennedys, Robesons, Einsteins, Chaplins, and Roosevelts. Surprisingly, only limited family descriptions are available for many of history's most interesting personalities. I trust that future biographers will be more aware of family systems and use genograms to broaden their perspective on the individuals and families they describe.

Monica McGoldrick

ACKNOWLEDGMENTS

I (MM) am grateful to many people for their help in the development of this project. First of all, I owe special thanks to my colleague, Randy Gerson, for the formative efforts he made to describe genogram patterns and make them universally accessible through his creativity in computer applications. I thank Randy's widow, Sylvia Shellenberger, for her continued support and effort on this book. She brought her own intuitions, intelligence, and excellent abilities to this second edition, which were a great boon. I thank my friend and colleague Michael Rohrbaugh, who challenged my assumptions and helped me clarify my thinking during our discussions over many years about genograms and their potential as a research and clinical tool.

My editor, Susan Barrows Munro, has been an enthusiastic promoter of genograms for many years and I thank her for her support and interest. My sister, Neale McGoldrick, offered helpful consultation on genograms over the years from both a graphic and a psychological point of view. At many critical times, my nephew, Guy Livingston, who has great graphic ability and intuition, helped me with the genograms in between his life adventures. My lifemates, Betty Carter, Froma Walsh, Carol Anderson, Nydia Preto, Rhea Almeida, Paulette Hines, Charlee Sutton, John Folwarski, Fernando Colon, Miguel Hernandez, Marlene Watson, Jayne Maboubi, Vanessa Mahmoud, and Ken Hardy, have also been of immeasurable support to me in thinking about genograms and their implications for understanding families. My refound friend and soulmate, Fernando Colon, provided inspiration, help, and affirmation, particularly regarding the importance of non-biological kin networks. I thank my dearest friend Robert Jay Green for challenging my unquestioning belief in the relevance of genograms, helping me to clarify for myself the deepest meanings of family and of "home." I thank Deborah Buurma for her creative work on family play genograms and her help on the discussion of their value for therapy. Mary Ann Broken Nose has generously offered her ideas, creativity, hard work, and good cheer with the research on this book. I also thank Mary Jean Battistella, who has helped make life at our office flow smoothly, and Rene Campbell, who has made coming to work every day a great pleasure for the past four years (Please don't ever leave me!).

Finally, my deepest thanks go to the closest members of my own genogram,

Sophocles Orfanidis, my husband of 28 years, and John Daniel Orfanidis, my son, whose birth coincided with the first edition of this book, and who is almost in high school as this edition goes to press. I cannot finish without thanking my parents and all my other family who have gone before me—whether connected through biology, legal ties, or spiritual affinity, who are a part of my genogram (see Genogram 1.3). And I write for all those who will come after— whether connected through biology or through other intellectual, emotional, and spiritual ties.

Monica McGoldrick

I (SS) would like to acknowledge Monica McGoldrick and Randy Gerson for their dedication to development of the genogram for use in assessment and intervention. Their dream of the many ways the genogram could contribute to the enhancement of families and society has moved this work forward. Susan Munro, our editor, has also contributed to the advancement of this work through her gentle prodding and astute editing. I would also like to thank Randy Gerson for five magical years of marriage and his many legacies that live on in me, others, and his work.

Sylvia Shellenberger

Genograms
Assessment and Intervention

1
Genograms: Mapping Family Systems

The intent of this book is to establish the genogram as a practical and useful framework for understanding family patterns. This standardized genogram format will, hopefully, become a common language for tracking family history and relationships. Despite the widespread use of genograms by family therapists, family physicians, and other health care providers, until the 1980s there was no generally agreed-upon format for a genogram. Even among clinicians with similar theoretical orientations, there was only a loose consensus about what specific information to seek, how to record it, and what it all meant. The standardized genogram format presented here was worked out by a committee of leading proponents of genograms from family therapy and family medicine, including such key people as Murray Bowen, Jack Froom, and Jack Medalie. They became part of a committee organized in the early 1980s by the North American Primary Care Research Group to define the most practical genogram symbols and agree on a standardized format. This format records information about family members and their relationships over at least three generations. Genograms display family information graphically in a way that provides a quick gestalt of complex family patterns; as such they are a rich source of hypotheses about how a clinical problem may be connected to the evolution of both the problem and the family's context over time.

In addition to presenting this standardized format, this book describes the interpretive principles upon which genograms are based, as well as recent applications in many clinical areas. Guidelines presented here for genogram assessment and application have been developed over the past several decades in collaboration with many colleagues. These guidelines are still evolving, as our thinking about families in context progresses.

Genograms appeal to clinicians because they are tangible and graphic representations of complex family patterns. They allow the clinician to map the family structure clearly and to note and update the family picture as it emerges. For a clinical record, the genogram provides an efficient summary, allowing a clinician unfamiliar with a case to grasp quickly a large amount of information about a family and to have a view of potential problems. While notes written

1

in a chart or questionnaire may become lost in a record, genogram information is immediately recognizable and can be added to and corrected at each clinical visit as more is learned about a family.

Genograms make it easier for clinicians to keep in mind the complexity of a family's context, including family history, patterns, and events that may have ongoing significance for patient care. Just as our spoken language potentiates and organizes our thought processes, genograms, which map relationships and patterns of family functioning, help clinicians think systemically about how events and relationships in their clients' lives are related to patterns of health and illness.

Gathering genogram information should be seen as an integral part of a comprehensive, clinical assessment. There is no quantitative measurement scale by which the clinician can use a genogram in a cookbook fashion to make clinical predictions. Rather, the genogram is a subjective, interpretive tool that enables the clinician to generate tentative hypotheses for further evaluation in a family assessment.

Typically, the genogram is constructed from information gathered during the first session and revised as new information becomes available. Thus, the initial assessment forms the basis for treatment. It is important to emphasize, however, that clinicians typically do not compartmentalize assessment and treatment. Each interaction of the therapist with the family informs the assessment and thus influences the next intervention.

Genograms help a clinician get to know a family. They thus become an important way of "joining" with families in therapy. By creating a systemic perspective that helps to track family issues through space and time, they enable an interviewer to reframe, detoxify, and normalize emotion-laden issues. Also, the genogram interview provides a ready vehicle for systemic questioning, which, in addition to providing information for the clinician, begins to orient the family to a systemic perspective. The genogram helps both the clinician and the family to see the "larger picture," that is, to view problems in their current and historical context. Structural, relational, and functional information about a family can be viewed on a genogram both horizontally across the family context and vertically through the generations.

Scanning the breadth of the current family context allows the clinician to assess the connectedness of the immediate players in the family drama to each other, as well as to the broader system, and to evaluate the family's strengths and vulnerabilities in relation to the overall situation. Consequently, we include on the genogram the nuclear and extended family members, as well as significant non-blood "kin" who have ever lived with or played a major role in the family's life. We also note relevant events and problems. Current behavior and problems of family members can be traced on the genogram from multiple perspectives. The index person (the "I.P." or person with the problem or symptom) may be viewed in the context of various subsystems, such as siblings, triangles, and reciprocal relationships, or in relation to the broader community, social institutions (schools, courts, etc.), and sociocultural context.

By scanning the family system historically and assessing previous life cycle transitions, the clinician can place present issues in the context of the family's evolutionary patterns. Thus, the genogram usually includes at least three generations of family members, as well as nodal and critical events in the family's history, particularly as related to the life cycle. When family members are questioned about the present situation in relation to the themes, myths, rules, and emotionally charged issues of previous generations, repetitive patterns become clear. Genograms "let the calendar speak" by suggesting possible connections between family events over time. Patterns of previous illness and earlier shifts in family relationships brought about through changes in family structure and other critical life changes can easily be noted on the genogram, providing a framework for hypothesizing about what may be currently influencing a crisis in a particular family. In conjunction with genograms, we usually include a family chronology, which depicts the family history in chronological order.

Family systems applications range from multigenerational mapping of the family emotional system using a Bowen framework (see bibliographic section on Assessment, Genograms, and Systems Theory), to systemic hypothesizing for strategic interventions, to developing "projective" hypotheses about the workings of the unconscious from genogram interviews, to simply depicting the basic demographic information about a family. Some have suggested modifications of the genogram (see bibliography section on Genogram Variations and Sociograms), such as color-coded genograms (Lewis, 1989), Friedman, Rohrbaugh, and Krakauer's (1988) "time-line" genogram, Watts Jones' (1998) genogram to depict the "functional" family, Friesen and Manitt's (1991) attachment diagrams, or Burke and Faber's (1997) genogrid to depict the networks of lesbian families. Some clinicians have stressed the usefulness of genograms for working with families at various life cycle stages (see bibliography on Family Life Cycle), keeping track of complex relational configurations seen in remarried families (see bibliography on Divorce and Remarriage), and for engaging and keeping track of complex, culturally diverse families (see Culture and Race section of bibliography), exploring specific issues such as sexuality (Hof & Berman, 1986), and making family interventions, as with family play genograms (see Chapter 7). Some have even used genograms as the basis for teaching illiterate adults to read, interviewing them about their genograms, transcribing their stories and then teaching them to read what they have spoken (Darkenwald & Silvestri, 1992). Others have used genograms to facilitate career decisions (Moon, Coleman, McCollum, Nelson, & Jensen-Scott, 1993), or to illustrate organizations such as a medical practice (McIlvain, Crabtree, Medder, Strange, & Miller, 1998). Some have creatively expanded the genogram concept with what they call a gendergram, to map gender relationships over the life cycle (White & Tyson-Rawson, 1995). Hardy and Laszloffy (1995) suggest using genograms to expand cultural exploration with families. McMillen and Groze (1994) and others have developed special ways for showing the genograms of children in child welfare practice.

The genogram has been used to elicit family narratives and cultural stories (Hardy & Laszloffy, 1995; McGill, 1992; Sherman, 1990), to identify therapeutic strategies such as reframing and detoxifying family legacies (Gewirtzman, 1988), to discover families' strengths and exceptions to usual problems (Kuehl, 1995), and to work with special populations, such as children (Fink, Kramer, Weaver, & Anderson, 1993), the elderly (Ingersoll-Dayton & Arndt, 1990), and caregivers of the elderly (Shellenberger, Watkins Couch, & Drake, 1989).

Many of these authors have called for more research using genograms. For example, research could be conducted to assess interventions with groups of unrelated older adults (Ingersoll-Dayton & Arndt, 1990), to evaluate the use of the sexual genogram with couples with specific sexual dysfunctions (Hof & Berman, 1986), or to assess those supporting caregivers of the elderly who are feeling burdened with their role (Shellenberger, Watkins Couch, & Drake, 1989).

Although structural and strategic family therapists, such as Minuchin, Watzlawick, Weakland, and Sluzki, have not used genograms in their approaches, preferring to focus on the relationships in the immediate family, even they share a concern about hierarchical structures, particularly coalitions where generational boundaries are crossed.

Some family therapists have actually eschewed the use of genograms. Haley, for example, has said he does not believe in ghosts, and Michael White (1995) believes that gathering genogram information is actually unhelpful, because it "privileges" certain historical information over other knowledge.

We, on the other hand, believe this is precisely one of the magical aspects of genograms—they can reveal aspects of the family that have been hidden from family members—secrets of their history. Such revelations help families understand their current dilemmas and provide solutions for their future. Indeed, one of the most exciting aspects of genograms is the way they lead families beyond the unidimensional linear perspectives that have so often characterized psychological explanations. They actually teach people to think systemically, because, as soon as family members and clinicians notice one pattern, their vision is expanded by seeing another as well. The very richness of the genogram graphic itself facilitates noticing more than one pattern at a time.

Family physicians have used genograms to record family medical history efficiently and reliably (Crouch & Davis, 1987; Jolly, Froom, & Rosen, 1980; Medalie, 1978; Mullins & Christie-Seely, 1984; Rakel, 1977; Rogers & Holloway, 1990; Sloane, Slatt, Curtis, & Ebell, 1998; Taylor, David, Johnson, Phillips, & Scherger, 1998; Tomson, 1985). It was they who proposed the standardization of genogram symbols (Jolly et al., 1980) and who developed efficient procedures for using genograms in medical practice (Rogers, Durkin, & Kelly, 1985). Indeed, Crouch (1989), one of the most influential family physicians in the promotion of genograms, constructed a genogram depicting the field of family practice and family medicine (Genogram 1.1), showing the

Genogram1.1 Family practice and family medicine:
Modification of Michael Crouch's genogram of family practice and family medicine (1989)

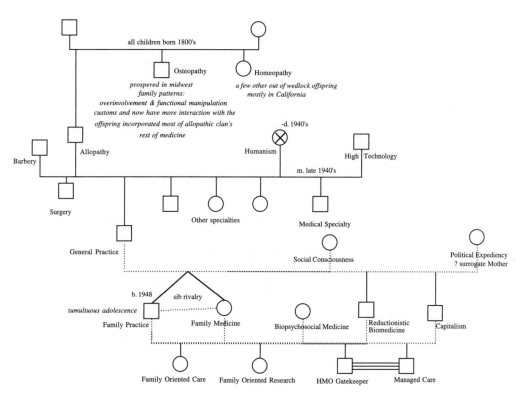

Genogram 1.2 Family therapy's history

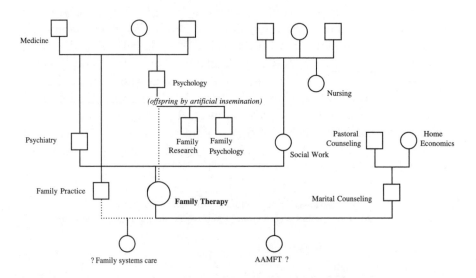

potential of genograms to illustrate the history of systems other than families. Following Crouch, we have, for fun, made a tentative genogram for the history of family therapy (Genogram 1.2). Crouch (1986) has also written about the value of working with one's own family for the sake of professional development, an approach that has been widely promoted by Bowen and his followers for many years (see bibiliography on Coaching). Meanwhile, as we have been expanding genograms to illustrate in greater depth the context around the immediate family, the concept of the genogram has been evolving. For example, Genogram 1.3 illustrates the informal kinship network of friends that has surrounded my own (MM) immediate family. Genograms have even been used to show the relationships and historical connections of national and cultural patterns. Scharwiess (1994) used a genogram most creatively to illustrate the multigenerational, stepsibling and half-sibling relationships involved in the reunification of Germany. This historical genogram even included "Uncle Sam" and "Mother Russia" to illustrate the multigenerational international connections that may impinge on the "sibling" relationships of East and West Germans today. We look forward to the continued evolution of genograms.

A Family Systems Perspective

We begin by reviewing the systemic assumptions that guide us in using genograms in our work. A family systems perspective views families as inextri-

Genogram 1.3 McGoldrick family and network

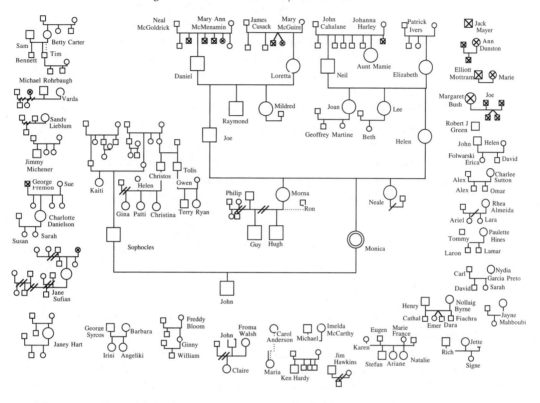

cably interconnected. Neither people nor their problems or solutions exist in a vacuum. All are inextricably interwoven into broader interactional systems, the most fundamental of which is the family. The family is the primary and, except in rare instances, most powerful system to which we humans ever belong. In this framework, "family" consists of the entire kinship network of at least three generations, both as it currently exists and as it has evolved through time (Carter & McGoldrick, 1998b). Family is, by our definition, those who are tied together through their common biological, legal, cultural, and emotional history and their implied future together. The physical, social, and emotional functioning of family members is profoundly interdependent, with changes in one part of the system reverberating in other parts. In addition, family interactions and relationships tend to be highly reciprocal, patterned, and repetitive. The existence of these patterns allows us to make tentative predictions from the genogram.

A basic assumption here is that problems and symptoms reflect a system's adaptation to its total context at a given moment in time. The adaptive efforts of members of the system reverberate throughout many levels of a system—from the biological to the intrapsychic to the interpersonal, i.e., nuclear and extended family, community, culture, and beyond. Also, family behaviors, including problems and symptoms, derive further emotional and normative meaning in relation to both the sociocultural and historical context of the family. Thus, a systemic perspective involves assessing the problem on the basis of these multiple contextual levels.

Families are organized within biological, legal, cultural, and emotional structures, as well as according to generation, age, gender, and other factors. Where you fit in the family structure can influence your functioning, relational patterns, and the type of family you form in the next generation. Gender and birth order are key factors shaping sibling relationships and characteristics. Given different family structural configurations mapped on the genogram, the clinician can hypothesize possible personality characteristics and relational compatibilities. Ethnicity, race, religion, migration, class, and other socioeconomic factors, as well as a family's time and location in history (Elder, 1992), also influence a family's structural patterns (Carter & McGoldrick, 1998a; McGoldrick, 1995, 1998a; McGoldrick, Giordano, & Pearce, 1996). These factors, too, become part of the genogram map.

Families repeat themselves. What happens in one generation will often repeat itself in the next; that is, the same issues tend to be played out from generation to generation, though the actual behavior may take a variety of forms. Bowen termed this the "multigenerational transmission" of family patterns. The hypothesis is that relationship patterns in previous generations may provide implicit models for family functioning in the next generation. On the genogram, we explore patterns of functioning, relationship, and structure that continue or alternate from one generation to the next.

Clearly, this systems approach involves an understanding of both the current and historical context of the family. The "flow of anxiety" (Carter, 1978) in a family system occurs along both vertical and horizontal dimensions (see Figure 1.1) (Carter & McGoldrick, 1998b; McGoldrick & Carter, 1998a). For the individual the vertical axis includes the biological heritage and intricate programming of behaviors from temperament, possible congenital disabilities, and genetic make-up. The horizontal axis relates to the individual's emotional, cognitive, interpersonal, and physical development over the life span within a specific historical context. Over time, the individual's inherent qualities can become either crystallized into rigid behaviors or elaborated into broader and more flexible repertoires.

At the family level, the vertical axis includes the family history, the patterns of relating and functioning that are transmitted down the generations, primar-

Figure 1.1
Flow of stress through the family

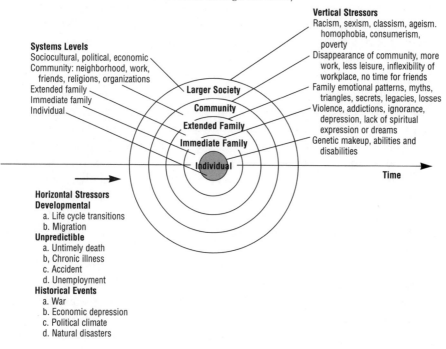

Vertical Stressors
Racism, sexism, classism, ageism, homophobia, consumerism, poverty
Disappearance of community, more work, less leisure, inflexibility of workplace, no time for friends
Family emotional patterns, myths, triangles, secrets, legacies, losses
Violence, addictions, ignorance, depression, lack of spiritual expression or dreams
Genetic makeup, abilities and disabilities

Systems Levels
Sociocultural, political, economic
Community: neighborhood, work, friends, religions, organizations
Extended family
Immediate family
Individual

Larger Society
Community
Extended Family
Immediate Family
Individual

Time

Horizontal Stressors
Developmental
   a. Life cycle transitions
   b. Migration
Unpredictible
   a. Untimely death
   b, Chronic illness
   c. Accident
   d. Unemployment
Historical Events
   a. War
   b. Economic depression
   c. Political climate
   d. Natural disasters

ily through the mechanism of emotional triangling (Bowen, 1978). It includes all the family attitudes, taboos, expectations, labels, and loaded issues with which we grow up. These aspects of our lives are the hand we are dealt. What we do with them is the question. The horizontal flow at a family level describes the family as it moves through time, coping with the changes and transitions of the family's life cycle. This horizontal flow includes both the predictable developmental stresses and those unpredictable events, "the slings and arrows of outrageous fortune," that may disrupt the life cycle process—untimely death, birth of a handicapped child, migration, chronic illness, job loss, etc.

At a sociocultural level, the vertical axis includes cultural and societal history, stereotypes, patterns of power, social hierarchies, and beliefs, all of which have been passed down through the generations. A group's history, in particular a legacy of trauma, will have an impact on families and individuals as they go through life (e.g., the holocaust on the Jews and the Germans, slavery on African Americans and on colonizing, slave-owning groups, homophobic crimes on homosexuals and heterosexuals, etc.). The horizontal axis relates to community connections or lack of them, current events, and social policy, as they impact the family and the individual at a given time. This axis depicts the consequences in people's present lives of the society's "inherited" (vertical) norms of racism, sexism, classism and homophobia, as well as ethnic and religious prejudices, as these are manifested in social, political, and economic structures that limit the options of some and support the power of others (McGoldrick & Carter, 1998a). With enough stress on this horizontal axis, any family will experience dysfunction. Furthermore, stressors on the vertical axis may create additional problems, so that even a small horizontal stress can have serious repercussions on the system. For example, if a young mother has many unresolved issues with her mother or father (vertical anxiety), she may have a particularly difficult time dealing with the normal vicissitudes of parenthood (horizontal anxiety). The genogram helps the clinician to trace the flow of anxiety down through the generations and across the current family context.

Coincidences of historical events or of concurrent events in different parts of a family are viewed not as random happenings but as occurrences that may be interconnected systemically, though the connections may be hidden from view (McGoldrick, 1995). In addition, key family relationship changes seem more likely to occur at some times than at others. They are especially likely at points of life cycle transition. Symptoms tend to cluster around such transitions in the family life cycle, when family members face the task of reorganizing their relations with one another in order to go on to the next phase (Carter & McGoldrick, 1998a). The symptomatic family may become stuck in time, unable to resolve its impasse by reorganizing and moving on. The history and relationship patterns revealed in a genogram assessment provide important clues about the nature of this impasse—how a symptom may have arisen to preserve or to prevent some relationship pattern or to protect some legacy of previous generations.

There are many types of relationship patterns in families. Of particular interest are patterns of relational distance. People may be very close or very distant or somewhere in between. At one extreme are family members who are very distant from or in conflict with each other. The family may become so distant that it breaks apart. At the other extreme are families who seem almost stuck together in "emotional fusion." Family members in fused or poorly differentiated relationships are vulnerable to dysfunction, which tends to occur when the level of stress or anxiety exceeds the system's capacity to deal with it. The more closed the boundaries of a system become, the more immune it is to input from the environment, and consequently, the more rigid family patterns become. In other words, family members in a closed, fused system react automatically to one another, practically impervious to events outside the system that require adaptation to changing conditions. Fusion may involve either positive or negative relationships; i.e., family members may feel very good about each other or experience almost nothing but hostility and conflict. In either case, there is an overdependent bond that ties the family together. With genograms clinicians can map family boundaries and indicate which family subsystems are fused and thus likely to be closed to new input about changing conditions.

As Bowen (1978) has pointed out, two-person relationships tend to be unstable. Under stress two people tend to draw in a third. They stabilize the system by forming a coalition of two in relation to the third. The basic unit of an emotional system thus tends to be the triangle. As we shall see, genograms can help the clinician identify key triangles in a family system, see how triangular patterns repeat from one generation to the next, and design strategies for changing them (Fogarty, 1973; Guerin, Fogarty, Fay, & Kautto, 1996).

The members of a family tend to fit together as a functional whole. That is, the behaviors of different family members tend to be complementary or reciprocal. This does not mean that family members have equal power to influence relationships, as is obvious from the power differentials between men and women, between parents and children, between the elderly and younger family members, and between family members who belong to different cultures, classes, or races (McGoldrick, 1998a). What it does mean is that belonging to a system opens people to reciprocal influences and involves them in each other's behavior in inextricable ways. This leads us to expect a certain interdependent fit or balance in families, involving give and take, action and reaction. Thus, a lack (e.g., irresponsibility) in one part of the family may be complemented by a surplus (overresponsibility) in another part. The genogram helps the clinician pinpoint the contrasts and idiosyncrasies in families that indicate this type of complementarity or reciprocal balance.

A Caveat

Throughout this book, we make assertions about families based on their genograms. These observations are offered as tentative hypotheses, as is true for genogram interpretations in general. They offer suggestions for further exploration. Predictions based on the genogram are not facts. The principles for interpreting genograms should be seen as drawing a roadmap that, by highlighting certain characteristics of the terrain, guides us through the complex territory of family life—nothing more.

Sometimes exact dates for family events are not known. We have inserted question marks beside dates when sources have provided inexact information.

Many of the genograms shown here include more information than our discussion can cover. We encourage readers to use these illustrative genograms as a departure point for further developing their own skills in using and interpreting genograms.

Clearly, a genogram is limited in how much information it can display. Clinicians gather a great deal more important information on people's lives than can ever appear on genograms. Therefore, genograms should not be used out of the context of family members' experience of their history and relationships. The genogram is just one part of an ongoing clinical investigation and must be integrated into the total family assessment.

2

Developing a Genogram to Track Family Patterns

Gathering family information and constructing a genogram should always be part of a more general process of joining, assessing, and helping a family. The information is gathered and organized as family members tell their story. While basic genogram information can be collected in a structured format as part of a medical record, the information should always be treated with respect and gathered for a purpose. Sharing a family's history is a sacred relationship, not a matter of technical fact-gathering.

Genogram information can be obtained by interviewing one family member or several. Clearly, getting information from several family members increases reliability and provides the opportunity to compare perspectives and observe interactions directly. By interviewing several family members, we get many points of view, and together these versions become a whole story.

Since family patterns can be transmitted from one generation to the next, the clinician should scan the genogram for patterns that have repeated over several generations. Such repetitive patterns occur in functioning, relationships, and family structure. Recognizing such patterns often helps families avoid repeating unfortunate patterns or transmitting them into the future. Tracking critical events and changes in family functioning allows us to notice anniversary reactions, make systemic connections between seeming coincidences, assess the impact of traumatic changes on family functioning, its resources and vulnerability to future stresses, and then try to understand such events in the larger social, economic, and political context. This tracking enables the clinician to seek ways to promote resilience based on past sources of strength and modify adaptive strategies that in the past have proved dysfunctional.

Of course, seeing several family members is not always feasible, and often the genogram interview is used with one person. The time required to complete a genogram assessment can vary greatly. While the basic information can usually be collected in 15 minutes, a comprehensive family assessment interview involving several family members may take one to two hours. Clinicians often prefer to spread the interviewing over a number of sessions or to develop the genogram as they go along in their work with families.

Mapping the Family Structure

The backbone of a genogram is a graphic depiction of how different family members are biologically and legally related to one another from one generation to the next. This map is a construction of squares and circles representing people and lines delineating their relationships.

Each family member is represented by a box (male) or circle (female), depending on his or her gender (Genogram 2.1). For the index person or identified patient (IP) around whom the genogram is constructed, the lines are doubled, as for Woody Allen and Mia Farrow on this genogram. For a person who is dead, an X is placed inside the symbol, as indicated for Mia's brother Michael and her parents John and Maureen. Birth and death dates are indicated to the left and right above the symbol. The person's current age or age at death is usually indicated within the symbol, as indicated for Mia's oldest brother Michael, who died in 1958 at the age of 19. The figures representing family members are connected by lines that indicate their biological and legal relationships. Two people who are married are connected by lines that go down and across, with the husband on the left and the wife on the right, as indicated on Genogram 2.1 for Martin and Nettie. "m." followed by a date indicates when the couple was married. Sometimes only the last two digits of the year are shown (e.g., met

Genogram 2.1 Woody Allen and Mia Farrow

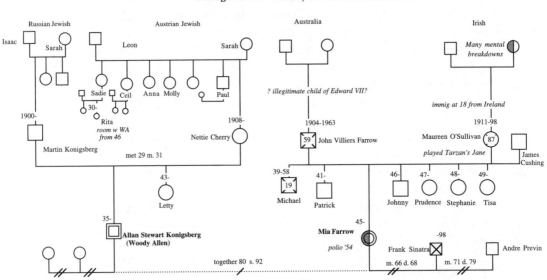

29 m. 31) when there is little chance of confusion regarding the appropriate century. The marriage line is also the place where separations or divorces are indicated. The slashes signify a disruption in the marriage—one slash for separation (as in Mia Farrow's separation line from Woody Allen, which occurred in 1992 (indicated by s. 92) and two for a divorce (as in the divorces of Mia from Frank Sinatra and Andre Previn and of Woody from his previous wives. In extended genograms that go back more than three generations, symbols for individuals in the distant past are not usually crossed out, since they are presumably dead. Only relevant deaths are indicated on such genograms. Other

Genogram 2.2 Foster and adopted children, twins, miscarriages, stillbirths, abortions, pregnancies

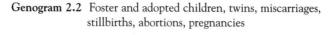

symbols are used to indicate twins, foster and adopted children, pregnancies, miscarriages, abortions, and stillbirths (Genogram 2.2). Converging lines connect twins to the parental line. If the twins are identical, a bar connects them to each other (Genogram 2.2). A dotted line is used to connect a foster child to the parents' line, while a dotted and a solid line connect an adopted child to the parents' line (Genogram 2.2).

Genogram 2.3 Husband with many wives: Henry VIII

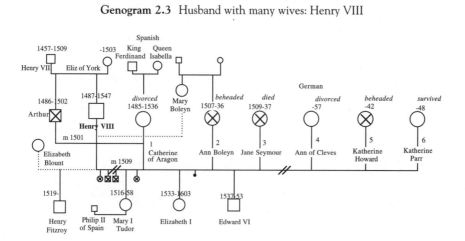

Genogram 2.4 Husband (Ted Turner), wife (Jane Fonda), and several partners of each

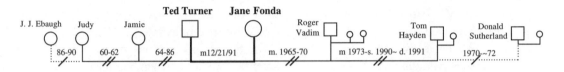

Multiple marriages add a degree of complexity that is challenging to depict. Genogram 2.3 shows one way of indicating several wives of one husband (the wives of King Henry VIII). The rule of thumb is that, when feasible, the different marriages follow in order from left to right, with the most recent marriage coming last. The marriage and divorce dates should also help to make the order clear. However, when each spouse has had multiple partners (and possibly children from previous marriages), mapping the complex web of relationships can be very difficult indeed. One solution is to place the relationship you are focusing on in the center and the partner's other spouses off to the side, as in Genogram 2.4 (Jane Fonda and Ted Turner). Of course, such situations can get very complicated, as they do for Jackie Kennedy's sister Lee Bouvier (Genogram 2.5), because Lee's first husband, Michael Canfield, went on to marry a woman, Laura Dudley, whose first husband, Eric Dudley, went on to marry Stas Radziwell's previous wife, Grace Kolin.

Genogram 2.5 The Bouvier family

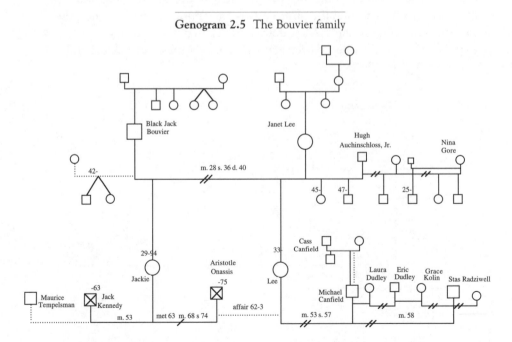

Genogram 2.6 Fonda marriages

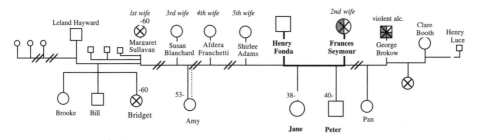

If previous spouses have had other partners, it may be necessary to draw a second line, slightly above the first marriage line, to indicate these relationships. For example, in Genogram 2.6 (Henry Fonda), each spouse has been married several times. Henry's first wife, Margaret Sullavan, had been married once before she married him, and she remarried afterwards. Fonda's second wife, Frances Seymour, had earlier been married to George Brokaw, who himself had previously been married to Clare Booth, who in turn later married Henry Luce.

Whenever possible it is preferable to show children from different marriages in their correct birth order (oldest on the left, youngest on the right). But sometimes, when there are many partners, this becomes impossible, as with Genogram 2.6, where Jane and Peter Fonda are shown after Amy, their adopted half-sister, who was 13 years younger than Peter, but who grew up with them for the first two years. Their older half-sister, Pan, who was five years older than Jane and lived with them from age five until she went to college, is also not shown in birth order, since, in fact, she was the oldest of all. An alternative genogram showing all the Fonda siblings in birth order (Genogram 2.7) could be relevant for understanding the siblings in relation to each other. Notice that in this case Brokaw's next wife, Clare Booth Luce, has been omitted to keep the graphic clear. With complex families like this, choices always have to be made between clarity, accuracy, and level of detail.

Genogram 2.7 Fonda children in birth order

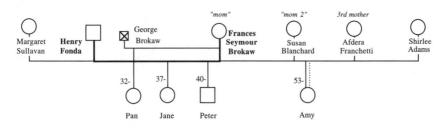

Genogram 2.8 Heterosexual and homosexual couple relationships:
Jodie Foster's family

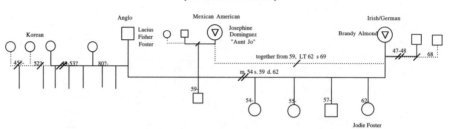

If a couple are involved in a love affair or living together but not legally married, their relationship is depicted as with married couples, but a dotted line is used (as shown for Mia Farrow and Woody Allen in Genogram 2.1). When spouses have had partners of both sexes, it may be necessary to draw separate connecting lines to clarify who had a relationship with whom. Genogram 2.8 shows the family of Jodie Foster. Her father Lucius fathered children by five partners: three wives and two other partners. The dates for Jodie's mother, Brandy Almond's marriage to Lucius are indicated by "m. 54 s. 59 d. 62." Recording the specific dates to track couple relationships can be significant in tracking family patterns. Jodie, for example, was conceived and born three years after the parents separated, indeed shortly before the divorce came through. It turns out she was the product of the father's financial, emotional, and physical abuse of the mother, conceived under pressure from the father for sex in return for owed child support.

Jodie's mother was in a committed couple relationship with Jo Dominguez from 1959. The couple began living together in 1962 ("LT 62"). Jo's prominence in the family is indicated by depicting the couple line for Brandy and Jo just above that of the biological father. "Aunt Jo" became a haven of stability to the children, providing financial, physical, and emotional support to them for many years. They separated in 1969. Jo's husband is shown smaller and higher, along with the woman he spent the rest of his life with. He never divorced Jo and was thus not free to marry again, so his other relationship is indicated with a dotted line.

If a couple has children, each child's symbol hangs down from the line that connects the couple. Children are drawn left to right, going from the oldest to the youngest, as in Genogram 2.1, with the index person shown lower than the others, to distinguish him or her. If there are many children in a family, an alternate method (depicted for Margaret Sullavan and Leland Hayward's three children, Brooke, Bill, Bridget, on Genogram 2.6) may be used to save space. Parents of the index person are also depicted larger and lower than their siblings to clarify their importance (see Woody and Mia on Genogram 2.1).

Genogram 2.9 Mia Farrow's children: Biological and adopted

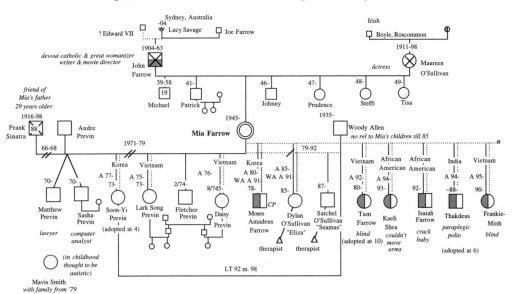

Single parent adoption can be indicated as in Genogram 2.9. This genogram shows the family of Mia Farrow, who had biological children (including twin sons, Matthew and Sasha) and interracially adopted children (Soon-Yi, Lark, and Daisy) with her second husband, Andre Previn. She then adopted another interracial child (Moses) and one who was American born (Dylan/Eliza) during her relationship with Woody Allen, after which they had a biological child together (Satchel, now called Seamus), and finally she adopted five more children on her own, Tam, Kaeli Shea, Isaiah, Thakdeus, and Frankie-Minh Farrow. If at all possible, we indicate the cultural background, since it is an important part of anyone's history.

Where living situations are complicated, a line can be drawn to encircle the household(s). This is especially important in multi-nuclear families, where children spend time in various households, as in Genogram 2.10 for Jackie Bouvier Kennedy and her sister Lee after their parents' separation when Jackie was seven. During the school year they lived with their mother, maternal grandparents, and maternal great-grandmother. During the summers they spent time with their father, paternal grandparents, and all their paternal cousins on Long Island.

When the "functional" family is different from the biological or legal family, as when children are raised by a grandparent or in an informal adoptive family, it is useful to create a separate genogram to show the functional structure

Genogram 2.10 The family of Jackie Bouvier (Kennedy)

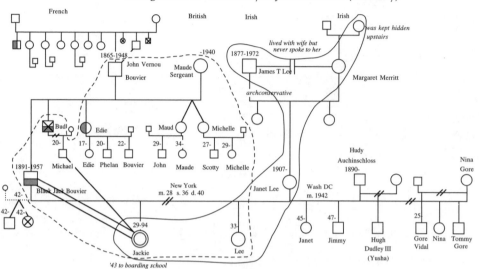

(see Watts Jones, 1998). Where children have lived as part of several families—biological, foster, and adoptive—separate genograms may help to depict the child's multiple families over time (Genogram 2.11; see also Colon's genograms in Chapter 3). McMillen and Groze (1994), who have suggested another way to show children who have grown up in multiple placements, suggest accompanying the graphic with a chronology, as shown in Genogram 2.12.

We can also indicate on a genogram (Genogram 2.13) a lesbian couple with a child born to one of them and adopted by the other. The very small square indicated as the biological parent of Meg is a sperm donor. Fran and Martha, the parents of Meg, had previous couple relationships that are also indicated on Genogram 2.13. Burke and Faber (1997) have suggested using a "gendergrid," an adaptation of the genogram, to help to depict the liaisons, long-term bonds, communities, and social networks of lesbian couples. The gendergrid provides for three levels of relationship: historical influences, primary emotional and social influences, and primary intimate relationships for an individual or a couple.

Constructing the Genogram

Using the basic symbols and procedures for mapping the family structure on a genogram, we can illustrate the construction of a genogram for Sigmund Freud. Neither Freud nor his biographers ever did extensive research into his family, and the details of his family life are sketchy. Nevertheless, we do know the basic structure of the Freud family.

Genogram 2.11 Multiple living situations of child raised in foster care and adoption

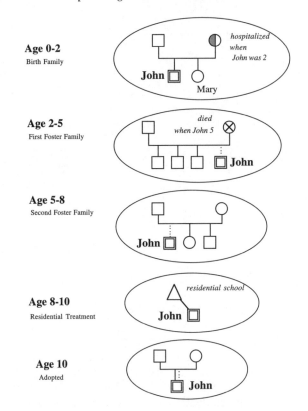

If we map a basic three-generational genogram for Freud (Genogram 2.14) we can see Sigmund and his siblings, and then we can look back a generation and include Sigmund's parents with their siblings and parents (Sigmund's grandparents). To highlight his central importance, the figure for Sigmund is lowered out of the sibling line. The same has been done for the parents, Jacob and Amalia. In general, siblings are shown in a horizontal line, except for any who have died early; they, like Sigmund's brother Julius, are depicted higher and smaller.

In taking a genogram we usually go back to the grandparents of the index person, including at least three generations on the genogram (four or even five generations if the index person has children and grandchildren). The spouses of siblings are also usually placed slightly lower than the siblings themselves, to keep the sibling patterns clear.

The year that a genogram depicts is usually written in the upper lefthand corner. Usually the genogram depicts the current year, but a clinician might also use the genogram to freeze-frame a moment in the past, such as the time

Genogram 2.12 Placement genogram

based on McMillen & Groze (1994)

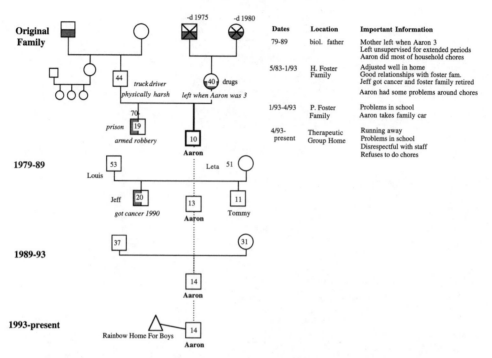

Dates	Location	Important Information
79-89	biol. father	Mother left when Aaron 3 Left unsupervised for extended periods Aaron did most of household chores
5/83-1/93	H. Foster Family	Adjusted well in home Good relationships with foster fam. Jeff got cancer and foster family retired Aaron had some problems around chores
1/93-4/93	P. Foster Family	Problems in school Aaron takes family car
4/93-present	Therapeutic Group Home	Running away Problems in school Disrespectful with staff Refuses to do chores

of symptom onset or critical change in a family. When we choose one date in a person's life, other information, deaths, ages, and important events are calculated in relation to that date. It is then useful to put each person's age inside his or her figure. If the person is dead, the age at death is used instead (Chapter 6 shows a number of Freud genograms for different dates in the family's life cycle, indicating the ages of family members at each point).

Genogram 2.13 Lesbian family

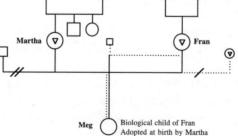

Genogram 2.14 Sigmund Freud family

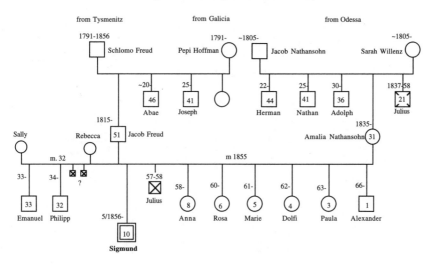

When only partial information can be unearthed, that is included. For instance, Sigmund's father was married three times. We know that he had four children with his first wife, two of whom died early, but nothing is known about these two children or about his second wife, Rebecca. The third wife, of course, was Sigmund's mother, Amalia Nathansohn.

Tracking Family Patterns on the Genogram

Once the basic family structure or skeleton of the genogram is drawn, we can start adding information about the family, particularly about demographics, functioning, relationships, and critical family events. At times it may be useful to make several different genograms to show the different kinds of information.

Demographic Information: Getting the "Facts"

In fleshing out the history of the nuclear and extended families, our initial concern is with getting the "facts" on each family member. These are the vital statistics of the family, the type of objective data that can usually be verified by public record. Demographic information includes ethnic background, ages, dates of birth and death, whereabouts, income, occupation, and educational level. There is a specific place to put some of this information: current age or age at death (inside the symbol); birthdate (above left); deathdate (above right); income (above birth and death dates). The other demographic informa-

Genogram 2.15   Fonda family: Demographics

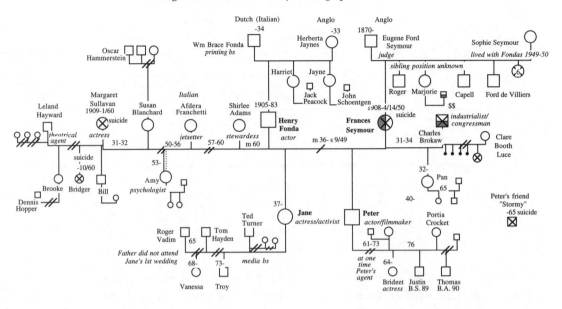

tion goes near the person's symbol wherever there is room (see Genogram 2.15 for Fonda family demographic information). The following information would be relevant for each family member:

- dates of birth, marriage, separation, divorce, illness, and death (including cause)
- sibling position
- ethnic, class, and religious background
- any changes in class through education, income, or marriage
- current religious practices
- occupation and education
- current whereabouts

As the clinician collects more and more "facts" about family events, certain gaps will appear in the history. The clinician can use the genogram to map the family's evolution through time and to broaden the historical perspective on the family. At times family members themselves become so interested in their story that they begin historical research to expand their perspective. Family members may learn more information by speaking to relatives, consulting family bibles, reading local or regional histories, or obtaining medical and genealogical records.

Genogram 2.16 Fonda family: Functioning

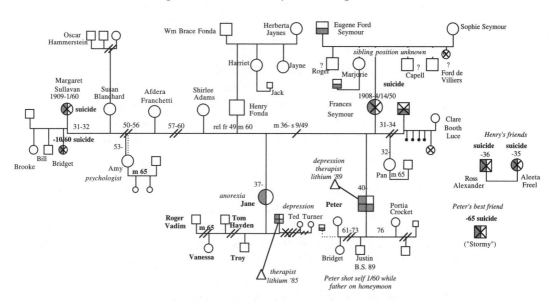

Information about functioning includes more or less objective data on the medical, emotional, and behavioral functioning of family members. Objective signs, such as absenteeism from work and drinking patterns, may be more useful indications of a person's functioning than vague reports by family members that someone is "weird." Signs of highly successful functioning should also be included. The information collected on each person is placed next to his or her symbol on the genogram. Addictions are shown by filling in the bottom half of the square or circle. Those in recovery from addiction have only the lower left half filled in, while the lower right half has only slash marks (as shown for Ella on Genogram 2.21). If they have attended therapy, AA, or another recovery program, or indeed if they have any strong institutional affiliation, such as with a church, fraternal organization, or other group, this can be indicated by a line out to a triangle. On Genogram 2.16 triangles linked to Ted Turner and Peter Fonda indicate these relationships with their therapists. The dates of treatment can also be shown. Suspected alcohol or drug abuse can be indicated by slanted lines on the bottom half of the symbol, as indicated for Peter Fonda on Genogram 2.16. In Peter's case, he has acknowledged using drugs over many years, but sees himself as lucky that it never became an addiction (Fonda, 1998).

Serious mental or physical illness can be indicated by filling in the left half of the symbol. In general, the nature of the illness should also be indicated near the symbol. Where a person has both an addiction and a mental illness, three-quarters of the symbol is filled in, and where he or she is mentally ill but in recovery from addiction, the left half is filled in, and the lower right has light dots. Genogram 2.16 shows the functioning information for the Fonda family.

Patterns of Functioning

The functioning of family members may repeat itself across several generations. In such cases, a particular style of functioning (whether adaptive or maladaptive) or of dealing with problems is passed down from one generation to the next. This transmission does not necessarily occur in linear fashion. An alcoholic father may have children who become teetotalers, and their children may again become drinkers.

Often the presenting problem of the family will have occurred in previous generations. Numerous symptomatic patterns, such as alcoholism, incest, physical symptoms, violence, and suicide, tend to be repeated in families from generation to generation. By noting the pattern repetition, the clinician may be helped to understand the family's present adaptation to the situation and to short-circuit the process. For example, let's look again at the Fonda genogram (Genogram 2.16). Margaret Sullavan's daughter Brigit Hayward committed suicide less than a year after her mother did the same. Given the evidence that one suicide seems to make suicide an option for others in the family, specific efforts at suicide prevention may well be indicated in such families. The same can be said for preventive intervention in families with a history of such symptoms as alcohol abuse and incest. For example, Ted Turner (Genogram 2.17) reached a crisis at age 53, the same age at which his father had shot himself in the head with the gun with which he had taught Ted to shoot years before. Ted, like his father, had led a driven life of work and hard drinking. But in this case Ted managed not to repeat his father's pattern, and, in fact, that age became for him a time of critical transformation of his life. It was the year he married Jane Fonda. Both of them gave up drinking, and Ted committed himself to expanding his life rather than letting his obsession with work drive him over the edge, as it had with his father.

Clinicians can track multigenerational patterns of resilience, strength, and success as well as failure (Walsh, 1995, 1998). All families should be assessed for their resilience as well as their problems. Among the most amazing in this book are the Hepburns (Genogram 3.6), who illustrate the repeated trauma of suicide and depression along with the resilience and power of strong women on their own; the Fonda/Turner families, which show an amazing ability to survive and transform themselves beyond the trauma of loss, suicide, silence, and mental illness, turning hardship into productivity and self-regeneration; the Bell family (Genogram 5.4), in which deafness is complemented by inventiveness and resourcefulness with sound; and the genogram of Frida Kahlo and Diego Rivera (Genogram 5.5), which illustrates an amazing ability to transform cul-

Genogram 2.17 Ted Turner family: Functioning

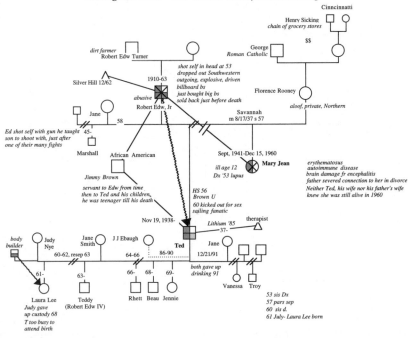

tural difference and disruption, loss, trauma, and physical disability into transcendent strength and creative energy. The Blackwell family genogram (Genogram 2.18) shows a pattern of strong and successful women. Included in this remarkable family were the first woman physician and the first woman minister in the U.S., as well as numerous other successful woman physicians, ministers, artists, and suffragettes. Yet patterns of success and failure may coexist in the same family and in each succeeding generation. Looking again at the Blackwell family, we see that among all these successful women, one daughter in each generation appears to have been an invalid.

Another common functioning pattern is success in one generation followed by remarkable failure in the next. This may be particularly true of the families of famous people, where children may rebel against pressure to live up to the reputations of their parents. The Adams family (Genogram 3.13) is a powerful example of that phenomenon, with all but one of the children of John Adams having serious problems. The same was true for the one successful son in that second generation, John Quincy Adams, whose first two sons had serious problems. Only in the next generation did the one successful son, Charles Adams, manage to produce a group of children who were, all but one, relatively functional.

Specific patterns of functioning may also be repeated across the generations. A good example would be the family of Carl Gustav Jung (Genogram 2.19). A

Genogram 2.18 Blackwell family

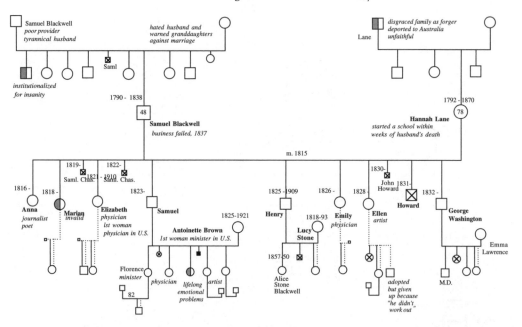

quick glance at his genogram shows the preponderance of ministers: Jung's father, two paternal uncles, all six maternal uncles, the maternal grandfather, and two maternal granduncles. Next one sees that both his paternal grandfather, for whom he was named, and his paternal great-grandfather were physicians; finally, one can note several family members who believed in the supernatural: his mother, maternal grandfather, and maternal cousin, Helena Preiswerk, who claimed to be a medium and whose seances Jung attended in his youth. Thus, his becoming a physician with a profound interest in religion and in the supernatural very much fit with the predominant patterns in his family.

Family Relationships and Roles

The third level of genogram construction is the most inferential. This involves delineating the relationships between family members. Such characterizations are based on the report of family members and direct observations. Different lines are used to symbolize various types of relationship between two family members (Genogram 2.20). Although such commonly used relationship descriptors as "fused" or "conflictual" are difficult to define operationally and have different connotations for clinicians with various perspectives, these symbols are useful in clinical practice. Relationships in a family do, of course, change over time, so this aspect of genograms is one of the most subjective and most

Genogram 2.19 Jung family

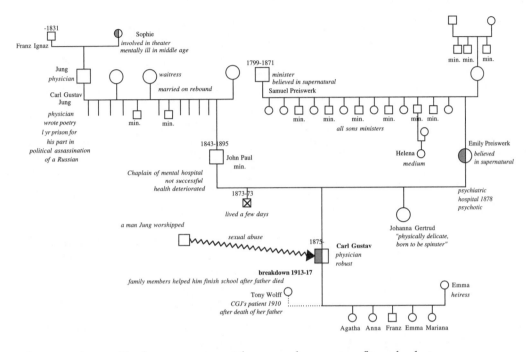

subject to change. Furthermore, one might argue that any conflictual relationship implies underlying connection, so that any highly conflictual relationship by definition reflects fusion as well as conflict. However, the fused/conflictual lines are usually used to illustrate a relationship that shows a high degree of connection as well as conflict at an overt level. Cut-offs can also involve great conflict or silent distancing. Dominance or relationships in which one person focuses an enormous amount of energy on another may be illustrated by a heavy straight line with an arrow in the direction of the one who is focused upon, as in Genogram 2.20. Other important relationships, such as hostile/dependent and ambivalent ones, are harder to depict on a genogram. Relationships involving physical or sexual abuse are depicted by a zigzag line ending in a filled-in arrow, indicating who was abused by whom (Genogram 2.20).

Since relationship patterns can be quite complex, it is often useful to represent them on a separate genogram. Questions on relationships include:

- Are there any family members who do not speak to each other or who have ever had a period of not speaking? Are there any who were/are in serious conflict?
- Are there any family members who are extremely close?

Genogram 2.20 Relationship lines on a genogram

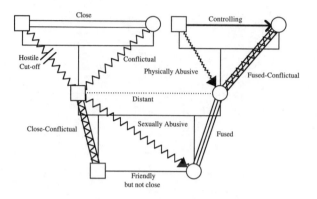

- Who helps out when help is needed? In whom do family members confide?
- All couples have some sort of marital difficulties. What sorts of problems and conflicts have you encountered? What about your parents' and siblings' marriages?
- How do you each get along with each child? Have any family members had particular problems dealing with their children?

The clinician should get as many perspectives on family relationships as possible. For example, the husband may be asked, "How close do you think your mother and your older brother were?" The wife might then be asked for her impression of that relationship. The goal is to uncover differences, as well as agreements, about family relationships and to use the different perceptions of the family to enrich the genogram picture for both the clinician and the family.

From the relationships between family members, the clinician also begins to get a sense of the complementarity of roles in the family. Questions that elucidate the role structure include:

- Has any family member been focused on as the caretaker? The problematic one? The "sick" one? The "bad" one? The "mad" one?
- Who in the family is seen as the strong one? The weak one? The dominant one? The submissive one?
- Who in the family is seen as the successful one? The failure?
- Who is seen as warm? As cold? As caring? As distant?

Labels or nicknames used by family members are particularly instructive. Often, each family member has a family-wide label that describes and even circumscribes his or her position in the family, e.g., the tyrant, the supermother, the star, the rebel, or the baby. Labels are good clues to the emotional patterns in the system.

Sometimes it is useful to ask how members of the present family would be characterized by other family members, e.g., "How do you think your older brother would describe your relationship with your wife?" or "How would your father have described you when you were 13, the age of your son now?" Again, gathering as many perspectives as possible enriches the family's view of itself and introduces channels for new information.

Relationship patterns of closeness, distance, conflict, etc., may also repeat themselves over the generations. Genograms often reveal complex relational patterns that would be missed if not mapped across a few generations. Recognizing such patterns can, it is hoped, help families avoid continuing the repetition in future generations. One example of such a repetition would be a family in which mother and son in each generation have a special alliance while father and son have a negative conflictual relationship. Realizing the predictability of such a pattern and the multigenerational programming involved, a son might choose consciously to change his relationship with his parents to vary this pattern.

The O'Neill family (Genogram 2.21) shows a multigenerational pattern of estrangement between father and children. James O'Neill's father deserted his

Genogram 2.21 O'Neill family: Repetitive patterns

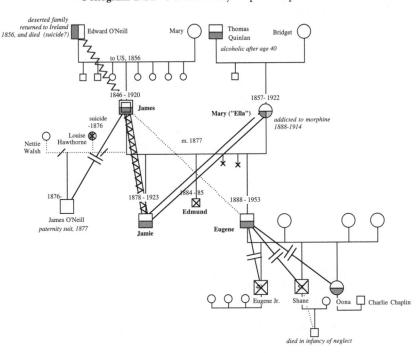

family, returned to Ireland and probably committed suicide. Both Eugene and his older brother Jamie felt estranged from their father, although they were both totally dependent on him emotionally and financially, and all of them blamed each other for the mother's drug addiction. In the next generation, the play-wright refused to see or even mention the name of his daughter Oona after her marriage to Charlie Chaplin or his son Shane after Shane's son died of neglect. O'Neill never even saw his oldest son, Eugene, Jr., until he was 12, and he was estranged from him at the time of this son's suicide.

In the family of Eleanor Roosevelt, the pattern was one of mother-daughter resentment and close feelings between father and daughter (Genogram 2.22). Although both her parents had died by the time she was 11, Eleanor remem-bered having a special relationship with her father while feeling her mother was harsh and insensitive to his predicament. Her father was in fact an alcoholic and irresponsible, and her mother had to have him committed to an asylum and later she separated from him. In the next generation, the daughter, Anna, an oldest like Eleanor, preferred her father and saw her own mother as overly harsh. Throughout her adolescence she had a stormy relationship with Eleanor, which did not change until her father contracted polio. Eleanor felt the ulti-mate betrayal in her daughter Anna's entertaining FDR and his girlfriend behind Eleanor's back at the White House and Camp David. But in later life Eleanor and Anna reversed this pattern of mother-daughter cut-off and became very closely connected (see McGoldrick, 1995).

Genogram 2.22 Eleanor Roosevelt's family: Repeated patterns

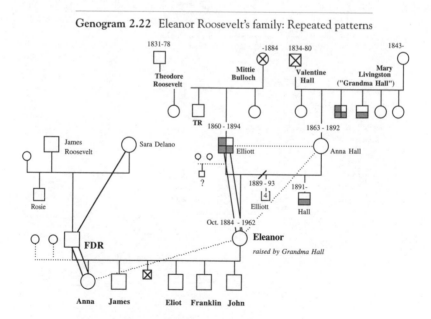

Critical Life Events

Predictable life cycle transitions and unpredictable nodal life events are tracked on a genogram; they include important family transitions, job changes, entrances and exits of family members, relationship shifts, moves or migrations, losses and successes. These give a sense of the historical continuity of the family and of the effect of the family history on each individual. Some of these events will have been noted as demographic data, e.g., family births and deaths. Others include new romances, marriages, separations, divorces, moves, and job changes. Critical life events are recorded either in the margin of the genogram or, if necessary, on a separate attached page.

There are certain critical life events that may be important to explore in detail.

- How did other family members react when a particular family member was born? Who attended the christening ceremony or bris? Who was named after whom and who "should have been"?
- How did the family react when a particular family member died? Who took it the hardest? The easiest? Who attended the funeral? What was the effect when the will was read? Who wasn't there? Who "should have been"?
- When and why did the family migrate to this country? How did they cope with the multiple losses of migration? How many generations of the family have lived in the U.S.? What was the context into which they came and how did they fit into it? How did the initial generations manage the adaptation to these new circumstances? How did they survive? Which members of the immigrant generation learned the language?
- What gender constraints have the women and men in the family experienced?
- What cultural prejudices have family members experienced?

Family Chronologies

It is useful to keep a family chronology (or listing of important family events) with the genogram (Weber & Levine, 1995). A timeline of important family dates is an excellent way to track family patterns. I (MM) remember being stunned the first time I did my own chronology to see that the only two major health threats of my life before midlife were breast tumors that occurred at ages 17 and 20, within six months after the only two major deaths I had ever experienced. Recognition of this time sequence led me to track my own family's patterns of handling loss and later to make a concerted effort to deal as fully as possible when deaths occurred. At times it is beneficial to make a special chronology for a critical time period, to track a family member's illness in relation to other concurrent significant events or to events at the same point in the life cycle of other family members (Barth, 1993; Huygen, 1982).

An individual chronology may also be useful for tracking a particular family member's functioning, transitions, and symptoms within the context of the family. Generally each occurrence is listed with the date of its occurrence. When family members are unsure about dates, approximate dates should be given, preceded by a question mark, e.g., ?84 or ~84 (see Freud's maternal grandparents in Genogram 2.14). A chronology of family events may be written on the side of the genogram or, if necessary, on a separate sheet of paper. The following chronology illustrates key dates indicated on the genogram for Ted Turner (Genogram 2.17). All the items on the chronology are shown on the genogram, but the pattern of family events gains clarity from the chronology. On the other hand, the family structure would be hard to envision without the genogram.

Short Chronology for Ted Turner: Critical Events

1953   Ted's sister, Mary Jean, age 12, diagnosed with lupus erythematosus followed by encephalitis, which left her with brain damage.

1957   Parents separate. There are conflicts over sister's care. Mother does not want her institutionalized. Sister is suffering horribly—racked with pain.

1960   (Dec. 15) Sister dies age 19. Neither Ted nor his father's new wife knew she was still alive at the time.

1961   (July) Ted's daughter Laura Lee is born.

1961   (July) Father, Ed Turner, goes to Silver Hill, a psychiatric hospital, to withdraw from alcohol.

1962   (September) Father, Ed Turner, makes multimillion dollar deal of a lifetime, turning his advertising business from middling company to largest outdoor advertising business in the south.

1962   (December) Ed Turner goes back to Silver Hill.

1963   (January) Ed Turner leaves Silver Hill.

1963   (March 5) Ed Turner, age 53, shoots himself in the head with gun with which he taught Ted to shoot, following one of the many fights father and son had had over the years. Son Ted is 25.

1991   Ted Turner, age 53, suffering from depression, and having felt that as his father died tragically at that age he would do the same, instead changes the pattern. He is stabilized by therapy and medication. He marries Jane Fonda, whose mother committed suicide when she was 17.

Clearly, a family chronology will vary in length and detail, depending on the breadth and depth of the information on demographics, functioning, relationships, and critical events available or needed for a particular assessment.

Assessing genograms also requires an understanding how life events and changes in family functioning are interconnected. Since the genogram records many critical dates in the family's history, it is useful to the clinician for looking at coincidences of various life events and changes in family functioning. Often seemingly unconnected events that occur around the same time in a family's history are systematically related and have a profound impact on family functioning.

It is particularly helpful to track changes in a family's long-term functioning as they relate to critical family life events. We examine the genogram carefully for a pileup of stresses, the impact of traumatic events, anniversary reactions, and the relationship of family experiences to social, economic, and political events. Thus, we can assess the impact of change on the family and its vulnerability to future changes.

Coincidences of Life Events

Whenever several critical family experiences occur around the same time, it is wise to request details. It is particularly important to notice the coinciding dates on the genogram, which may indicate hidden connections and reveal emotional and systemic patterns. Such "coincidences" may indicate a stressful time in the family's history. If nothing else, they pinpoint the critical periods in a family history, which are likely to have left an emotional legacy. We are not talking here about one event "causing" another, but about the association of events that may be influential in the development of family patterns. Queen Elizabeth referred to the year 1992 as the "annus horribilis" due to the multiple traumas that had plagued the royal family that year: the separation of one son, Andrew, from his wife, Sarah Ferguson; the divorce of Princess Anne from Captain Mark Philips; the ongoing rumors of marital problems between Charles and Diana; and a horrendous fire at Windsor Castle that had done $60 million dollars in damage (Genogram 2.29). In situations where there is such a pileup of stressful life events, one must be on the lookout for emotional reactivity among all family members as well as other hidden stressors influencing the family. The stress of such a pileup may show itself in physical symptoms as well, and indeed, when the Queen gave her speech on the topic she had a severe cold and had almost lost her voice, perhaps a coincidence or perhaps a physical indicator of the stress she was describing, and it was reported that she had difficulty sleeping for many months that year. As the Queen noted, her family's stress was compounded by stress in the country at the time. There had been months of worldwide turmoil and uncertainty, and Britain had had three years of severe recession, with millions unemployed and a record number of personal bankruptcies and homes repossessed.

In other situations the coincidences take place over time, perhaps on anniversaries or at the same life cycle transition. For example, Gregory Bateson's genogram (Genogram 2.23) depicts a number of interesting coincidences. First, Gregory's parents were married shortly after the death of his mother's father. Second, the middle son, Martin, committed suicide on the birthday of the oldest brother, John, who had died four years earlier. And finally, Gregory met Margaret Mead shortly after he cut off from his mother.

Viewed systemically, these events may be more than coincidence. Gregory's parents' engagement was called off by Beatrice's mother when W. B. Bateson got drunk. This was a reaction to Beatrice's father's alcoholism. However, three months after the alcoholic father died, Beatrice put a notice in the newspaper, hoping to reconnect with W.B., who then recontacted her. They were married shortly afterward. In the next generation, Gregory happened to meet and fall in love with Margaret just after becoming estranged from his mother. She and her second husband were doing anthropological work in a remote area of the world

Genogram 2.23 Bateson family

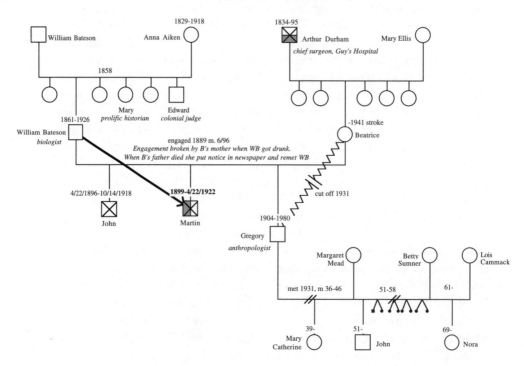

at that time. We might speculate that the children in this family could only connect to their spouses after disconnecting, through death or cut-off, from a parent.

Gregory Bateson, the youngest of three sons of a famous British geneticist, was considered the least promising of the three, sickly in childhood and not an outstanding student. The oldest son, John, was supposed to be the leader. He and the middle brother, Martin, two years apart in age, were extremely close. Gregory, four years younger, grew up somewhat separately. When John was 20 he was killed in World War I. A few days later his mother wrote to Martin that "You and Gregory are left to me still and you must help me back to some of the braveness that John has taken away" (Lipset, 1980, p. 71).

Following John's death a rift developed between Martin and his father, whose own mother had died two months before John (another coincidence). The father now began to pressure this second son, Martin, who was a poet, to become a zoologist. Relations between father and son deteriorated. When, in addition, Martin felt rebuffed by a young woman he admired, he took a gun and shot himself in Trafalgar Square on his brother John's birthday, April 22, 1922, in what was described as "probably the most dramatic and deliberate suicide ever witnessed in London" (Lipset, 1980, p. 93). Martin's choosing to kill himself on his brother's birthday is also an example of an anniversary reaction, which will be discussed below.

Genogram 2.24 Kennedy family

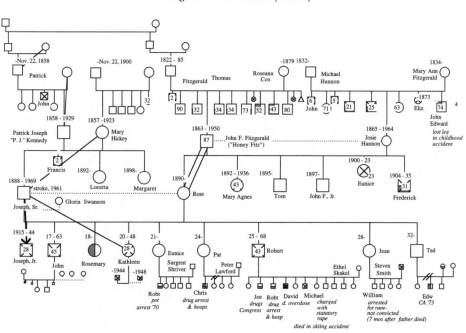

Critical Life Changes, Transitions, and Traumas

Critical life changes, transitions, and traumas can have a dramatic impact on a family system and its members. Our own experience has led us to pay particular attention to the impact of losses (see bibliography on Loss). Families are much more likely to have difficulty readjusting after a loss than after other family changes. We have already seen the impact that John Bateson's death had on Martin Bateson, who shot himself four years later. Both deaths had an impact on the youngest brother, Gregory. As Bateson's biographer notes, "Gregory had grown up unnoticed. His had been a vicarious, hand-me-down sort of youth. In part he had felt John and Martin were more able. . . . Death now made Gregory sole heir to an ambiguous intellectual heritage in the natural sciences—personified by his father—and made him a central member of his family" (Lipset, 1980, p. 90).

The Kennedy family has had more than its share of traumas and losses, as can be seen in Genogram 2.24. What is most striking about this family is the extraordinary number of premature deaths or tragedies. Four of the nine Kennedy children, as well as the spouse and the fiancé of one of them, died before middle age; John had been previously given up for dead on at least three occasions; Rosemary had a lobotomy in her twenties; Kathleen and her fiancé were killed taking a dangerous plane ride just after a cut-off from her mother; and Ted broke his back in a plane crash (seven months after John was shot) and

Genogram 2.25 Kennedy family: The next generation

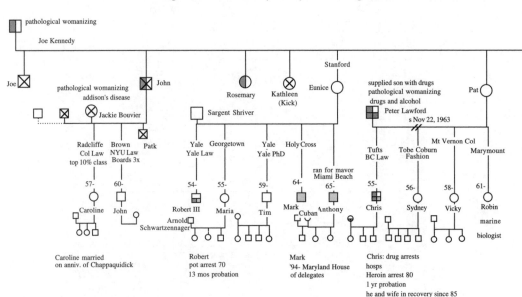

was involved in an accident at Chappaquidick in which one person drowned (12 months after Robert was killed). Two grandchildren were responsible for car accidents in which someone was permanently paralyzed or seriously injured.

Often, critical life events in a family will send ripples throughout the family system, having an impact on the family in many different ways. This certainly seems to be the case in the Kennedy family following the assassinations of John and Robert. In addition to Ted's accidents mentioned above, Pat separated from her husband on the day of Jack's assassination. Of the 29 grandchildren (Genogram 2.25), one died of an overdose of drugs, one lost a leg through cancer, one died in a skiing accident, two were accused of rape or statutory rape, and at least four others have had drug arrests and/or psychiatric hospitalizations. This group includes four of the six oldest sons, perhaps suggesting the importance of sons and the pressures on the oldest in this family.

That traumatic pattern was also characteristic of Rose Kennedy's own family of origin (Genogram 2.24). In her father's family only three out of 12 siblings survived in good health. The only two daughters died in infancy, as did the eldest son. Five others had severe alcohol problems and the other son had brain damage from malaria and barely functioned. On her mother's side, out of nine siblings, two sons died of childhood illnesses, one had his leg crushed by a train in childhood, two others died very early of alcoholism, and most tragic of all, the youngest daughter and her friend drowned, while Rose's mother, Josie,

---

Genogram 2.25 Kennedy family: The next generation

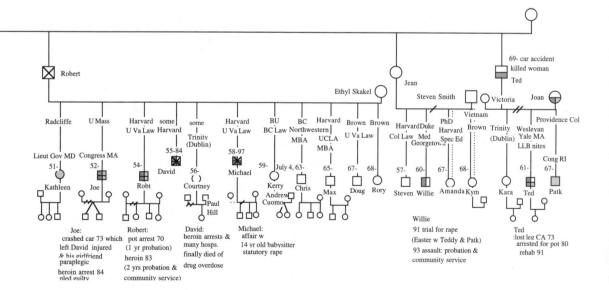

who was only eight herself, was supposed to be watching them. The devastating loss any family naturally would feel about the death of a child was compounded by a complex web of guilt and self-reproach that they—Josie in particular—had contributed to the death by failing to protect the children adequately (McGoldrick, 1995).

There were at least two coincidences of the type mentioned above in the Kennedy family. Ted Kennedy had two life-threatening traumas. Both events took place within the year following the death of his brothers: John in 1963 and Robert in 1968. While such events could be totally unrelated, research has shown that stressful life events increase one's susceptibility to accidents (Holmes & Rahe, 1967; Holmes & Masuda, 1974).

The Roosevelt family (Genogram 2.26) provides an example of a family that experienced multiple traumatic losses at a critical time in a child's (Eleanor's) development. The time of Eleanor's birth was a hard one for her father's family. Her paternal grandmother had died a few months earlier on Valentine's Day, and on the same night in the same house, Theodore Roosevelt's wife Alice died giving birth to a daughter Alice. (Alice grew up to be deeply resentful of Eleanor for having gotten their cousin Franklin to marry her.) During Eleanor's early years, her father's drinking and hospitalizations, as well as her parents' separation, were traumatic for her. Her brother died when she was five, her mother died when she was eight, and her father died when she was nine.

Genogram 2.26   Theodore Roosevelt's family: Multiple traumatic losses

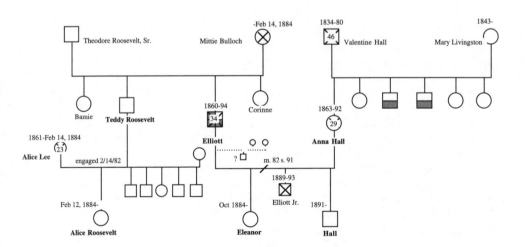

Seeing so many tragic events on the genogram leads us to speculate about the impact these events had on Eleanor's later development. Sometimes those born around the loss of grandparents may be more vulnerable to later dysfunction, especially if they become the special focus of parental attention. Eleanor's experiences instead seemed to strengthen her resilence, while at the same time making her more sensitive to the tragedy of others. Eleanor later discussed having an awkward, isolated adolescence and a strong desire to have a family of her own to make up for the one she lost. This she was able to do when she met Franklin Roosevelt. Perhaps her early experience of loss and isolation propelled her to reach out to the world as she became an internationally known figure.

Tracking the impact of family events must occur within the context of normative expectations (Carter & McGoldrick, 1998a; Gerson, 1995; Walsh, 1994, 1995). The ages and family structure at the time of the event are important to consider. For instance, how children are affected by a critical event such as a loss of a parent depends on their level of emotional and cognitive development. An older child will have a different experience than a younger child. For example, Eleanor Roosevelt, as the oldest, took on a good deal of responsibility for her younger brother after her parents died.

Particularly traumatic for a family is the death of an infant or a young child. In preparing the genograms of famous people, we noticed that quite a few were born shortly before or after the death of a sibling: Beethoven, Ben Franklin, Sigmund Freud, Henry Ford, Thomas Jefferson, C. G. Jung, Franz Kafka, Gustav Mahler, Eugene O'Neill, and Harry Stack Sullivan. One might attribute this solely to the higher child mortality rates of the past or speculate that the death of a child makes the surviving child even more "special" to the parents. In any case, their siblings were less likely to have the same connection to a loss.

Finally, a "good" event can also have a powerful impact on a family. In fact, in many of the families we studied, the fame of one individual had profound repercussions for other members of the family. Not only was privacy often lost, but the children in the next generation also had a difficult legacy—a tough act to follow. Martin, the son of Sigmund Freud, said it well: "I have never had any ambition to rise to eminence. . . . I have been quite happy and content to bask in reflected glory. . . . The son of a genius remains the son of a genius, and his chances of winning human approval of anything he may do hardly exist if he attempts to make any claim to fame detached from that of his father" (Wallechinsky & Wallace, 1975, p. 948). This has not, however, stopped many from trying!

Anniversary Reactions

Certain so-called coincidences can be understood as anniversary reactions, i.e., family members react to the fact that the date is the anniversary of some critical or traumatic event. For example, a family member might become depressed at the same time each year around the date when a parent or sibling died, even though he or she often makes no conscious connection. This appears to have been the case in the suicide of Martin Bateson, who killed himself on his dead brother's birthday. Possibly this anniversary intensified his plight and feeling of loss to the point of suicide.

Both Thomas Jefferson and John Adams died on the 50th anniversary of the signing of the Declaration of Independence, July 4, 1826. It was almost as if both of them waited until that anniversary to die. An event occurring on the anniversary of another event can intensify the meaning of both events.

One of the best documented examples of an anniversary reaction is that of George Engel (1975), a noted psychiatrist and internist who has written in detail about his own anniversary reactions following the fatal heart attack of his twin brother. The temporal connections become evident on the genogram shown in Genogram 2.27. Engel suffered a serious heart attack one year minus one day after the death of his twin, seemingly responding to the stress of the anniversary. Engel reports experiencing another type of anniversary reaction, an anniversary of age rather than date. Engel's father died of a heart attack at the age of 58. As Engel approached this age, he found himself becoming more anxious. He reports repeatedly misremembering his father's age at his death, fearing he would die at the same age. His experience led him to explore the psychological components of such family experiences and the mystifying way families often dissociate themselves from such emotional processes, e.g., forgetting the day or the year of significant events.

In other words, a type of anniversary reaction may be set up for corre-

---

Genogram 2.27 George Engel: Anniversary reaction

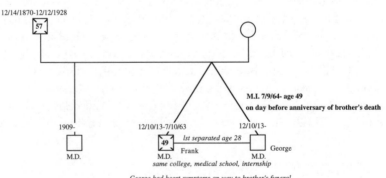

sponding events in the next generation of the family's life cycle. That is, as family members reach a certain point in the life cycle, they may expect the same thing to happen as happened at that point in the previous generation. For example, if a man's father cut off from his father when he left home, and then the man did the same with his father, he may expect his son to cut off when he reaches young adulthood. Another example is a family in which the death of a key family member has followed shortly after a marriage for two generations. That particular life cycle transition will probably become a toxic point for the next generation, with members consciously or unconsciously fearing to repeat the events yet again.

Thus, it is important to scan the genogram not only for coincidences in time, but in date, age, and point in the family life cycle. Such coincidences point to the interconnectedness of events and the impact of change on family functioning. Once these are recognized, the family can be warned of the potency of particular anniversary reactions.

Locating the Family in Historical Time: Social, Economic, and Political Events

Of course, family events do not occur in a vacuum. Family development must always be viewed against the background of its historical context, that is, the social, economic, and political events that have influenced the well-being of the family. These include war, migration, economic depression, etc. It is important to connect the family events that appear on the genogram to the context in which they occur (Cohler, Hosteler, & Boxer, 1998; Elder, 1977, 1986, 1992).

It is important not only to track important family events, but also to locate the family's development in historical time. For example, a suicide in 1929 might suggest certain hypotheses, such as a crisis related to the stock market crash; a marriage in 1941 might suggest other historical circumstances that would influence the couple's relationship, such as the husband's absence because of World War II. Men who came of age during the Vietnam war, whether they participated in the war or not, were profoundly affected by the ethos of that era.

It would be impossible to understand the families of Frida Kahlo and Diego Rivera (Genogram 5.5) apart from the politics and culture of the era in which they lived. Frida's father was a Hungarian Jew who migrated to Germany and then to Mexico, where he married first a Mexican woman and then a woman of half Mexican Indian and half Spanish origin. Frida Kahlo so identified herself with her political era that she used to say she had been born in 1910, the year of the Mexican revolution, although in reality she was born three years earlier. But her life was fully caught up in the sociopolitical struggles of her culture and times, as her work reflects.

Many of the later tragic events in the Kennedy family, of course, took place against the backdrop of the historical and political era in which the family played such an important role. On a private level, the deaths of John and Robert were a tremendous loss for their families, but these tragic assassinations of two important leaders were also shared by the whole nation. It is likely that this merging of the private and personal experience of the family with the public historical experience of the Vietnam era had a profound impact on the Kennedy's family adjustment to its loss, as shown by the next generation's evident difficulties.

Migration is another event that has great impact on a family (see bibliography section on Migration). It is important to evaluate sibling relationships, for example, in the context of the timing of a family's migration. A family that migrates in the middle of the mother's child-bearing years may have two different sets of children, those born before and those born after the migration. The children born after the migration may have been raised in a much more hopeful context or, on the other hand, in a much more economically disadvantaged situation, as happened with many of the children from the first wave of the Cuban migration to the U.S. in the late fifties.

Maria Callas (Genogram 2.28) is an example of a child who was the first child born after migration. The immigration appeared to have a major impact on the Callas family. Maria's parents had precipitously left Greece shortly before her birth because an older brother had died of typhoid fever. In the new coun-

Genogram 2.28 Maria Callas: Immigration child

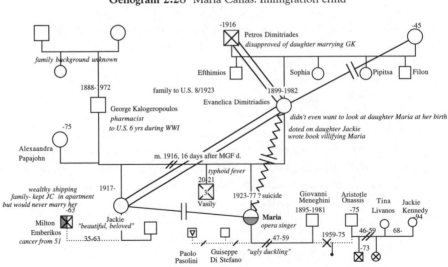

try they did not know the language and their adjustment was stressed further by the separation from their family and country. Under the circumstances, Maria's father focused all his energy on making a living and her mother focused her energy on the most recently born child, Maria. Maria became a "special" child to her mother in part because her birth coincided with the stresses of the migration experience, in addition to the loss of their son shortly before.

In the Blackwell family, discussed earlier (Genogram 2.18), only the youngest child, George Washington Blackwell, was born after the family's migration from England to the U.S. And, according to the information we have on the family, he was the only sibling not bound by the family's moralistic ideals and not involved in reform activities. Instead he was a pragmatic, financially successful businessman, who became the investment manager for the rest of the family (Horn, 1980, pp. 138-9).

Complex Genograms

Since genograms can become very complex, there is no set of rules that will cover all contingencies. Let us show some of the ways we have dealt with a few common problems. First, it helps to plan ahead. Obviously, if three-fourths of the page is filled with the father's three siblings, a problem will emerge when it is discovered that the mother is the youngest of 12. It helps to get an overview of the number of siblings and marriages in the parental generation before starting. The following questions will help in anticipating complexities and planning the graphic from the start:

- How many times was each parent married?
- How many siblings did each parent have and where was he or she in the birth order?

For example, in mapping the structure of Jane Fonda's family of origin, the basic framework might look like Genogram 2.15. The genogram shows Jane's parents and grandparents. Each of her parents had previous marriages and her father, Henry, had subsequent marriages. The other marriages are shown to the side of each parent and are dated to indicate the order.

Generally, the index person is the focal point of the genogram and details about others are shown as they relate to this person. The complexity of the genogram will thus depend on the depth and breadth of the information included. For example, if we were to include Jane's nuclear family, more detail on her mother's, father's, and siblings' various marriages, as well as the patterns of suicides, psychiatric hospitalizations and traumatic events, the genogram might look something like Genogram 2.16. This complex and crowded genogram reveals such important details as:

- Multiple marriages are common in this family.
- Henry Fonda's first two wives committed suicide.
- Henry Fonda separated from his second wife, Jane's mother, only a few months before she committed suicide. He had already started a relationship with his future third wife, Susan Blanchard, whom he married eight months later.
- During the honeymoon of Henry's third marriage, Peter Fonda shot himself and nearly died.
- Henry Fonda had two close friends who committed suicide, as did Peter's "secret love" Bridget Hayward in 1960, 10 months after her mother, Henry Fonda's first wife.
- In 1965 Peter's best friend committed suicide, his father married for the fifth time, and his sisters Pan and Jane both married for the first time.

Nevertheless, there are limits to what the genogram can show, particularly regarding complex relationships and multiple marriages. Sometimes, in order to highlight certain points, the arrangement must be reorganized. For example, the Fonda family genogram has been arranged to highlight the marriage of Henry Fonda and Frances Seymour Fonda as parents of Jane and Peter. Henry was actually married five times. His first wife, Margaret Sullavan, was married four times; Henry was her second husband. Margaret's third husband, Leland Hayward (who was also Henry Fonda's agent), was married five times, including twice to the same wife. Some of the spouses were married numerous times as well. At a certain point this kind of complexity becomes impossible to depict on a genogram.

Some complex family situations may require more than one genogram. Genograms are necessarily schematic and cannot detail all the vicissitudes of a family's history. For example, the Fonda genogram does not include the following information.

- Frances Seymour Fonda was in a mental hospital when she killed herself. Peter's close friend, Bill Hayward, was hospitalized for four years at the Menninger Clinic as a young adult, which had a strong influence on Peter, who feared mental illness for years. A woman with whom Peter had an affair (Tahlita Getty) later committed suicide as well.
- Henry Fonda's first wife, Margaret Sullavan, lived very near the Fonda family in California with her third husband, Leland Hayward, Fonda's agent. After she separated from Leland Hayward, she moved with her children to Connecticut, where she again lived very near the Fondas. Peter Fonda's first wife later married his former agent!
- Jane Fonda and Brook Hayward, Margaret's daughter, were best friends growing up and hoped that their parents would reunite.

- Jane found out about her mother's death in a movie magazine. Peter didn't learn for five years that her death was a suicide. He learned this the same week that he learned that his much loved stepmother was separating from his father. Not until ten years later did Peter learn that his mother's death had occurred in a mental hospital.
- Henry reportedly never discussed his wife's suicide with Peter or Jane.
- Henry Fonda and his mother-in-law held a private funeral for Jane's mother, which only the two of them attended. Henry went on stage that same night.
- Although Peter shot himself in the stomach during his father's honeymoon, eight months after his mother's suicide, Henry never asked him if he was upset about his mother's death, which Peter had been told was due to a heart attack.
- During Henry Fonda's fourth honeymoon in 1957, Peter became so troubled that his boarding school asked him to leave. His sister sent him to his aunt's in Nebraska. She arranged for him to get psychiatric treatment.
- Just after Henry Fonda's fifth honeymoon in 1965, Peter was involved in a drug arrest. His trial ended in a hung jury.
- For years, Peter Fonda kept the gun his friend Stormy, who committed suicide in 1965, had given him. He finally gave it to his therapist in 1972, feeling suicidal and not wanting to use it.
- Peter had certain extremely important resources growing up, including his sister Jane, though she thought she had been very mean to him; his aunt Harriet, who saved him at several critical times; Harriet's husband, his uncle Jack, whose smile was "like Santa Claus"; his first stepmother, Susan Blanchard, with whom he has stayed close all his life; his half-sister Pan, who was his godmother and a support from a distance; and several teachers and therapists.

It is clear that Fonda family members have been greatly influenced by suicides and remarriages and that the Hayward and Fonda families were closely intertwined. Perhaps the extraordinary strength and force of personality that Peter and Jane have shown in their careers reflect the many traumas they managed to overcome in their childhood. Furthermore, the relationship Jane and Ted Turner (Genogram 2.17) have developed, however successful in the long run, would indicate another coming together of resourceful people who have worked hard to transform and reinvent themselves and their lives many times in the face of suicides and other traumas.

Given the toxicity of suicide, the most traumatic of all deaths, the relevant facts surrounding the suicides would be critical to an understanding of the

Fonda family. Such additional family information should be noted on a family chronology or, where possible, indicated on the genogram.

Multiple Marriages and Intermarriages: Richly Cross-Joined Families

Other problems arise where there are multiple intermarriages in the family, e.g., cousins or stepsiblings marrying. There comes a point when the clinician must resort to multiple pages or special notes on the genogram to clarify these complexities. Sometimes a genogram may be confusing because of the multiple connections between family members, as when two members of one family marry two members of another [see Freud (Genogram 2.14), Einstein (Genogram 3.15), Kennedy (Genograms 2.24, 2.25), and Roosevelt (Genogram 3.10)]. The British Royal family provides one of the most challenging examples of this, and soon becomes so complex it cannot be shown on one page. It has been said that everyone on earth is connected within "six degrees of separation," that is, that within six connections each person becomes connected to each other. Indeed, we know that the Fondas are connected to the Adams family and to Henry VIII, as well as to the Churchills.

The multiple connections of the royal families of Europe would be impossible to indicate on one genogram. The suggestion is that the Windsors are even connected to Pushkin through Prince Philip's uncle George's wife, to the Nehru family (Genogram 3.9) and the Robeson family (Genogram 3.7), through Edwina Montbatten, Prince Philip's uncle's wife. They are reputed to be connected to the Bouvier family, through Lee Bouvier Radziwell's first husband Michael Canfield (Genogram 2.5), which would connect them to the Kennedy family. It is also said that Mia Farrow and, therefore, Woody Allen are connected to the Windsors through Edward VII, Queen Victoria's philandering son, who was reputed to be Mia's paternal grandfather (Genogram 2.9). Creating a genogram to show just the British Royal family (which appears to be mostly German) since the time of Queen Victoria, including all the immediate royal connections, proved quite a challenge (Genogram 2.29).

Children Raised in Multiple Households

Genograms may become complex when children have been adopted or raised in a number of different households, or where children have shifted residences many times to foster homes or to various relatives or friends, as in Genogram 2.30, which shows Peter Fonda's 11 living constellations from the time he was born until he reached adulthood. It is useful to make the genogram show as much of the information on the transitions and relationships as possible. Yet many situations are very complicated. In such cases let practicality and possi-

Genogram 2.29 The Windsors (after Victoria and Albert)

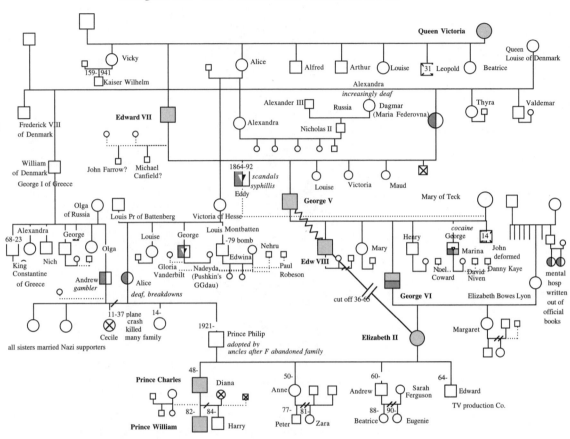

bility be your guides. Sometimes the only feasible way to clarify where children were raised is to take chronological notes on each child.

Missing Information

Of key interest in developing genograms is the missing information. Why does a person know nothing about his father? Why are aunts and uncles omitted from the mother's side? What does missing information tell us about cut-offs, conflicts, or painful losses in a family? Often, filling in the missing information can lead to opening up new options for the client in terms of potential resources and clarification of the family drama that has eluded understanding. In the Fonda family, for example, in spite of scanning many biographies on Peter, Jane, and Henry, it was actually impossible to do even a minimal nuclear family

Genogram 2.30 Peter Fonda's living situations before adulthood

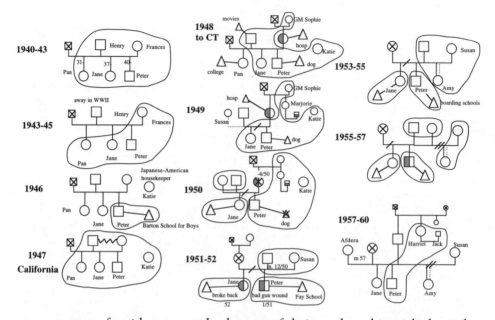

genogram for either parent. In the case of their mother, this might be under-
standable because of her mental illness and early death, although surely her history must have profoundly affected all her siblings, and their children as well.
Yet, as far as could be ascertained, Frances' father, her siblings, and Henry's siblings did not even attend her funeral, even though two of them were involved
in the lives of the children! Although Henry's sister Harriet and her husband
Jack played a critical role in Peter's life, as mentors, guardian angels, and
parental replacements when Henry and his wives were inaccessible, the other
sister, Jayne, is almost never mentioned. Nevertheless, if one were trying to
help Peter or Jane learn about their history, this aunt (and potentially her husband and children) would be key resources. Peter writes about his inability to
learn the truth of his family history, which had been "sanitized" over the generations, and which he felt blocked from discovering, though he was sure there
were explanations there for the mystifying experiences he had growing up. He
says about going to live with his aunt Harriet at age 20, "I wanted to say good-
bye to the dark, silent, booby-trapped thing that had been my 'family'" (Fonda,
1998, p. 133). Of his father's seemingly inaccessible history he says, "Things
happened to him that we will never know. He was never beaten. But something
happened to him that made him very quiet, very shy, and he let those qualities
define his personality. They were the makeup and costume that he wore in real
life. Somewhere, he found it was easier to say nothing. Easier on his heart, I

mean. . . . The deeper the emotion, the deeper he hid it. I say more about our father, because I know more about him. But I'll never know enough" (p. 496). Discussing his difficulty learning his family history he says:

> Such deafening privacy extended to my mother's family, of course. All I knew of my maternal grandparents—and they were both alive until I was in my late twenties—is that my grandfather was a debilitated (and debilitating) alcoholic, who would come home some nights completely blasted, and mow the lawns, stumbling around and screaming invectives at the injustices of civilized people. My grandmother was patient to a fault with him, as she was with us during the years of our mother's gradual disappearance. . . . I doubt I would believe a story told me by any remaining elder from either side. Too much time has passed, with too much opportunity to revise and sanitize the truth, and I hardly want to bother Harriet with my questions, now that she's in her nineties. My father's autobiography, as told to someone else, was full of so much sanitation that it had little base in reality. . . . Dad was too shy, too intensely private, to truly expose the part of his history that mattered to him. (p. 116)

From a systems perspective, one might help Peter do a genogram and explore in detail the missing information (some of which could, of course, be recovered through genealogical sources), to try to break through the "sanitized" versions. Such missing information often becomes the very focus of clinical investigation, since it is precisely what has been left out of the story that is central to understanding the participants. As one of Nabokov's characters once put it: "Remember that what you are told is really threefold, told first by the teller, retold by the listener, and concealed from them both by the deadman of the tale."

Discrepancies

Finally, there may be a problem with discrepant information. For example, what happens if three different family members give different dates for a death or conflicting descriptions of family relationships? It is best to note important discrepancies whenever possible. Genogram 2.31 shows the discrepancies about Bill Clinton's parenthood. His mother, Virginia Clinton, said he was the son of her first husband, Bill Blythe, Jr., for whom he was named, and who died in a car accident before Bill was born. Virginia said her husband returned from the service in November 1945, but his military records say he was discharged from the army on December 7, making it unlikely that he could have fathered Bill, and thus there is a question about Clinton's actual parentage. Bill Blythe was apparently a mysterious charmer; he was constantly reinventing himself, and there are many discrepancies about his life. Even his birthdate is open to question. His family said

Genogram 2.31 Discrepancy about Bill Clinton's father

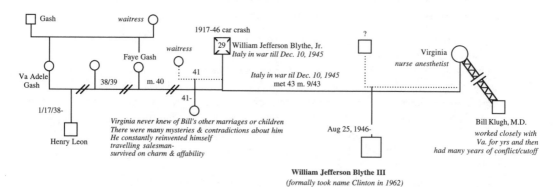

William Jefferson Blythe III
(formally took name Clinton in 1962)

he was born February 27, 1918; his military records say he was born February 21, 1917. His wife, Virginia, said she met him when he was passing through Shreveport, but military records show he had been there for two months before they met. He did not tell Virginia that he had married in December 1935 and filed divorce papers the following year, or that a birth certificate for a son, Henry Leon Blythe, was filed on January 17, 1938. Nor did she know that he was married again on August 11, 1938, and divorced a second time nine months later by a judge's ruling listing "extreme cruelty and gross neglect of duty" (Maraniss, 1995). Virginia also did not know about a third marriage in 1940 to his first wife's younger sister, apparently to avoid marrying a fourth woman who claimed to be pregnant with his baby. There is even another birth certificate, filed in Kansas City in 1941, for a daughter, born to a Missouri waitress, to whom he may also have been married. Indeed, living with conflicts over discrepancies, as the U.S. has done with President Clinton, seems to have a long history in his family.

Not only did Bill Blythe live by reinventing himself with new versions of his history, covering over the discrepancies and contradictions, but Virginia Kelley Clinton had conflicts in her workplace and community for years over her actions as a nurse anesthetist, and suits brought against her regarding the death of two patients. There were accusations and counter-charges over her behavior, and on her part over the behavior of others with whom she had worked. She held on for years but was eventually pressured out of her job. The conflicts, which are very hard to get clear, caused great turmoil for many years. Virginia's father also always denied that he was in the illegal liquor business with her second husband, Roger Clinton, although he was. And he always denied his wife's continuous accusations of marital infidelity. The mysteries and discrepancies over the facts in their family are numerous, and yet the family remained very closely connected over the years (see Genogram 3.2).

So many discrepancies in a family are extreme, but discrepancies are common and need to be indicated somehow on a genogram, where their implications might have emotional significance for the family. Bradt (1980) has suggested using color-coded genograms to distinguish the source of information.

In sum, large, complex families with multiple marriages, intertwined relationships, many transitions and shifts, and/or multiple perspectives challenge the skill and ingenuity of the clinician trying to draw a genogram within a finite space. Improvisation and additional pages are often needed.

The Genogram Interview

The Family Information Net

The process of gathering family information can be thought of as casting out an information net in larger and larger circles to capture relevant information about the family and its broader context. The net spreads out in a number of different directions:

- from the presenting problem to the larger context of the problem;
- from the immediate household to the extended family and broader social systems;
- from the present family situation to a chronology of historical family events;
- from easy, nonthreatening queries to difficult, anxiety-provoking questions;
- from obvious facts to judgments about functioning and relationships to hypothesized family patterns;

The Presenting Problem and the Immediate Household

In family medicine, genogram information is often recorded as it emerges in office visits. In family therapy, family members usually come with specific problems, which are the clinician's starting point. At the outset, families are told that some basic information about them is needed to fully understand the problem. Such information usually grows naturally out of exploring the presenting problem and its impact on the immediate household. It makes sense to start with the immediate family, and the context in which the problem occurs:

- Who lives in the household?
- How is each person related?
- Where do other family members live?

The clinician asks the name, age, gender, and occupation of each person in the household in order to sketch the immediate family structure. Other revealing information is elicited through inquiring about the problem:

- Which family members know about the problem?
- How does each view it? And how has each of them responded?
- Has anyone in the family ever had similar problems?
- What solutions were attempted by whom in those situations?
- When did the problem begin? Who noticed it first? Who is most concerned about the problem? Who the least?
- Were family relationships different before the problem began? What other problems existed?
- Does the family see the problem as having changed? In what ways? For better or for worse?

This is also a good time to inquire about previous efforts to get help for the problem, including previous treatment, therapists, hospitalizations, and the current referring person.

The Current Situation

Next the clinician spreads the information net into the current family situation. This line of questioning usually follows naturally from questions about the problem and who is involved:

- What has been happening recently in your family?
- Have there been any recent changes in the family (e.g., people coming or leaving, illnesses, job problems)?

It is important to inquire about recent life cycle transitions as well as anticipated changes in the family situation (especially exits and entrances of family members—births, marriages, divorces, deaths, or the departure of family members).

The Wider Family Context

The clinician looks for an opportunity to explore the wider family context by asking about the extended family and cultural background of all the adults involved. The interviewer might move into this area by saying, "I would now like to ask you something about your background to help make sense of your present problem."

Dealing with a Family's Resistance to Doing a Genogram

When family members react negatively to questions about the extended family or complain that such matters are irrelevant, it often makes sense to redirect the focus back to the immediate situation, until the connections between the present situation and other family relationships or experiences can be established. An example of such a genogram assessment for a remarried family whose teenage daughter's behavior was the presenting problem has been produced in the videotape *The Legacy of Unresolved Loss* (available from Norton). This tape also illustrates how to deal with a family's resistance to revealing genogram information. Gentle persistence over time will usually result in obtaining the information and demonstrating its relevance to the family.

The clinician inquires about each side of the family separately, beginning, for example, with the mother's side:

- Let's begin with your mother's family. Your mother was which one of how many children?
- When and where was she born?
- Is she alive?
- If not, when did she die? What was the cause of her death?
- If alive, where is she now?
- What does she do?
- Is she retired? When did this happen?
- When and how did your mother meet your father? When did they marry?
- Had she been married before? If so, when? Did she have children by that marriage? Did they separate or divorce or did the spouse die? If so, when was that?

And so on. In like fashion, questions are asked about the father. Then the clinician might ask about each parent's family of origin, i.e., father, mother, and siblings. The goal is to get information about at least three or four generations, including grandparents, parents, aunts, uncles, siblings, spouses, and children of the IP.

Ethnic and Cultural History

It is essential to learn something about the family's socioeconomic, political, and cultural background in order to place presenting problems and current relationships in context. When the questioning expands to the extended family, it is a good point to begin exploring issues of ethnicity, since the birthplace of the grandparents has now been established. Exploring ethnicity and migration history helps establish the cultural context in which the family is operating and offers the therapist an opportunity to validate family attitudes and behaviors determined by such influences. It is important to learn what the family's cultural traditions are about problems, health care and healing, and where the current family members stand in relation to those traditional values. It is also important to consider the family's cultural expectations about relationships with health care professionals, since this will set the tone for their clinical responses.

Furthermore, class differences among family members or between family members and the health care professional may create discomfort, which will need to be attended to in the meeting. Questions to ascertain class assumptions pertain not just to the family's current income but to cultural background, education, and social status within their community. Once the clinician has a clear picture of the ethnic and cultural factors influencing a family (and hopefully keeping his or her own biases in check), it is possible to raise delicate questions geared to helping families identify any behaviors that—while culturally sanctioned—may be keeping them stuck (see McGoldrick et al., 1996).

The Informal Kinship Network

The information net extends beyond the biological and legal structure of the family to encompass common law and cohabiting relationships, miscarriages, abortions, stillborns, foster and adopted children, and anyone else in the informal network of the family who is an important support. Inquiries are made about godparents, teachers, neighbors, friends, parents of friends, clergy, caretakers, doctors, etc., who are or have been important to the functioning of the family, and this information is also included on the genogram. In exploring outside supports for the family, the clinician might ask:

- To whom could you turn if in need of financial, emotional, physical, and spiritual help?
- What roles have outside people played in your family?
- What is your relationship to your community?
- Who outside the family has been important in your life?
- Did you ever have a nanny or caretaker or babysitter to whom you felt attached? What became of her or him?
- Has anyone else ever lived with your family? When? Where are they now?
- What has been your family's experience with doctors and other helping professionals or agencies?

For particular clients certain additional questions are appropriate. For example, the following questions would be important in working with gay and lesbian clients (see Burke & Faber, 1997; Laird, 1996; Scrivner & Eldridge, 1995; Shernoff, 1984; Slater, 1995).

- Who was the first person you told about your sexual orientation?
- To whom on your genogram are you out?

- To whom would you most like to come out?
- Who would be especially easy or difficult to come out to?

Tracking Family Process

Tracking shifts that occurred around births, deaths, and other transitions can lead the clinician to hypotheses about the family's adaptive style. Particularly critical are untimely or traumatic deaths and the deaths of pivotal family members. We look for specific patterns of adaptation or rigidification following such transitions. Assessment of past adaptive patterns, particularly after losses and other critical transitions, may be crucial in helping a family in the current crisis. A family's past and the relationship family members have to it provide important clues about family rules, expectations, patterns of organization, strengths, resources, and sources of resilience (Walsh, 1998).

The history of specific problems should also be investigated in detail. The focus should be on how family patterns have changed at different periods: before the problem began, at the time of the problem's onset, at the time of first seeking help, and at present. Specific genograms can be done for each of these time periods (computerized genograms, which can be generated for any given date can be enormously helpful in this process—see Chapter 8). Asking how family members see the future of the problem is also informative.

Questions may include:

- What will happen in the family if the problem continues? If it goes away?
- What does the future look like? What changes do family members imagine are possible in the future?

Seeing the family in its historical perspective involves linking past, present, and future and noting the family's flexibility in adapting to changes.

During the mapping on the genogram of the nuclear and extended family and gathering of facts on different family members, the clinician also begins to make inquiries and judgments about the functioning, relationships, and roles of each person in the family. This involves going beyond the bare facts to clinical judgment and acumen. Inquiries about these issues can touch sensitive nerves in the family and should be made with care.

Difficult Questions about Individual Functioning

Assessment of individual functioning may or may not involve much clinical judgment. Alcohol abuse, chronic unemployment, and severe symptomatology are facts that directly indicate poor functioning. However, many family members may function well in some areas but not in others or may cover up their dysfunction. Often, it takes careful questioning to reveal the true level of functioning. A family member with a severe illness may show remarkable adaptive strengths and another may show fragility with little apparent stress. Questions about individual functioning may be difficult or painful for family members to answer and must be approached with sensitivity and tact. The family members should be warned that questions may be difficult and they should let the clinician know if there is an issue they would rather not discuss. The clinician will need to judge the degree of pressure to apply if the family resists questions that may be essential to dealing with the presenting problem.

Clinicians need to exercise extreme caution about when to ask questions that could put a family member in danger. For example, if violence is suspected, a wife should never be asked about her husband's behavior in his presence, since the question assumes she is free to respond, which is unlikely to be the case. It is clinicians' responsibility to take care that their questions do not put a client in jeopardy.

Serious Problems

- Has anyone in the family had a serious medical or psychological problem? Been depressed? Had anxieties? Fears? Lost control? Has there been physical or sexual abuse?
- Are there any other problems that worry you? When did that problem begin? Did you seek help for it? If so, when? What happened? What is the status of that problem now?

Work

- Have there been any recent job changes? Unemployment? Do you like your job? Who else works in your family? Do they like their work?

Finances

- How much income does each member generate? Does this create any imbalance in family relationships? How does the economic situation compare with that of your relatives?
- Is there any expected inheritance? Are there family members who are expected to need financial help or caretaking at some time?
- Are there any extraordinary expenses? Outstanding debts? What is the level of credit card debt?
- Who controls the money? How are spending decisions made? Are these patterns different from the ways money was handled in the families of origin?

Drugs and Alcohol

- Do any family members routinely use medication? What kind and for what?

- Who prescribed it? What is the family's relationship with that physician?
- Do you think any members drink too much or have a drug problem? Has anyone else ever thought so? What drugs? When? What has the family attempted to do about it?
- How does the person's behavior change under the influence of the drug? How does the behavior of others change when a member is drug involved?

Trouble with the Law

- Have any family members ever been arrested? For what? When? What was the result? What is that person's legal status now?
- Has anyone ever lost his or her driver's license?

Physical or Sexual Abuse

- Have you ever felt intimidated in your family? Have you or others ever been hit? Has anyone in your family ever been threatened with being hit? Have you ever threatened anyone else in your family or hit them?
- Have you or any other family members ever been sexually molested or touched inappropriately by a member of your family or someone outside your family? By whom?

Given that physical battering has been called the number one health problem for women in the United States (McGoldrick, Broken Nose, & Potenza, 1998), it is critical for clinicians to take extreme care in inquiring about power relationships in families. It is estimated that over the course of the life cycle, 11 to 21% of husbands are physically violent toward their wives, and the prevalence of sexual violence is estimated to be as high as 30% (Burge, 1989; Hamberger, Saundes, & Harvey, 1992; McCowley et al., 1995). Couple relationships have many dimensions, and abuse may be a part of any of these in a couple's relationship (Almeida, Messineo, Woods, & Font, 1998):

- *Economic:* continuum from shared responsibility and accountability to execution of control and threats.
- *Emotional:* continuum from communication, intimacy, to mind control and dependence.
- *Power arrangements:* continuum from partnership and equity to male privilege and dominance.
- *Physical power:* continuum from belief in sanctity of each individual to intimidation, abuse, and threats.
- *Boundaries around the couple in relation to all other connections:* (a) friends, (b) extended family, (c) work, (d) children, (e) religion. In each area the boundary may be flexible or tight and controlled by one partner.

- *Sexuality:* continuum from sexual intimacy to sexual objectification to rape and exploitation.
- *Child rearing:* continuum from shared parenting to view of this as solely one parent's, namely the woman's, responsibility.
- *Chores and leisure activities:* home care, food, priorities for vacation and leisure time: continuum from shared to defined as exclusively one spouse's responsibility or right.

The breadth, depth, and complexity of these dimensions give us a clue as to how carefully and thoroughly the clinician must proceed with his or her inquiries, since abuse is likely to be denied or minimized unless it is brought to the surface. We have found that in addition to the genogram, the Power Wheel (Figure 2.1), adapted by Almeida et al. (1998), is an extremely useful tool for assessing both violence and psychological abuse in the multiple domains of couple and family relationships. The wheel can be given to partners (in separate meetings) to help them the power dimensions of their relationship. The clinician might ask:

- Who is making the decisions?
- Who is managing the money?
- How are conflicts being resolved?
- What is each partner's attitude toward violence or intimidation in marriage?

Setting Priorities for Organizing Genogram Information

One of the most difficult aspects of genogram assessment remains setting priorities for inclusion of family information on a genogram. Clinicians cannot follow every lead the genogram interview suggests. Awareness of basic genogram patterns can help the clinician set such priorities. As a rule of thumb, the data are scanned for the following:

- Repetitive symptoms, relationship, or functioning patterns across the family and over the generations. Repeated triangles, coalitions, cut-offs, patterns of conflict, over- and under-functioning are central to genogram interpretation.
- Coincidences of dates: e.g., the death of one family member or anniversary of this death occurring at the same time as symptom onset in another, or the age at symptom onset coinciding with the age of problem development in another family member.
- The impact of change and untimely life cycle transitions: particularly changes in functioning and relationships that correspond with critical

family life events and untimely life cycle transitions, e.g., births, marriages, or deaths that occur "off schedule."

Awareness of possible patterns makes the clinician more sensitive to what is missing. Such missing information about important family members or events and discrepancies in the information offered frequently reflect charged emotional issues in the family. The clinician should take careful note of the connections family members make or fail to make to various events.

Figure 2.1 Power Wheel

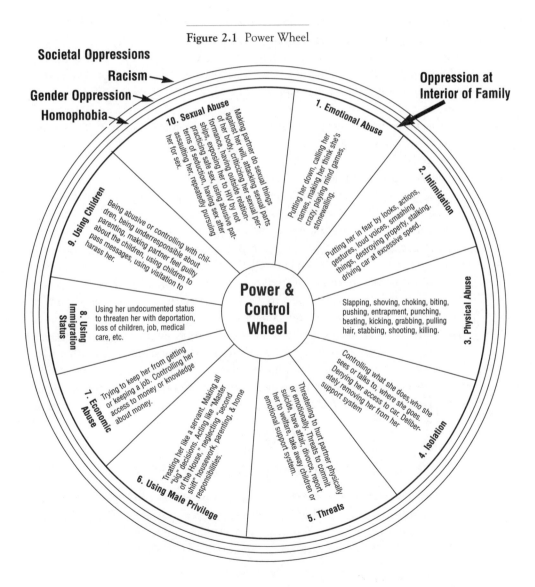

3

INTERPRETING FAMILY STRUCTURE FROM GENOGRAMS

By examining relational structure, family composition, sibling constellations, and various family configurations, clinicians can make many hypotheses about themes, roles, and relationships that can be checked out by eliciting further information about the family. The interpretive principles for evaluating genograms are based on the principles of family systems theory. For further elaboration of ideas outlined here, the reader is referred to literature on Bowen theory (see bibliography section on Assessment, Genograms, and Systems Theory) and sibling constellation (see bibliography on Siblings), as well as the writings of other family theorists who affirm the value of understanding family history in solving current problems.

The first area to explore on a genogram is the basic family structure, that is, the structural patterns revealed by the lines and symbols on the diagram. Examining this graphic structure allows us to make hypotheses about likely family issues, patterns, roles, and relationships based on normative expectations for household composition, sibling constellation, and unusual family configurations.

It is also common for family patterns to intensify when there is a repetition of structure from one generation to another. In particular, people in a similar structural pattern as the previous generation are likely to repeat the patterns of that generation. Thus, as we look for repetition of functioning and relationships, we also look for repetition of family structure. For example, a mother who is the youngest of three sisters will probably find herself overidentifying with her youngest if she also has three daughters. Or, if one comes from a family of three generations of separation and divorce, one's expectations may be that divorce is almost a norm.

Household Composition

One glance at the structure of the genogram usually tells the clinician the family's composition, i.e., whether there is a traditional nuclear family household, a single-parent household, a multi-household family, an extended family household, or a multi-family household.

Traditional Nuclear Family Household

The percent of U.S. households that are traditional nuclear families (a couple in their first marriage and their children) has been steadily declining; currently it is less than 25%. By itself, this family structure might not attract the clinician's attention. However, if the family is under severe stress or there is serious marital conflict, the clinician will want to explore what factors and strengths have helped to keep the family together and what additional resources may be needed or accessible, since such structures tend to be less flexible under stress than more extended family units. In addition, nuclear family structures can be expected to have certain predictable parent-child triangles, such as mothers joining with children in relation to the father, parents joining in relation to a "sick" or "bad" child, or children joining in relation to fighting parents.

Single-Parent Families

A single-parent household, in which only one parent is raising children, may be formed by a single parent bearing or adopting children or after the death, divorce, separation, or desertion of one of the parents. Seeing a single-parent structure on the genogram should cue the clinician to explore the reasons for single parenthood, the difficulties in raising children alone, economic problems, and available resources, such as extended family, godparents, and friends. Genogram 3.1 shows the first years of Bill Clinton's life with his mother, Virginia, who was 23 when he was born and lived as a single parent with her own parents. Newly widowed, with no real job skills and no money, she had few resources. Luckily, her parents were available, although the most common triangle of such three-generational households soon developed: The parent feels like an outsider living in the grandparents' household, while the grandparents develop a tight relationship with her child. As Virginia Clinton (1994) put it:

Genogram 3.1 Clinton: Living changes

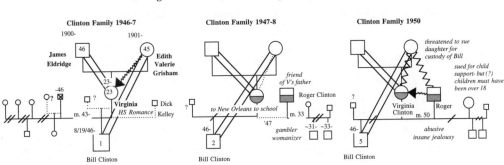

> Mother, meanwhile, was totally involved in showing me how mothering
> was done. She meant well, but I felt like a lowly student nurse again, . . .
> while. . . my mother played God. . . . When mother wasn't monopolizing
> him, I would take him out for a spin in his carriage. (pp. 61-63)

Virginia decided to spend the next year in New Orleans to finish school, leaving Bill at home with her parents. The relationship problems intensified, even
after she returned and was living at home again:

> Mother increasingly rubbed me the wrong way. I was 25, 26, even 27, and
> still living with my parents. It was a blessing, of course, that I had some-
> body to take care of Bill during the day. But there's always a price to be
> paid for such a service. Mother had already grown incredibly attached to
> Bill while I was in anesthetist school, and now, with me working, she still
> held sway over him. She would dress him and feed him and walk him and
> buy him things. Nothing was too fine or too expensive for her beloved
> grandson. (pp. 77-8)

Such problems are predictable in single-parent structures, and clinicians should
inquire about such typical patterns whenever they see them on a genogram.
Also of interest would be the impact on the family (particularly on the children) of the loss of the other parent and associated relational patterns and triangles. Often such households are part of larger multi-household networks,
sometimes called binuclear families (Ahrons, 1994) or multi-nuclear families,
in which children are part of several different family structures.

Remarried Families

When one or both parents remarry following a divorce or death, bringing a
stepparent into the household, a remarried family is formed. The children of
the previous marriages may all live in the same household, they may be divided among households, or they may move back and forth between households.

Remarried families have to deal with particular issues, such as custody, visitation, jealousy, favoritism, loyalty conflict, and stepparent or stepsibling problems. The clinician should also explore the impact of the divorce and remarriage on each family member and the relational patterns and triangles inherent
in this type of family situation. Genogram 3.2 shows some of the complications
of Bill Clinton's family. His father, William Jefferson Blythe, Jr., had been married several times before marrying Clinton's mother, Virginia Cassidy, though
she did not know about these previous marriages. She married William Blythe
in 1943. As mentioned earlier, there is question about whether he is actually
Bill Clinton's father, because he was away in the army until December 10, 1945,
and Bill was born, not prematurely, on August 19, 1946, two months after
William had died in an auto accident.

Genogram 3.2 Bill Clinton's Family

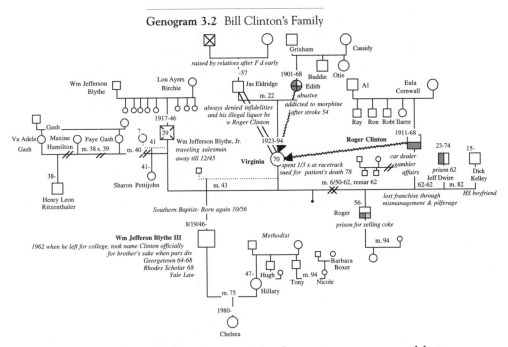

Clearly, it can be a challenge to map the fluctuating structure and living arrangements in such families. Virginia Cassidy married again in 1950, when Bill was four. Her second husband, Roger Clinton, had also been married before. Virginia Cassidy later divorced him, but then remarried him in 1968. In midlife Bill Clinton became aware that he had two other half-siblings from Bill Blythe's earlier relationships. (He has chosen not to connect with them.)

Extended Family Networks

Ethnic groups vary tremendously in their definitions of family (McGoldrick et al., 1996). It is important to attend to structures that include godparents or other kinship networks and to assess how the relationship patterns may be affected by these structures. Aunts, uncles, cousins, foster children, and housekeepers may be part of the household. Babysitters, close friends, or other "outsiders" who are especially important to the family often become members of the informal extended kinship network and should be included in the genogram.

A nuclear family may live with grandparents. This is particularly common for single parents where, for example, a mother might live with her mother for aid and support, as Virginia Blythe Clinton did (Genogram 3.1). With a three-generational household the clinician should explore issues around cross-generational boundaries, alliances, and conflicts, asking, for example, who does the parenting. In the case of Virginia Clinton, she had always adored her father but found her mother quite overpowering. Once she had her son, she seems to have let her mother run things and be his primary caretaker for the first couple of years, although she adored him and missed him when she was away studying.

The clinician should explore the roles and relationships of extended family members living in the household. Relationship issues will vary according to the individual's role and structural position in the family. A spouse's parent, brother, sister, aunt, uncle, or cousin may seem like an intruder to the other spouse, while a foster or adopted child is likely to become involved in predictable triangles as the special one or the problem one, depending on the child's own qualities and those of the host family. It is important to consider the reverberations in both the immediate and extended family caused by the entry of an extended family member or other person into the household.

Sibling Constellation

The importance of birth position, gender, and distance in age from other siblings has long been discussed in the literature, although there has not always been agreement on the role sibling constellation plays in development (see bibliography on Siblings). Many factors influence sibling patterns, including timing of a child's birth, sibling position, ethnicity, and life circumstances. In addition, in certain situations, such as chronic family disruption, siblings may become each other's main protector and resource. When Bill Clinton's parents divorced in 1962, Bill, who had never been adopted by his stepfather, decided to change his name officially. The change was not to connect with his abusive, alcoholic stepfather, whom his mother was just leaving, but in order to have the same name as his young half-brother, to whom he felt a deep loyalty and sense of protection.

At present, sibling patterns are undergoing significant changes, primarily because of the different child-bearing, child-rearing, and family structural patterns that have followed the increased availability of birth control, the women's movement, the entry of more women into the work force, and increased divorce and remarriage.

Sibling experiences vary greatly. An important factor is the amount of time brothers and sisters spend together when young. Two children who are close in age, particularly if they are of the same gender, generally spend a lot of time together. They share their parents' attention and are usually raised under similar conditions. Siblings born farther apart obviously spend less time with each other and have fewer shared experiences; they grow up in the family at different points in its evolution, and in many ways are like only children. In general, siblings who are more than six years apart are more like only children than like siblings, since they have gone through each phase of development separately (Toman, 1976). Jung (Genogram 2.19) is an example of a functional only child due to this factor. Since his older brother died before he was born and his sister was born nine years later, Jung's experience was probably more like an only child than a sibling.

In today's world of frequent divorce and remarriage, families often have a combination of siblings, stepsiblings, and half-siblings, who may live in different households and only come together occasionally. There are also more only children, whose closest sibling-like relationships will be their playmates. In addition, there are more two-child families than in previous generations, where the relationship between the two children tends to be more intense for the lack of other siblings. Clearly, the more time siblings have with one another, the more intense their relationships are likely to be. In large sibling groups, subgroups tend to form according to sex and distance in age. Two brothers born 18 months apart may form a dyad, and their two younger sisters born five and seven years later may form a second subsystem.

Siblings often come to rely on each other, especially where parents are unavailable or unable to provide for the nurturing needs of their children. From early childhood Jane and Peter Fonda had to fend much for themselves. They experienced the early emotional loss of both parents, then their mother's very traumatic suicide, and being shifted to multiple family and other constellations before adulthood. They became for each other the anchor in a traumatic and unstable world. From earliest childhood, Peter says, his father was away most of the time "and forgot or didn't notice that our mother increasingly spent time in her bedroom with the curtains drawn. . . . Jane and I pulled together. . . . We began to carve holes in the wall between our rooms so we could talk at night. We had (still have) our very secret word that we could whisper into our little holes" (Fonda, 1998, pp. 14-15). "Moving a family, uprooting and relocating, no matter how close or great the distance is one of the most stressful things in life. . . . I felt that Jane and I had been sent into exile from our Paradise, hauled along on some unspoken crusade of our parents" (p. 35). He says, "Jane became my savior. And though she says she hated me and treated me meanly, she was there for me at every critical moment. Sister and brother, brother and sister" (p. 39).

It was Jane who was there for him when at age 10 he shot and injured himself while his father was away on his honeymoon. It was Jane, then just starting college, who came for him when at 16 he was expelled from prep school and had no other guardian. He says of her "I really didn't have anyone else but Jane. She meant everything to me" (p. 54). He describes her importance in his life many years later: "I needed her approval as much as I needed anything. Jane had always been just slightly below Dad on the need-of-approval scale and as we were closer and more in touch with each other, her blessing was the more important one" (pp. 292-293).

At one crisis in her life, when she was over 50, Jane made Peter promise to spend five days alone with her. She said she needed to talk about their childhood together, to know all the little details he remembered, so she could try to put the crazy, broken pieces of the puzzle of their early life together, and she feared she might lose him before she could do it (p. 474).

Birth Order

Sibling position can have particular relevance for a person's emotional position in the family of origin and future relations with a spouse and children. For example, an oldest child is more likely to be overresponsible, conscientious, and parental, while the youngest is more likely to be child-like and carefree. Jane Fonda, two years older than her brother, was always the responsible child, following in her father's footsteps into acting at an early age, while Peter for many years played the role of rebel against authority. Often, oldest children will feel special and particularly responsible for maintaining the family's welfare or carrying on the family tradition. They may feel they have a heroic mission to fulfill in life. In addition, sometimes the oldest will resent younger siblings, feeling they are an intrusion on his or her earlier exclusive possession of the parents' love and attention. The oldest child's experience is very different from that of the youngest, while middle children may feel caught in between or have a need to find their niche and define themselves as different (Sulloway, 1996). Birth order can also profoundly influence later experiences with spouses, friends, and colleagues, though, of course, it does not guarantee a particular type of person. There are many other factors that influence sibling roles, such as temperament, disability, physical appearance, intelligence, talent, gender, and the timing of each birth in relation to other family experiences—deaths, moves, illnesses, and changes in financial status.

Twins

The ultimate shared sibling experience is between identical twins. Twins and other multiple births are becoming more common. About one person in 50 is a twin, although about one in eight pregnancies begins as twins (Wright, 1995). When one twin dies the other may experience lifelong guilt. They have a special relationship that is exclusive of the rest of the family. The grip twins hold on our imagination perhaps relates to the fact that their very existence challenges our sense of our own uniqueness (Wright, 1995). They have been known to develop their own language and maintain an uncanny, almost telepathic sense of each other. Even fraternal twins often have remarkable similarities, because of their shared life experiences.

The major challenge for twins is to develop individual identities. Since they do not have their own unique sibling position, there is a tendency for others to lump twins together; twins may have to go to extremes to distinguish themselves from each other.

Different Roles for Brothers and Sisters

Brothers and sisters generally have very different roles in the family. Because of our society's preference for sons, sisters of sisters tend to have very different sibling patterns than sisters of brothers. Indeed, the research indicates that, because of society's preference for boys, the segregation of boys and girls in their socialization is quite extreme from early childhood (Maccoby, 1990). In co-ed situations boys tend to ignore or mistreat girls, whose wishes do not get equal attention. If a brother is older, he is often favored and catered to. If the brother is younger, he may be envied and resented by the sister for his special status.

The example of Princess Diana, while particular to her family's situation, also reflects general gender problems that exist the world over (Genogram 3.3). She was the third daughter in a family whose status depended on producing a son who would become, on the death of his father, the seventh Earl of Althorp,

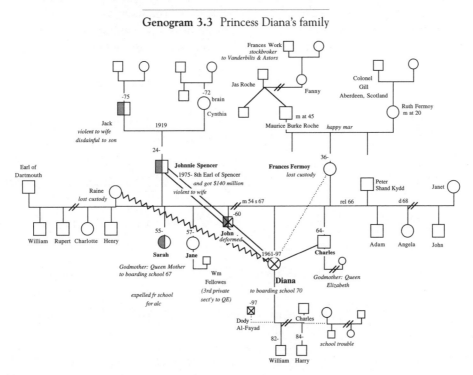

Genogram 3.3 Princess Diana's family

inheriting an estate worth about $140 million dollars. The parents were desperate for a son, since they would have to leave the family home if they did not have one. The one son they had had, born the year before Diana, had been deformed and died soon after birth. Indeed, the parents were so disappointed when she was born that they did not bother to register her birth, and she is the only one of her siblings who did not have a royal godparent. As Diana said, "I was a disappointment. My parents were hoping for a boy. They were so sure I'd be a boy they hadn't even thought of a (girl's) name for me." (Campbell, 1998, p. 1). Although she was finally given the name of the one ancestor who almost married into the royal family, her positon probably led to both her sense of inadequacy and her carefully cultivated aura of being special. As the third girl in a family that required a son and had just lost one, she would definitely need to be "different" to find a niche, and different she became. Her position was greatly relieved, of course, when her younger brother was born three years later. Indeed, he became, not surprisingly, her favorite (the more so because the parents divorced soon after) and the youngest two became each other's primary refuge, as we have just seen with Jane and Peter Fonda.

In early childhood, sisters are often caretakers of one another and of their brothers, as well as rivals and competitors for parental attention. Parents may, with the best of intentions, convey very different messages to their sons than to their daughters. Here, for example, is a description by Jackie Robinson, the remarkably versatile baseball player who integrated the sport, written about his daughter, Sharon, the middle child with two brothers (Genogram 3.4), and the role of his wife, Rachel, who had had the same sibling constellation.

Genogram 3.4 Robinson family

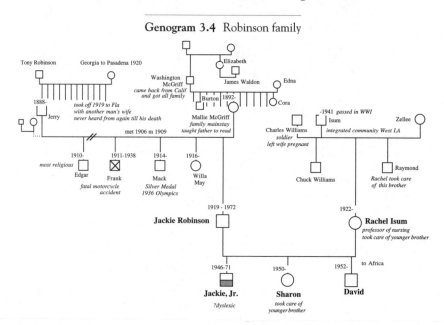

> She was just such an ideal and perfect child in our eyes and in the opinion of virtually everyone who came in touch with her that she sometimes seemed a little too good to be true. While fathers may be crazy about their sons, there is something extraordinarily special about a daughter. It's still the same—our relationship—perhaps even deeper. . . . Rachel had been brought up with the same family pattern—a girl in the middle of two boys. She was the busy, loving, but not necessarily always happy, mainstay of her family, who took care of her younger brother. With a kind of grim amusement, I recall our assumption that Sharon was strong enough to cope well with whatever confronted her. We took her development for granted for many years. She rarely signaled distress or called attention to her problem by being dramatic. (Robinson, 1972, p. 242)

Sharon herself fell into many of the typical sister behaviors, in spite of both parents' efforts to the contrary and in spite of the fact that her mother was a highly dynamic and successful woman in her own right and a role model of strength:

> At times [the older brother, Jackie], would hold me down and tickle me until I cried. Despite all this, I easily fell into the role of my brother's protector. . . . In spite of my mother's warnings to the contrary, I was running up and down the hill in our backyard fetching water and food for my brothers while they sat on the bank of the lake fishing. (S. Robinson, 1996, p. 88)

There are many reasons for the complexity of sister relationships: the familial bonds, the length of these relationships, the caretaking responsibilities sisters share, and their competitiveness for male attention and approval. There is also a special intricacy and intimacy in sister relationships. Our society has generally denied the importance of sister relationships. In most of our legends and stories a man stands between sisters, who compete for his attention (Berkinow, 1980). Mothers are, of course, hardly mentioned at all, unless divisively, as in Cinderella. Older sisters in literature are usually depicted as evil, while the youngest is the infantilized baby and favorite, "Daddy's Girl," receiving his love and wealth in return for her loyalty and willingness to be his "love object." The influence of this negative mythology on how women in families see each other is an important issue in clinical assessment. Conflict between women should never be accepted at face value, but should be asessed in terms of who benefits when women cannot be each others' allies (McGoldrick, 1989).

It is also important to assess sibling gender roles (and all other gender roles) in relation to culture. In many cultures daughters are more likely to be raised to take care of others, including their brothers. Some groups, such as Irish and African American families, may, for various historical reasons, overprotect their sons and underprotect their daughters (Watson, 1998). Other groups have less specific expectations. Anglos, for example, may believe in brothers and sisters having equal chores. In any case, it is essential to notice how gender roles influence sibling patterns.

Unlike oldest sons, who typically have an unacknowledged feeling of entitlement, oldest daughters often have feelings of ambivalence and guilt about their responsiblities. Whatever they do, they may feel that it is not quite enough and that they can never let up in their efforts to caretake and to make the family work right.

Oldest Sons and Daughters

In general, oldest children are likely to be the overresponsible and conscientious ones in the family. They make good leaders, since they have experienced authority over and responsibility for younger siblings. Being the first-born can be a mixed blessing. As the answer to parents' dreams and beginning of a new family, the first-born may receive an intensity of interest and devotion denied to the children that follow. But the burden may be heavy. A major characteristic of the oldest is liking to lead others and assume responsibility for them, working hard to elevate the group to an elite position. George Washington, our first President (Genogram 3.5), is an outstanding example of this.[1] Washington's leadership ability was surely a major factor in the formation of the United States. At the

Genogram 3.5 Washington family

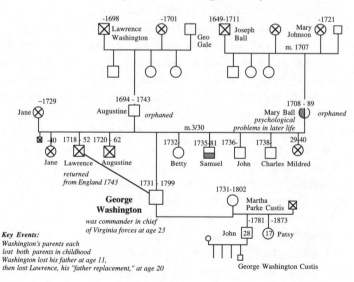

[1] Like Freud, Washington had two very much older half-brothers. They were educated abroad and he did not get to know them until adolescence, when the older of them, Lawrence, 14 years his senior, became his guardian upon their father's death.

age of 20 Washington joined the Virginia Militia; he quickly distinguished himself, becoming Commander in Chief of all Virginia forces by the age of 23. He had a seemingly miraculous ability to lead his men into battle and emerge unscathed. A brilliant leader, he kept a singleminded focus on his objectives and his obligation to duty, regardless of the sacrifices involved.

The oldest daughter often has a similar sense of responsibility, conscientiousness, and ability to care for and lead others as her male counterpart. However, daughters generally do not receive the same advantages, nor are there generally the same expectations for them to excel. Thus, they are often saddled with the responsibilities of the oldest child without the privileges or enhanced self-esteem. When siblings are all female, oldest sisters may have certain privileges and expectations urged on them that would otherwise go to sons.

When a boy follows an oldest girl in the family line-up, he may become a functional oldest. Thomas Jefferson (Genogram 3.14), John Quincy Adams (Genogram 3.13), and Martin Luther King, Jr. (Genogram 4.16) all had older sisters but functioned as oldests.

A younger child may also be thrust into the oldest role by a sibling's illness or disability. Katherine Hepburn (Genogram 3.6) became the oldest surviving child in the family when she was 13, after her older brother hung himself at the

Genogram 3.6 Hepburn family

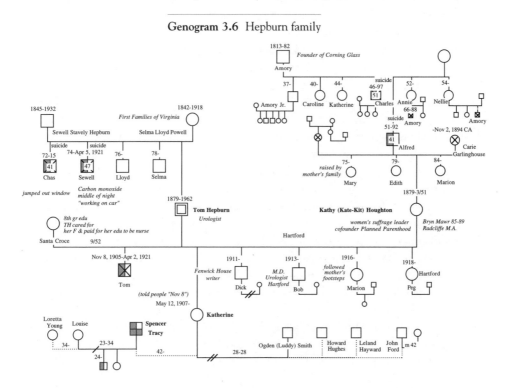

age of 16. She had become the functional oldest years earlier, when she was given the role of caretaker for this older brother, who had suffered from depression and various other problems in childhood. Several other factors may have influenced this role reversal, including many other suicides of men in her family and the heroism of the women who survived and reinvented themselves in the face of their losses. Indeed, Katherine Hepburn's mother, Kit Houghton, whose own father had killed himself when she was only 13, had been left an orphan two years later when her mother died as well, having struggled to ensure that her daughters would be able to have an education and thus not be dependent on men for their survival. Kit Houghton managed to wage a legal battle with her uncle and go to Bryn Mawr at 16, while supporting two younger sisters until they too began college.

The Youngest Child

The youngest child often has a sense of specialness, which allows self-indulgence without the overburdening sense of responsibility that comes with being the oldest. This sense may be more intense when there are several siblings. The younger of two probably has more a sense of "pairing" and twinship—unless there is a considerable age difference—than the youngest of ten. Freed from convention and determined to do things his or her own way, the youngest child can sometimes make remarkable creative leaps leading to inventions and innovations, as in the examples of Thomas Edison, Benjamin Franklin, Marie Curie, and Paul Robeson (for more detailed discussion of these families, see McGoldrick, 1995; Sulloway, 1996).

Given their special position as the center of attention, youngest children may think they can accomplish anything. The youngest may feel more carefree and content to have fun rather than achieve. Less plagued by self-doubt than their older brothers and sisters, they are often extremely creative, willing to try what others would not even consider. They can also be spoiled and self-absorbed, and their sense of entitlement may lead at times to frustration and disappointment. In addition, the youngest often has a period as an only child after the older siblings have left home. This can be an opportunity to enjoy the sole attention of parents but can also lead to feelings of abandonment by the siblings.

Other general characteristics of youngest children are readily apparent. Since the youngest has older siblings who have often served as caretakers, he or she is more used to following than leading. The youngest may remain the "baby," a focus of attention for all who came before, expecting others to be helpful and supportive. Youngest children may feel freer to deviate from convention. Youngests may even feel compelled to escape from being the "baby," which may cause a rebellion, as with Edison and Franklin, who both ran away in adolescence.

A younger sister tends to be protected, showered with affection, and handed a blueprint for life. She may either be spoiled (more so if there are older brothers) and have special privileges or, if she is from a large family, frustrated by always having to wait her turn. Her parents may have just run out of energy with her. She may feel resentful of being bossed around and never taken quite seriously. If she is the only girl, the youngest may be more like the princess, and yet the servant to elders, becoming, perhaps, the confidante to her brothers in adult life and the one to replace the parents in holding the family together.

Paul Robeson (Genogram 3.7), a brilliant and creative youngest, was the multi-talented star in his family, the more extraordinary because the family was African American, living in a racist society. Outstanding athlete in every sport, Phi Beta Kappa and valedictorian of his college class, lawyer turned world famous singer and actor and then political speaker, Robeson was deeply aware of the importance of each of his siblings in his life. He said everyone lavished an extra measure of affection on him and saw him as some kind of "child of destiny . . . linked to the longed-for better days to come" (1988, p. 16). This is a common role for a youngest, especially where the family has experienced hard times.

Genogram 3.7 Robeson family

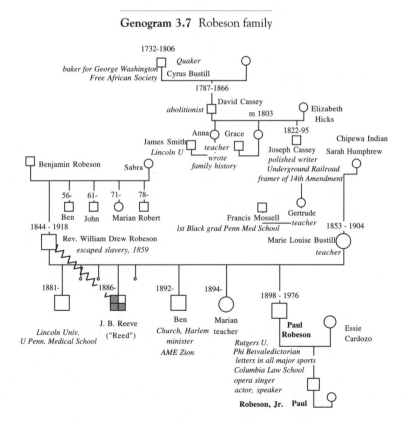

Middle Children

The middle child in a family is "in between," having neither the position of the first as the standard bearer nor the last as the "baby." Middle children thus run the risk of getting lost in the family, especially if all the siblings are of the same sex. On the other hand, middle children may develop into the best negotiators, more even-tempered and mellow than their more driven older siblings and less self-indulgent than the youngest. They may even relish their invisibility.

Middle children are under less pressure to take responsibility, but they need to try harder to make a mark in general, because they have no special role. In the Robeson family (Genogram 3.7) there were three middle children, who all played out variations of the middle child role. While the oldest brother, William Drew, was named for the father and followed in his footsteps, attending the same college, Lincoln University, before going to medical school, the second oldest, Reed, also brilliant but too overtly angry to survive easily as an African American in their community, became the "lost" middle child; Paul felt he learned the quality of toughness from this brother. The third son, Ben, an outstanding athlete and role model for Paul, became a successful minister like their father. The fourth child and only daughter, Marion, became a teacher like their mother and was noted for her warm spirit. For Paul, Ben and Marion—those closest to him in age—were the most important mentors—"reserved in speech, strong in character, living up to their principles—and always selflessly devoted to their younger brother" (p. 13). This support was all the more important because the children's mother died tragically in a fire when Paul was only five. Both Ben and Marion were willing to do without the limelight and to facilitate the relationships of others.

There were lessons also from Reed, who carried a little bag of stones for self-protection, should he encounter a dangerous situation. Robeson admired this "rough" second oldest brother and learned from him a quick response to racial insults and abuse. Robeson had a special feeling for this brother, who did not live up to the father's high expectations of the Robeson children. He later wrote:

> He won no honors in classroom, pulpit or platform. Yet I remember him with love. Restless, rebellious, scoffing at conventions, defiant of the white man's law. I've known many Negroes like Reed. I see them every day. Blindly, in their own reckless manner, they seek a way out for themselves; alone, they pound with their fists and fury against walls that only the shoulders of many can topple. . . . When. . . everything will be different. . . . the fiery ones like Reed will be able to live out their lives in peace and no one will have cause to frown upon them. (Robeson, 1988, p. 14)

Although Reverend Robeson disapproved of Reed's carefree and undisciplined ways and eventually turned him out for his scrapes with the law, Paul saw Reed as having taught him to stand up for himself. Reed, like many middle children, may have expressed feelings for the others, in his case the rage against racism. In the one-man play written about Robeson's life, the character of Robeson says there was one conversation he and his father could never finish—about this brother Reed. Remembering the night his father turned Reed out, fearing he would set a bad example for his younger brother, Paul imagines getting together with his father and brother Ben to go looking for Reed to bring him home. He imagines his response to his father on the subject:

> Aw Pop, don't change the subject. . . . Reed was not a bad influence. Only horrible thing he said to me was, "Kid, you talk too much." All he ever told me to do was to stand up and be a man. "Don't take low from anybody, and if they hit you, hit 'em back harder." I know what the Bible says, Pop, but Reed was your son too! You always said you saw yourself in me. Pop, you were in all your sons. (Dean, 1989)

This dramatization expresses eloquently the connectedness between siblings and how much it matters if one is cut off, even though others in the family may not realize the effects of the cut-off.

Not surprisingly, middle children may show characteristics of either the oldest or the youngest, or both combined. A middle child, unless he or she is the only girl or only boy, has to struggle for a role in the family. While the child may escape certain intensities directed at the oldest or the youngest, he or she may have to struggle to be noticed. Alfred Adler (Genogram 3.8) is a good example of a middle child. Adler was one of the first to theorize about the importance of sibling constellation for family development, and it is clear many

Genogram 3.8 Alfred Adler's family

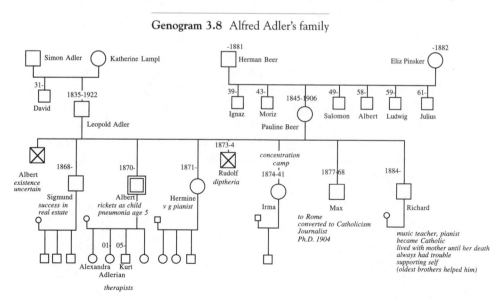

of his ideas derived from his personal experience. Ellenberger, a historian of psychiatry, describes Adler's ideas as follows:

> According to Adler, each one of the children in a family is born and grows up with a specific perspective according to its position in relation to the other siblings. From the outset the position of the oldest brother is better than that of the younger ones. He is made to feel that he is the stronger, the wiser, the most responsible. That is why he values the concept of authority and tradition and is conservative in his views. The youngest brother, on the other hand, is always in danger of remaining the spoiled and cowardly family baby. Whereas the oldest will take his father's profession, the youngest may easily become an artist, or then, as the result of overcompensation, he will develop tremendous ambition and strive to be the savior of the entire family. The second child in a family is under perpetual pressure from both sides, striving to outmatch his older brother and fearing to be overtaken by the younger one. As for the only child, he is even more exposed to be spoiled and pampered than the youngest one. His parents' preoccupation with his health may cause him to become anxious and timorous. Such patterns are subject to modifications according to the distance between siblings and according to the proportion of boys and girls and their respective position in the family. If the oldest brother is closely followed by a sister, there comes a time when he will fear being outdistanced by the girl who will mature more rapidly than he. Among many other possible situations are those of the only girl in a family of boys, and of the only boy among a constellation of girls (a particularly unfavorable situation, according to Adler). (1970, pp. 613-14)

This appears to fit with Adler's own family experience. Adler, who himself was sickly as a child (he had rickets, nearly died of pneumonia at age five, and was twice hit by moving vehicles), felt he grew up in the shadow of his older brother, Sigmund, who became a successful businessman, following in their father's footsteps. As can be seen on the genogram, Alfred was followed closely by his sister, Hermine, with whom he apparently had little relationship in adulthood. The third brother died in bed with Alfred when Alfred was four. The fourth brother, Max, who was apparently very envious of Adler, distanced from the family by moving to Rome and converting to Catholicism. The youngest brother, Richard, seems indeed to have been spoiled, living with his mother until her death, aspiring to be an artist and musician. He always had trouble supporting himself, living at times with Adler's family and receiving support from Adler.

Missing information is always of interest on a genogram. In Adler's case, in spite of his explicit belief about the importance of sibling relationships in determining behavior, his biographers have given only sketchy and conflicting information about his own sibling constellation (see bibliography section on Adler).

We know even less about the sibling or family patterns of Adler's parents, a fact that is true also for Freud, Horney, and Jung, in spite of the great interest there has been in their work and their psychological make-up. Clearly, biographers have yet to take a systemic view of history (McGoldrick, 1995).

Only Children

Only children may have the seriousness and sense of responsibility of the oldest and the conviction of specialness and entitlement of the youngest. At the same time they tend to be more oriented toward adults, seeking their love and approval, and in return expecting their undivided attention. Their major challenge is getting along with others their own age. They tend to be more socially independent, less oriented toward peer relationships, more adultlike in behavior at an earlier age, and perhaps more anxious at times as a result of the attention and protectiveness of their parents. They often maintain very close attachments to their parents throughout their lives, but find it more difficult to relate to friends and spouses.

Indira Gandhi, the second Prime Minister of India, is an example of an only child (Genogram 3.9). She grew up quite isolated and lived primarily in the

Genogram 3.9 Indira Ghandi's family

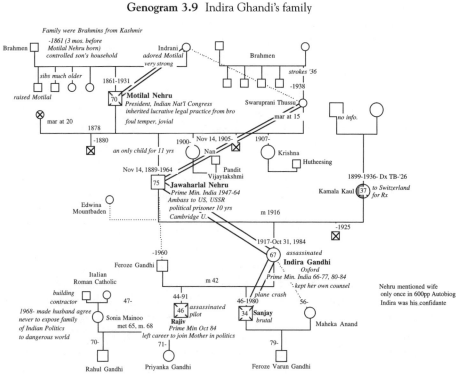

presence of older people, early becoming her father's confidante. She clearly had the sense of mission and responsibility of an oldest, but as a leader she was autocratic and led a rather isolated existence, keeping her own counsel. Both her father and paternal grandfather were functional only children. Her father, Jawaharlal Nehru, was eleven years older than his next sibling and his father, Motilal Nehru, also a leader of India, was much younger than his siblings and raised in the home of his older brother, because his father had died before he was born. The illnesses of both Jawaharlal's mother and Indira's mother may have compounded their independent roles as only children.

Sibling Position and Marriage

Sibling relationships can often pave the way for couple relationships—for sharing, interdependence, and mutuality—just as they can predispose partners to jealousy, power struggles, and rivalry. Since siblings are generally one's earliest peer relationships, a man or woman is likely to be most comfortable in other relationships that reproduce the familiar sibling patterns of birth order and gender. And generally speaking, marriage seems easier for partners who fit their original sibling pattern, e.g., if an oldest marries a youngest, rather than two oldests marrying each other. If a wife has grown up as the oldest of many siblings and the caretaker, she might be attracted to a dominant oldest, who offers to take over management of responsibilities. But as time goes along, she may come to resent his assertion of authority, because by experience she is more comfortable making decisions for herself.

All things being equal (and they seldom are in life!), the ideal marriage based on sibling position would be a complementary one where the husband was the older brother of a sister and the wife was the younger sister of an older brother. However, the complementarity of caretaker and someone who needs caretaking, or leader and follower, does not guarantee intimacy or a happy marriage.

In addition to complementary birth order, it seems to help in marriage if one has had siblings of the opposite sex. Most difficult might be the youngest sister of many sisters who marries the youngest brother of many brothers, since neither would have much experience of the opposite sex in a close way, and they might both play "the spoiled child" waiting for a caretaker.

Eleanor Roosevelt, an oldest, and her cousin Franklin (Genogram 3.10), an only, are a good example of two strong-willed spouses whose marriage seems to have survived because of their ability to evolve separate spheres. Leaders in their own separate worlds, they came to live apart except for holidays. Early in the marriage, Eleanor generally subordinated herself to Franklin and to his powerful mother, Sara Delano, who played a major role in their lives. However,

Genogram 3.10 Eleanor and Franklin Roosevelt

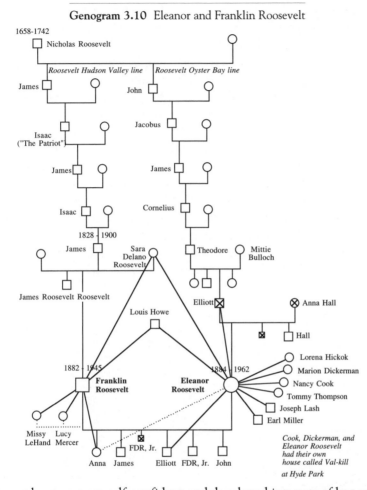

as Eleanor became more self-confident and developed interests of her own, she began to show the determination of an oldest. The crisis came when Eleanor discovered letters revealing Franklin's affair with Lucy Mercer. Apparently it was Franklin's mother Sara who negotiated a contract between them for Eleanor to return to the marriage. Since oldests and only children are oriented to parents, Sara may have been the only one who could have kept them from separating—and she did.[2]

The Roosevelts remained married but lived separate lives, with politics as their common ground. After Franklin's paralysis due to polio, Eleanor became essential to his political career. She nevertheless had her own intimate rela-

---

[2] This contract that Sara negotiated between Franklin and Eleanor is the only document in the Roosevelt archives that is unavailable to the public!

tionships, her own political views and activities, and her own living space in a separate house at Hyde Park which she shared with her friends.

Richard Burton and Elizabeth Taylor (Genogram 3.11), who married and divorced each other twice, provide a dramatic example of two youngest children who competed to be "junior," both seeking a caretaker. Burton was the second youngest of thirteen children, but was treated like a youngest, since he was reared apart from his younger brother. In very large families several of the younger children will often have the characteristics of a youngest. Elizabeth Taylor was the younger of two, with an older brother whose needs were often sacrificed to her stardom, which, of course, solidified her special position. Burton and Taylor were known for their histrionic love quarrels, each outdoing the other in their demanding and childish behavior.

There are, of course, many other possible sibling pairings in marriage. The marriage of two only children might be particularly difficult, since neither has the experience of intimate sharing that one does with a brother or sister. Middle children may be the most flexible, since they have experiences with a number of different roles.

Genogram 3.11 Burton/Taylor:
Marriage of two younger siblings

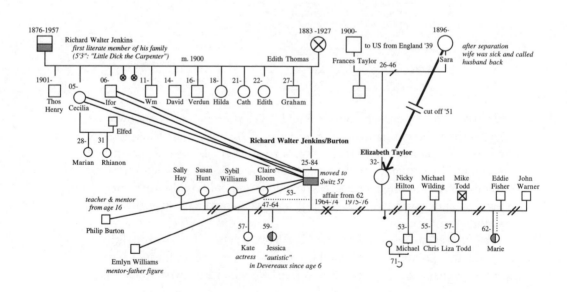

Genogram 3.12 Bateson/Mead family

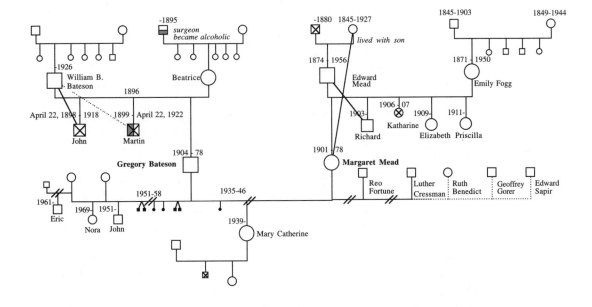

Of course, spouses from complementary sibling constellations may have problems, in which case it may be important to check the particular family more closely. A case in point is that of Margaret Mead, an oldest, and Gregory Bateson, a youngest (Genogram 3.12). Their sibling positions seem clearly reflected in their personality styles. As their daughter, Catherine, describes it:

> Margaret's approach must have been based on early success in dealing with problems, perhaps related to the experience of being an older child and amplified by years of successfully organizing the younger ones. Gregory's experience was that of a younger child with relatively little capacity for changing what went on around him. Instead he would seek understanding. Indeed, he had a kind of abhorrence for the effort to solve problems, whether they were medical or political. (Bateson, 1984, p. 176)

Mead's and Bateson's respective sibling positions and problem-solving styles did not lead, however, to a complementary helper/helped relationship, but to struggle and disappointment in the other. Margaret's role as the senior partner was emphasized by the fact that she was three years older than Gregory, as her mother, also an oldest, was three years older than her husband. Their daughter describes their relationship:

> In the marriage she was the one who set the patterns, for Gregory lacked this fascination with pervasive elaboration. . . . His life was full of loose ends and unstitched edges, while for Margaret each thread became an occasion for embroidery. (p. 27)
>
> It was Gregory, more than anyone else, who lashed back at her for try-ing to manage his life. . . . She would see a problem and her imagination would leap to a solution. (p. 111)
>
> (He) began with his rebellion against Margaret, a rebellion shot through with resentment against his family and especially against his mother. (p. 160)
>
> It may well be that the suicide of his brother Martin in 1922, which fol-lowed on heavy-handed parental attempts at guidance and led to a period of increasing efforts to shape Gregory's choices as well, was an ingredient in his anxiety about problem solving and indeed about any effort to act in the world. (p. 176)

This description of Bateson reflects well his position as a youngest, waiting to be taken care of, yet rebellious against the one (Margaret, an oldest) who does it. The expectations of his sibling position were changed by the traumatic deaths of his two older brothers, thrusting him at age 18 into the position of only child and replacement for the loss endured by his family. The shift in Gregory's sibling posi-tion in early adult life may thus have contributed to the incompatibility between him and Margaret, even though their birth positions were complementary.

There is some similarity between Gregory, whose role in his family as the only surviving child intensified to the point of toxicity in his relationship with his mother, and Margaret Mead's father, who was an only child doted on by his mother after his father's death when he was only six. While Bateson cut off from his mother, Edward Mead brought his mother with him into his marriage and she lived in the Mead household for the rest of her life.

Sibling Position and Parenting

A parent may overidentify with a child of the same sex and sibling position. One father who was an oldest of five felt that he had been burdened as a child with too much responsibility, while his younger brothers and sister "got away with murder." When his own children came along, he spoiled the oldest and tried to make the younger ones toe the line. A mother may find it difficult to sympathize with a youngest daughter if she always felt envious of her younger sister. Parents may also identify with one particular child because of a resemblance to another family member.

Intergenerational problems related to sibling position may arise when the identification is so strong that parents perpetuate their old family patterns or when their own experience is so different that they misread their children. Two sisters may get along quite well, although their mother expects them to fight the way she and her sister did. And a parent who was an only child may assume that normal sibling fights are an indication of trouble.

Sibling Relationships in Adult Life

Sibling relationships can be a most important connection in adult life, especially in the later years. However, if negative feelings persist, the care of an aging parent may bring on particular difficulty. At such times siblings, who may have been apart for years, have to work together in new and unfamiliar ways. The child who has remained closest to the parents, usually a daughter, often gets most of these caretaking responsibilities, which may bring long buried jealousies and resentments to the surface.

Once both parents are no longer living, siblings are truly independent for the first time. This is the time when estrangement can become complete, particularly if old rivalries continue. Strong feelings can be fueled by all the old unresolved issues and conflicts. But the better relationships the siblings have, the less likely it is that this or other traumatic family events will lead to a parting of ways.

Other Factors Influencing Sibling Constellation

It is important not to take the hypotheses about sibling constellations too literally. Many people fit the characterizations, but many do not. Also, the usual sibling constellation predictions may be influenced by a number of other factors. For example, how the sibling constellation fits into the constellation of cousins may modify or intensify certain sibling patterns. For instance, the role of Woody Allen (Genogram 2.1) as older brother of a younger sister was probably intensified by the fact that all his cousins in a large extended family, including his mother's five sisters, were female. Indeed, throughout his high school years he shared a room with a female first cousin five years older than himself, to whom he had always been close. Such a pattern would probably intensify to an extreme the pattern of older brother of a younger sister being somewhat special and more highly valued.

Jackie Bouvier Kennedy (Genogram 2.10) is another example of a family where it is essential to know how the sibling constellation is embedded in the cousin constellation. Jackie was not only the older sister of a younger sister, with whom she always had an intense, close, and competitive relationship, not only a half-sibling and stepsibling of many children to whom she became connected through her mother's second marriage, but also part of an extended family of cousins on her father's side, who spent much time together in the formative summers of her childhood. In this constellation she was one of three cousins born in the same year. Jackie always had a special preference for several older male cousins. Indeed, she most admired her cousin Michel, nine years older, whom she even remembered and mentioned in her will. This cousin's specialness in the family was intensified in his earliest childhod, when his mother divorced his alcoholic father, an event that created great distress throughout the entire family, because they felt they were losing the sole male Bouvier of that generation. This sense of the fragility of the male line had begun in the previous generation, when out of 12 children there were only four males and only one of these lived to marry and have children. Five of the siblings never married but lived a long time. This kind of "aunt and uncle power" can also influence a sibling constellation in the next generation, giving special extra care and attention. These relatives probably played an important role in conveying the strong sense of family to the children of the next generation.

Other experiences in a family's history may also modify sibling patterns. For example, Richard Burton (Genogram 3.11), here used to illustrate marital patterns of a youngest married to a youngest, grew up in a complex family situation after the early death of his mother. His oldest sister, Cis (Cecilia), 19 years older than he, had recently married and became the primary mother figure for him and for many of the other siblings; but, as Burton put it, "Cis was wonderful, but she was not my mother" (Bragg, 1990, p. 69). "His father had been replaced by an elder brother (Ifor), then by one teacher (Philip Burton), then another dominating man (Emlyn Williams). . . his younger sisters were his nieces [Cis's daughters], his older sisters more like aunts, the brothers like uncles, the cousins like brothers, the real aunts like mothers . . . he had many alternative worlds. . . . Complexity, elaboration, alternatives, parallel lives, that was the way it had always been; that was his 'norm'" (Bragg, 1990, p. 69).

Thus, we must always explore sibling constellation, like any single factor in family life, within the context of the complexity of multiple family patterns. Out of temperament or necessity, siblings may often play non-sibling roles and non-siblings may often play sibling roles, as they did for Burton. Indeed, the empirical research on sibling constellations is at best inconclusive, because there are so many other factors that can change or moderate the influence of sibling position. Nevertheless, an awareness of sibling constellation can provide clinically useful normalizing explanations of people's roles in their family, as well as indicating other factors to explore when the typical patterns are not found. In addition, adult siblings, often ignored by clinicians, can be extremely important resources in therapy and health care.

The timing of each sibling's birth in the family's history.

Sometimes, when a child is born at a critical point in a family history, there are special expectations for that child, in addition to those typical of his or her sibling position. These expectations may exaggerate a sibling position characterization (as with the oldest who acts super-responsible) or modify the usual sibling roles (as with a middle or youngest who functions as an oldest or only child). Particularly critical are family deaths and transitions. For example, a child born around the time one of the grandparents dies may play a special role in the family. Freud was born not only at the start of a remarried family, but also within a few months of the death of his paternal grandfather.

The child's characteristics.

A child with special characteristics may also shift the expected sibling patterns in a family. For example, children may become functional oldests if they are particularly talented or if the oldest is sickly, as appears to have happened with Katherine Hepburn in relation to her oldest brother. An older child may also be treated as a youngest if he or she has special problems (such as a psychological or physical disability).

The family's "program" for the child.

Parents may have a particular agenda for a specific child, such as expecting him or her to be the responsible one or the "baby," regardless of that child's position in the family. Children who resemble a certain family member may be expected to be like that person or to take on that person's role. Children's temperaments may be at odds with their sibling position. Noteworthy is the situation where a child cannot fulfill the sibling position role that is structurally ordained for him or her. Some children struggle so valiantly against family expectations—the oldest who refuses to take on the responsibility of the caretaker or family standard bearer or the youngest who strives to be a leader. And, of course, cultures differ tremendously in the expected roles of birth order and gender. Asian cultures, for example, tend to have highly stratified expectations for children, depending on their birth order and gender, while Jewish and Anglo families tend to be relatively democratic. In some families, it will be the child most comfortable with the responsibility—not necessarily the oldest child—who becomes the leader.

Naming patterns of siblings are often significant signals of family "programming." For example, Gregory Bateson, named for one of his father's heroes,

Gregor Mendel, though the youngest son, was perhaps being "programmed" to aim at great accomplishments as a natural scientist. On the other hand, John Quincy Adams (Genogram 3.13) broke a four-generational family tradition of naming the oldest son John to name his first son George Washington Adams, after his father's political rival. Although names or nicknames may give hints on the genogram as to the family's "programming," the clinician needs to look for other indications. For example, an examination of the Kennedy family's history (Genograms 2.24 and 2.25) suggests that the males were programmed to run for political office. As is well-known, the oldest son of Joseph P. Kennedy was slated by his father to run for president, but died before he could. Later, his three brothers all did run for president and two of his brothers-in-law ran for vice-president or governor. Not surprisingly, a number of the members of the next generation have also run for office.

Genogram 3.13   Adams family

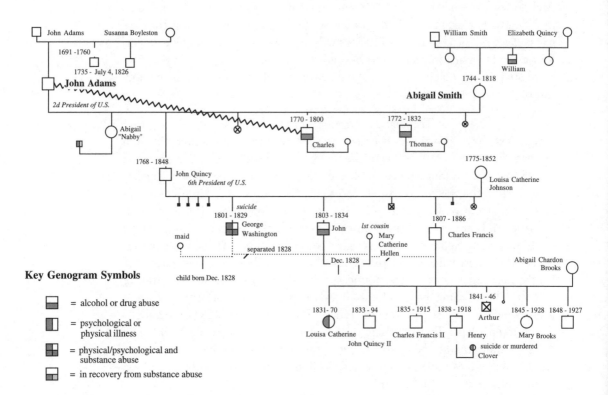

The child's sibling position in relation to that of the parent.
The child's position in the family may be particularly highlighted if it repeats the position of the same-sexed parent. Thus, a man who is the oldest son of an oldest son may have certain specific expectations placed on him that do not apply to his younger brother. If a man's relationship with his own father was charged, there is a good chance that in the next generation the relationship with his son in the same ordinal position may also turn sour. This is more likely, of course, in cultures with strong rules governing sibling functioning in relation to ordinal position (McGoldrick & Watson, 1998).

Unusual Family Configurations

As the clinician scans the genogram, sometimes certain structural configurations will "jump out," suggesting critical family themes or problems. At least three aspects of the graphic structural configuration are striking on the genogram of Elizabeth Blackwell, the first woman physician in the U.S. (Genogram 2.18): first, the preponderance of successful professional women; second, the fact that none of Samuel Blackwell's five sisters ever married, nor did any of his five daughters and only a few of the 14 women in the third generation; and third, the frequency of their adopting children.

This configuration opens up for further exploration the role of gender in this family of extraordinary feminists (several of them men!) and successful women. It would be fascinating to know the rules and attitudes in the family that influenced such a pattern. Some of these have been suggested by Horn (1983), who says that the family viewed marriage negatively and actively discouraged the daughters from marrying. Two of Elizabeth's three sisters-in-law, Lucy Stone, the famous suffragette, and Antoinette Brown, the first woman minister in the U.S., had become best friends in college at Oberlin. They had resolved with each other, long before meeting their future husbands in the Blackwell family, they would never marry but would adopt and raise children! Of the five Blackwell sisters, four were very successful (Elizabeth and Emily as physicians, Anna as a writer, and Ellen as an artist), and the fifth was an invalid. Of the five daughters of their brother Samuel, two also became physicians, two became ministers, and the fifth was also an invalid. This reveals a pattern of complementarity common in families where siblings or partners are polar opposites. One is forced to wonder whether deeper forces are at play in some families, where one person seems to take on a role for the others—maybe to absorb certain negative energy, which is lived out through sickness or anger, while others are freed for creativity and achievement.

Genogram 3.14 Jefferson family

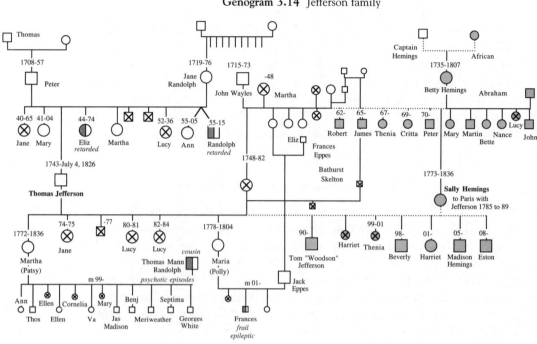

Thomas Jefferson, the third President of the United States (Genogram 3.14) has an extraordinarily convoluted genogram, involving marriages and liaisons from within the same few families, slave and white. Such configurations were a common occurrence in the convoluted and racist era of slavery, where white slave owners frequently fathered children with their slaves and then denied this parentage, making it very difficult for the African Americans to know their history (Pinderhughes, 1998). The cut-offs and conflicts produced by this exploitation of African Americans has been a shameful part of our national heritage, but facing this history is an important part of healing and changing such patterns of exploitation. Making sense of this interracial configuration is a challenge. As Pinderhughes has said:

> The invisibility of African Americans in the recorded history of the United States has led to a pervasive ignorance for everyone, Black or white, about African Americans and their contributions to the building of our country. . . . With no power to affect the writing of American history and few resources to disseminate our story, it has remained invisible or dis-

torted by negative stereotypes, and we have until recently remained unable or unwilling to challenge the distortions, untruths, and omissions that have been accepted about our past. . . . But we are coming to realize that knowledge of the past, even if painful, can nourish a people's strength. This realization has stimulated us to unseal these memories and reclaim the truth, no matter how cruel and shocking, so that the festering wound can begin to heal and so that we can better cope with the present and build the future. (1998, p. 170)

Historians have been extremely reluctant to face the truth of this history in families like that of Thomas Jefferson, in which there were many interconnected secret affairs and relationships. Jefferson's white family, along with numerous white historians, went to great lengths to cover up this part of the family history. It is often necessary to reassess carefully the history we have been told in order to understand the truth of the relationships in our families.

Indeed, Jefferson's father-in-law had a long secret relationship with his slave Betty Hemings, by whom he had six children, and Jefferson later had a long secret relationship and seven children with Betty's daughter, Sally Hemings, who was the half-sister of his wife, Martha Wayles. Furthermore, Jefferson's daughters both married cousins; Martha married a cousin on her paternal grandmother's side, and Maria married her maternal first cousin. In addition, Martha Jefferson's first husband was the younger brother of her stepmother's first husband. Jefferson seems to have believed quite directly in keeping things in the family!

Another example of an unusual family configuration would be a family in which two siblings married siblings from another family, such as the Freud/Bernays family (Genogram 6.5).

Interestingly, Albert Einstein (Genogram 3.15) left his first wife to marry a woman who was doubly related to him already. She was his first cousin on his mother's side and his second cousin on his father's side. He and his first wife Mileva also had a mysterious first child, Liserl, born in 1901, before their marriage in 1903 and never mentioned in any biographies until recently. Certain genogram information, particularly about births, liaisons, and traumatic deaths, is often concealed, though its importance is thus intensified. The discovery of Liserl's existence has led to much speculation about what happened to her and why her existence was kept a secret. Recently another possible child of Einstein has emerged. This man, now in his sixties, bears a remarkable resemblance to Einstein and has spent his life as a physicist. Apparently Einstein's second wife may have given up this child in infancy. Could it be that in both the Einstein and Jefferson families the secrecy and the closely cross-joined family members show a parallel process of fusion?

Genogram 3.15 Einstein family

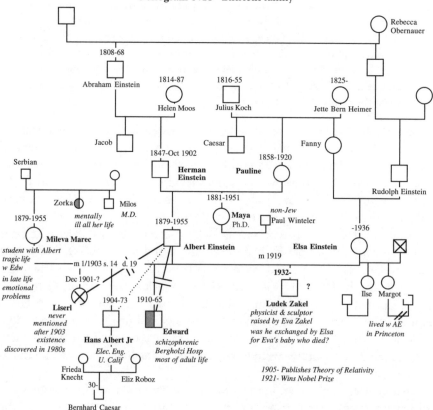

The unusual connections seen in the graphic configurations of the Jefferson, Freud/Bernays, and Einstein families might lead to a number of speculations about triangles set up by these intrafamily marriages and liaisons, as well as about possible family expectations influencing members against marrying outside the group. In Jefferson's case, for example, we know that his wife elicited from him a deathbed promise that he would not remarry, and he himself, having lost his wife and four children, was protective with his two daughters and apparently encouraged them, as well as many of his slaves, to marry within the family (Brodie, 1974, p. 47). In terms of relationships, we know that Jefferson was extremely close to his daughter Martha. Perhaps not surprisingly, he had many problems relating to her husband, Thomas Mann Randolph, and felt closer to his other son-in-law, John Wayles Eppes, the son of his wife's sister, Elizabeth. Randolph, in fact, became very jealous of Eppes, sensing Jefferson's preference.

Unusual family configurations on the genogram should also cue the clinician to the application of other interpretive principles. For example, repeated graphic patterns (e.g., multiple remarriages in each generation) might suggest pattern repetition across generations. Structural contrasts (e.g., one spouse coming from a large family and the other an only child) might suggest family imbalance.

Children Growing Up in Multiple Families: Foster Care, Adoption and Orphanage Experiences

Many children grow up in multiple settings, whether because their parents divorce, die, remarry, or have special circumstances that require the child to live for a while or even permanently in a different setting. Clinicians have often failed to make full use of genograms in such circumstances to track children through the life cycle, taking into account the multiple family contexts to which they belong. We consider that genograms can be a particularly useful tool for tracking children in multiple foster placements, where the many different family constellations a child lives in are otherwise extremely hard to keep in mind. The more clearly the clinician tracks the actuality of this history, however complex, the better able he or she is to validate the child's actual experience and multiple forms of belonging. Such a map can begin to make order out of the at times chaotic placement changes a child must go through when sudden transitions or shifts in placement are necessary because of illness, trauma or other loss.

This section draws on the experience of Fernando Colon, who has for many years been one of our most creative advocates for acknowledging the relevance of specific foster family history for children who have lived in foster care. Fernando grew up in several foster homes after the loss of his mother. As an adult, he became a psychologist and has put much effort into exploring his own genogram (1973, 1998) and helping others to think contextually about child placement and foster care as a valid and important aspect of a child's history, which should be attended to as any other experience (Colon, 1998). He has made it very clear how important the genogram of the foster family is for both the past and the future of a child through the life cycle. He himself still has ongoing connections with the biological grandchildren of his third foster mother, who were very close to him in age, and whom he knew growing up, because they shared holidays and other visits when they came to visit their grandmother, his foster mother. They share much history and have much in common through this shared history, a history that is so often not acknowledged in our individualistic society. One of the most powerful aspects of genograms is the way in which it can steer us to the rich ongoing possibilities of complex kin relationships, which continue throughout life to be sources of connection and

Genogram 3.16 Fernando Colon's childhood knowledge of his biological family

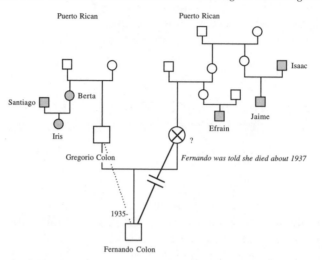

life support. It is not just our shared history that matters, but current connections that strengthen us and can enrich our future.

As he grew up, Fernando's knowledge of his biological family was very limited (Genogram 3.16). There were two visits from family members, indicated in gray on this genogram, which he enjoyed, but he was too young to appreciate who these relatives were. When he was six his father's sister, Berta, visited with her husband, Santiago, and daughter, Iris, and the next year his mother's maternal uncle, Isaac, visited with Fernando's first cousin, Efrain, and Isaac's son Jaimie. The map of all his living situations, including three foster homes, an orphanage, his family of origin, and his family of procreation is offered in Genogram 3.17. In order to better understand the sibling patterns with his brothers in the foster home where he spent most of his growing-up years, we might want to show the changing family constellations separately, as in Genogram 3.18. This genogram makes evident the multiple losses that Fernando and his foster family had throughout his childhood, but also the resilience and resourcefulness in their ability to deal with these losses, as well as with new relationships almost each year. As is evident, he had experience in virtually every sibling constellation during his childhood years, a factor that would probably increase his flexibility in multiple relationship situations. He was the youngest of three, the oldest of three, the middle of three, the older of two, the younger of two, but rarely an only child, although, as the one child who remained with the family for his entire childhood, he must have had a special position there. At the same time, the three brothers who stayed for long periods of time (four years each), Alvin, Stanley, and later Kenneth, would

Genogram 3.17 Tracking Fernando Colon's living situations

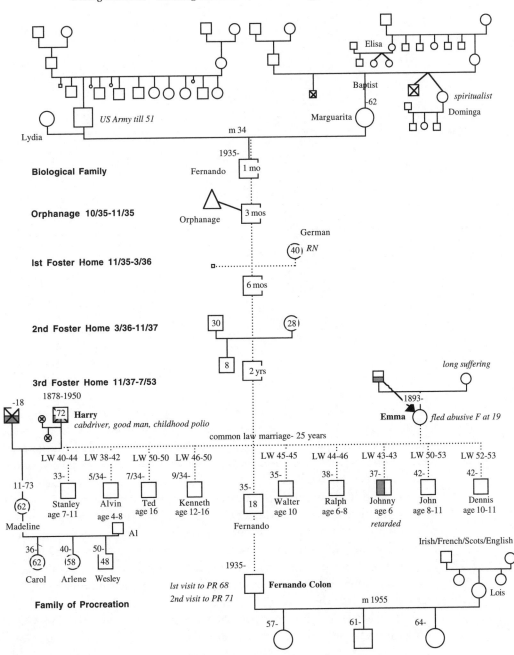

Genogram 3.18 Changing constellation of Colon's foster home, 1937–1953

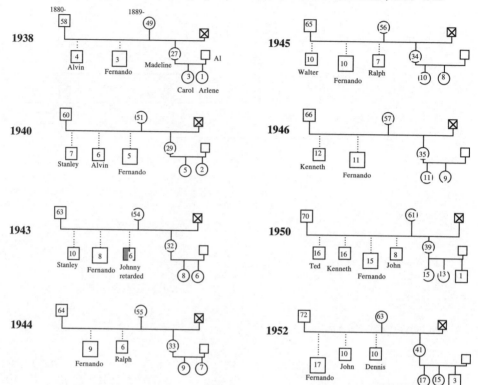

probably have had more significance for him, especially as they were all close to Fernando in age. Indeed, he reports that he and the first two, with whom he shared the foster home in his early years, were like the three Musketeers. Kenneth, who spent four adolescent years in the household, was a powerful role model, and Fernando believes his love for swimming and reading came from this relationship. Less evident from the ages alone was the extremely special relationship that Fernando and his foster mother had with his brother Johnny, who only lived in the family for four months, but to whom they became very attached. It was one of the most painful losses when they were forced to send him to an institution for the mentally retarded. Fernando remembers clearly how hard Johnny had tried to learn to say Fernando's name and how he and his mother cried when they had to let Johnny go.

As an adult Fernando undertook a remarkable endeavor to find and reconnect with his family in Puerto Rico and in the U.S., which has continued over the past 30 years (Genogram 3.19). The physical genogram, which is a highly condensed map of the rich and complex family he discovered, is an awesome lesson to anyone who is unable to see beyond the cut-offs that may occur in a family. Although the foster care system at that time operated on the principle that children were never to have contact with other family once they moved to a new home, he made great efforts to reverse that process of cut-off. Indeed, he remembers that in the early days of placement, one of his foster brothers, Kenneth, was especially depressed. Kenneth was one of five brothers, and in spite of the regulations, their foster mother asked Kenneth where the brothers were and took him to see them, after which he began to adjust to his new situation. Fernando has not as yet reconnected with his foster brothers, but he remains connected to his foster mother's grandchildren, Carol, Arlene, and Wesley. He has developed a strong conviction that no relationship is to be discarded.

Fernando has close, current, ongoing connections with family members on both sides of his biological family. For example, he has close connections with Elisita, Eugenito, and Fernando, who are second cousins on his mother's side (Genogram 3.19). One of these cousins is also named Fernando and bears a strong resemblance to Fernando Colon. This cousin, Fernando, now has a 16-year-old son who is also named Fernando. Fernando's older sister, Elisita, and his brother, Eugentio, inherited the family farm. Elisita is the first Puerto Rican woman licensed to artificially inseminate cows. Fernando currently enjoys rich connections with this part of his maternal family. Another cousin, Nancy, who

Genogram 3.19 Colon's family discovered through research

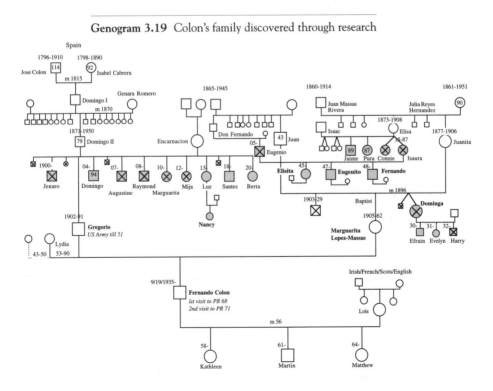

was still a child when Fernando began to research his family in Puerto Rico 30 years ago, has now become one of his closest relatives and keeps him connected with his paternal family. She herself received her Ph.D. in geography in the United States and teaches at the University of Puerto Rico, thus sharing many of his professional, political, and cultural interests, as well as many personal connections.

So, Fernando, by making creative use of his genogram, has stayed connected to his foster family and reconnected richly and rewardingly with his families of origin. His next goal is to identify a male cousin on each side of the family and to develop those relationships in the years to come.

The accepted practice of severing family ties, be they biological, adopted, foster, or blended, is, in our view, seriously pathological. It has often led to therapists' being drawn in to replace other relationships in a person's natural system. As Fernando Colon's own family demonstrates so well, such cut-offs leave us depressed, bereft, and weakened. A cut-off of one person tends to lead to multiple cut-offs of other family members and to the loss of many potentially rich relationships. It weakens the entire fabric of one's life. The use of genograms can counter this tendency to oversimplify and cut off, by making clear the enormity of the losses, as one scans the numerous people involved, and opening up the rich possibilities for connection and meaning.

As Fernando's story shows, connections with others who have grown up in the same foster family may last a lifetime and reconnections at later life cycle stages may be particularly meaningful. The same is, of course, true for orphanage experiences, as the touching memoir of John Folwarski (1998) illustrates.

Genogram 3.20 St. Hedwig's orphanage family

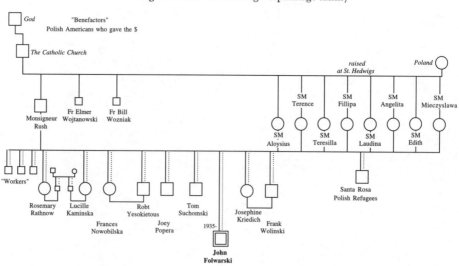

Folwarski figures that he had approximately 3,000 siblings, that is, 3,000 other children in one generation shared the same home (St. Hedwig's Orphanage in Chicago) and the same foster parents and grandparents—the nuns and priests who ran the home. Genogram 3.20 shows Folwarski's diagram for the family as he experienced it during the years he grew up (1937–1950). As adults many of his "siblings" have come together to share memories, have reconnected with some of their teacher/mothers, and have strengthened their sense of family through a realization that their genogram has real meaning for them all. Indeed, he describes that the experience of creating and looking at the diagram itself had a powerful meaning for him in terms of validating his history.

Clinical Illustration

Joe Petrucci was a successful 50-year-old businessman, recently married for the third time, having abandoned his previous children when he left his wives (Genogram 3.21). In his third family, he took on the responsibility of two sons who had lost their father, a successful and powerful lawyer, who had died after several years of a debilitating disease. Joe was very happy with his new wife and sons, but would find himself withdrawing from the very intimacy he sought, which led his wife, Barbara, to frustration and anger. When asked about his family of origin, Joe did not want to talk about it. He admitted that he had grown up in an often disrupted context, moving frequently as his mother moved from one relationship to another, having married seven times before he

Genogram 3.21 Petrucci family

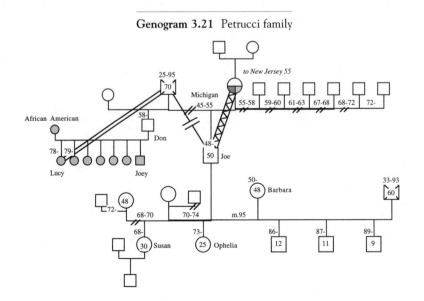

was 24. He had been cut off from his own father since age seven, when his mother packed him up and took him 1,000 miles away. In the previous years he vaguely remembered being "captured" back and forth by each parent, as they fought their bitter battles with each other. His mother was abusive and alcoholic and from an early age Joe had to take care not only of himself, but often also of her. Once, he remembered, his father tried to reconnect, but when he took out a picture of his son by his second wife, Joe got up in fury and left.

It took many months in therapy to move Joe from anger to curiosity about his genogram. Finally, he discovered through some detective work that his father had died the year before. He decided to go back to his home town and see the house where he was born and his father's grave. When he got to the house, he found a young African American woman living there. When he introduced himself, she gave a shocked response that her name was Lucy Petrucci. It turned out she was one of six children of Joe's half-brother, Don, who had married an African American woman. Their youngest child and only son was also named Joe Petrucci. The oldest was Lucy, who had been the closest to the grandfather, Joe's father, who had lived with the family until he died the previous year. That night the family took Joe out and, as he later described it, he experienced a love and connection he had never even realized he needed. His newly discovered niece, Lucy, was able to fill him in on much of the history of his father that he had never known, since she had been closest to him in his last years and the last one to speak to him the night he died. His new "brother" shared recollections of their father's longing for Joe over the years and his pain when Joe rejected him, the one time he had tried to connect. He was particularly shocked to feel so close to this Black family, since he had been a strong racist for as long as he could remember. His reconnection made him profoundly aware that he lost a lot more than just his father when the cut-off occurred in his childhood. And the reconnection affected more than just Joe—his family shared in it, and it helped him rethink his connections to the children he had left behind as well. It also "miraculously," as he thought, facilitated a shift in his relationship with his wife. As she said, one reconnection can't change a whole life, but somehow it seemed to her she now had "a softer, gentler, Joe."

4

FAMILY RELATIONAL PATTERNS AND TRIANGLES

The genogram allows the clinician to detect intense relationships in a family and, given the family's structure and position in the life cycle, to hypothesize about the important triangular patterns and boundaries of that family. Understanding such triangular patterns is essential in planning clinical interventions. "Detriangling" is an important clinical process through which family members are coached to free themselves from rigid triangular patterns. Relational patterns in families have been variously characterized as "close," "fused," "hostile," "conflictual," "distant," "cut off," etc. The complexity of family relationships is infinite. In addition, of course, relationships change over time. In spite of such complexity, the genogram can often suggest relational patterns to be further explored.

Obviously, the smallest human system is a two-person system. Genograms can be analyzed in terms of dyadic relationships, with relationship lines depicting these patterns in at least a crude way. Repeated dyadic patterns can be tracked throughout the system, as in Genogram 4.1.

If the focus is simply on the relationships in this genogram, it is apparent that in each generation all sons have conflictual relationships with their fathers

Genogram 4.1 Dyadic relationships and triangles

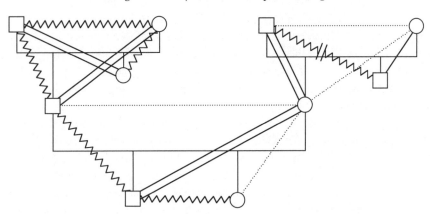

and close relationships with their mothers, while daughters have the opposite—distant or conflictual relationships with their mothers and close relationships with their fathers. Meanwhile, all the couples have distant or conflictual relationships. In other words, there is a complementary pattern of marital distance, same-sex conflicts, and cross-sex alliances between the generations. The prediction may be that the son and daughter in the third generation would repeat this pattern of distant marriages, conflict with same-sexed children, and closeness with the opposite-sexed children. This type of fixed intergenerational pattern of triangling is well illustrated in the cartoon by Jules Feiffer of the mother who says she hated her own mother and tried to do everything differently and now her daughter has turned out—just like her mother!

However, another level of analysis would link these dyadic relationships and see each as a function of the others. That is, we can look at the family system as a set of interlocking triangles. From this perspective father's closeness to his daughter is a function of his distance from his wife, as is the mother's conflict with the daughter. The same could be hypothesized for any threesome in this system: that the functioning of any two is bound up with the interrelationships of the three in a predictable way. One of these triangles is highlighted in the genogram. This brings us to the subject of triangles (Bowen, 1978; Caplow, 1968; Carter & McGoldrick, 1998a; Fogarty, 1973; Guerin et al., 1996; Kerr & Bowen, 1988).

Triangles

While it would be impossible in this short book to explain all the complexities of systemic thinking that underlie the interpretation of relational patterns on genograms, we offer a number of common relational configurations as schema for interpreting genograms. The genogram is a valuable interpretive tool for inferring possible triangles based on partial knowledge of family relationships.

Our primary focus is on triangles, or sets of three relationships in which the functioning of each is dependent on and influences the other two. The formation of triangles in families involves two people triangling or bringing a third into their relationship. This usually serves the function of lessening difficulties in the initial dyad. For example, two family members may join in "helping" a third, who is labeled "victim," or gang up against a third, who is in this case labeled "villain." It is the collusion of the two in relation to the third that is the defining characteristic of a triangle (Bowen, 1978). The behavior of any one member of a triangle is thus a function of the behavior of the other two.

Any triangle tends to be part of a larger systemic pattern as well. Thus, a child's tantrum with an overburdened mother is not only a function of the relationship between mother and child, but most likely a function of the relationship between the mother and father, or between those two and an over-involved paternal grandfather, or between one or several adults and a precocious older sibling, to mention just a few of the possibilities. In Bowen's conceptual framework, healthy development involves differentiation. Differentiation means functioning independently in each relationship and not automatically falling into a certain pattern of relating to one person because of that person's relationship with another person. When there is high tension in a system, it is common for two people to join in relating to a third to relieve stress. Differentiation means reaching the point of relating on an individualized basis to another person rather than on the basis of the relationship that person has to someone else. Thus, a daughter would be able to have a close relationship with her mother even if father is in conflict with mother.

Parent-child Triangles

While parental tension may be lowered by joining around a sick, brilliant, or misbehaving child, children are also often drawn into coalitions on the side of one of two parents. Eugene O'Neill's older brother, Jamie (Genogram 4.2), became locked in a triangle in which he was relentlessly hostile toward his father, while adoring his drug-addicted, dreamy mother. The third side of this triangle—the relationship between the parents—obviously set in motion Jamie's polarized parental relationships. Jamie and Eugene grew up in a deprived situation—their mother often in a dream state, their father trying to hold things together. The mother, Ella, could not forgive her husband for exposing her to his rough and tumble theatrical world, and he could not forgive

Genogram 4.2 O'Neill family relationships and triangles

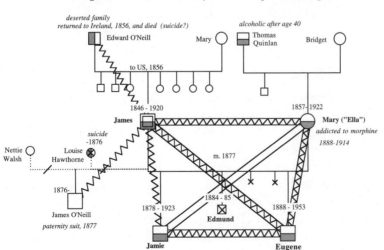

her for holding herself back from that world. While Eugene's interlocking parental triangle was different from Jamie's—he was never as negative to his father nor as adoring of his mother as Jamie, the brothers remained all their lives more children to their parents than mature adults themselves. They were opposites in many ways, yet always close in some covert way. As one biographer put it: "The brothers constantly bantered each other, one could sense a serious undertone in their relationship, a deep bond between them, as though they shared secrets they could never divulge to anyone else" (Sheaffer, 1973, p. 59), intimating, perhaps, the parental triangles into which the brothers were drawn.

Incidentally, the common mythology that a son having a close relationship with his mother is bad for his health is definitely not the case. Indeed, many of the famous people we investigated were extremely close to their mothers, including Bill Clinton, Franklin Roosevelt, Harry Truman, Frank Lloyd Wright, Douglas McArthur, and Jimmy Carter.

However, when a parent draws a child into a collusion against the other parent, whether as caretaker or "parental" child or as partner substitute, it creates a problematic triangle.

Eleanor Roosevelt (Genogram 4.3) seems to have been drawn into such a parental triangle by her father, who called her "Nell," the same name he had been called as a child. He spoke to her of making a home for him, leaving her unclear whether he expected her younger brothers to be their children or whether the brothers would be off on their own. This kind of triangling draws a child into a pathological collusion, which distorts parent-child boundaries and other relationships. Although the father was an irresponsible alcoholic, who abandoned his family, Eleanor thought of him as the center of her world for many years, while feeling there was an invisible barrier between her and her mother, who had been left to take responsibility for the children when her husband could not. Sadly, both parents died very early, making it all the more difficult for Eleanor to revise her distorted early parental relationships.

Common Couple Triangles

A couple may draw not only children, but also other people, animals (the family dog, for example), or things (such as TV or alcohol) into a triangle. Perhaps the most common couple triangle is the in-law triangle. Classically, this involves a favorite son, his mother, and his wife.

The in-law triangle may play itself out in a variety of ways. The spouses may divert their own conflicts by focusing on what is wrong with the husband's mother. Or the wife may blame the mother-in-law for her husband's inadequacies, while the mother-in-law blames the daughter-in-law for keeping her "darling boy" away. And the husband may enjoy letting his mother and his wife go

Genogram 4.3 Eleanor Roosevelt family triangle

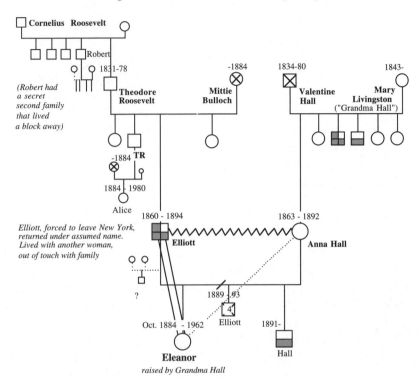

raised by Grandma Hall

at it; he probably has difficulty dealing with both of them. It is a case of "Let's you and her fight." Of course, in-law triangles can naturally occur between two spouses and any of their four parents, but the wife often takes a more central and involved emotional role and thus becomes the focus of stress in this situation.

Another common couple triangle involves an affair. Clearly, an extramarital relationship has implications for a marriage and can become a major triangle even if the marriage survives. The affair may relieve some of the tension of a conflictual relationship by giving one of the partners an outlet or it may divert the couple from underlying problems. Wilhelm Reich's genogram (4.4) shows how triangles can lead to tragedy when an affair is going on in a family. Wilhelm discovered his mother having an affair with his tutor and told his father, who then confronted the wife. She committed suicide in response. One might hypothesize that Reich's later espousal of sexuality in all forms was an attempt to make up for the disastrous results of his being drawn into that family triangle.

The investment of a spouse outside the marriage may be in an affair, work,

Genogram 4.4 Reich family

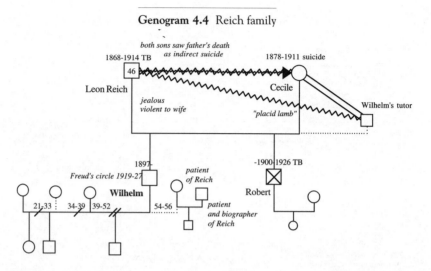

hobbies, the bottle, etc., but the impact is the same. For example, the closer the husband gets to the affair, the job, or the alcohol, the more negative the wife becomes toward both him and the object of his "affections." The more negative the wife becomes, the closer the husband moves to his girlfriend, his job, or his liquor. It is important to note that triangling occurs with objects as well as people. When this happens, it should be noted on the genogram. Family members may triangulate with the family dog or even with television, with one family member often becoming more involved with the TV as the other tries to pull him or her away (Genogram 4.5).

Triangles in Divorced and Remarried Families

When separation or divorce appears on a genogram, the possibility of certain predictable relational patterns should be explored. For example, children often

Genogram 4.5 Fonda triangle with dog

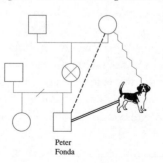

Genogram 4.6 Divorce and remarriage triangles: Fonda example

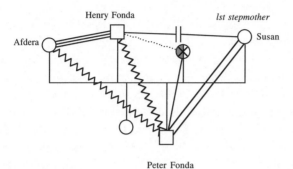

idealize the missing parent, blaming the present parent for the loss of the other, as Eleanor Roosevelt did.

When one or both parents remarry, there are additional triangles to explore (McGoldrick & Carter, 1998b). Perhaps one of the reasons such triangles are so easy to identify on the genograms of remarried families is that the structure of the family, rather than the personalities of the participants, usually defines the situation. This makes the triangles rather predictable. Children are basically never prepared to lose a parent, whether by death or divorce. Parents are not replaceable. And no parent ever ceases to matter, no matter how many years ago they died or disappeared. Thus the insider-outsider structural pattern in remarried families is endemic to the situation and tends to create triangles. How children respond to new stepparents will depend on many factors, including their gender and ages at the time of the divorce (McGoldrick & Carter, 1998b), but certain triangles are highly predictable. For example, Henry Fonda's remarriage to Susan Blanchard after his previous wife's suicide seems to have elicited a very different reaction from Peter, who was 10, than from Jane, who was 13. When Fonda redivorced four years later, Peter was heartbroken. Although it meant a great deal to Peter not to lose his second mother, his father argued that Peter's seeing Susan was insensitive to him and his new bride. Peter retorted that he hadn't divorced Susan and would see her whenever he wanted (Fonda, 1998, p. 84). We can easily see the patterns of interlocking triangles that get set in motion by the changing structures of remarried families (Genogram 4.6)

The following schematic genograms demonstrate some of the predictable triangles in remarried families. One possibility is that the children in a family with a biological father and a stepmother do not get along with the stepmother. This is not surprising. The stepmother can never replace the biological mother and the child's alliance will usually be with the biological parent rather than the stepparent. For the father in this situation the new wife offers hope after his loss. For the child she is a threat: She may take the remaining parent away.

Two different types of triangles are likely in this situation. One is a triangle involving the children, the biological father, and the stepmother (Genogram 4.7). There is hostility between the children and the new wife (the "wicked" stepmother). The stepmother often feels that her spouse gives more attention to his children than he does to her, and the husband is usually caught in a loyalty conflict between his wife and his children, making this an unstable triangle for him, because it is hard to stay connected to two others who are at war. The structure here shows clearly how he is likely to founder. But the structure also indicates the solution: He must position himself to stay connected first to his children, since the new marriage follows his historical commitment to his children.

The second triangle, usually interlocking with the first, involves the children, the stepmother, and the biological mother (Genogram 4.8). The children may resent the stepmother's efforts to replace their biological mother. The new wife feels unaccepted in her own home and the biological mother may feel threatened by the new wife. It is not uncommon for overt conflict to occur between the mother and stepmother in this triangle. Again, the structure implies the solution: The stepmother needs to avoid this triangle, that is, to avoid seeking a central position in the children's lives that would promote a loyalty conflict for them in relation to their own mother. Thus, the solution is for the stepmother to stay in a more distant relationship to the children, allowing their connection to their mother and to their father, as indicated on Genogram 4.9. The other requirement to keep this set of relationships in balance is for the divorced parents to maintain a working partnership that allows children to stay loyal to both parents, obviously not an easy task in many situations!

Indeed, interlocking triangles involving the husband, his ex-wife, and his new wife are very common. There is tension between the new couple and the ex-wife, with the ex-wife on the outside. Two types of triangles are likely here. The new couple may band together against the ex-spouse, seeing her as the cause of all their problems (Genogram 4.10). Or the new and old wife may have overt conflicts, with the husband perhaps even encouraging his new wife to fight the old battles for him (Genogram 4.11). Of course, triangles also occur with a biological mother, her children, and a stepfather. However, because our culture places greater expectations on motherhood than on fatherhood, stepmothers generally seem to have a more difficult experience (McGoldrick & Carter, 1998b).

Another relational pattern in a remarried family is seen on the genogram of

Genogram 4.7 Divorce and remarriage triangles: Children, father, and stepmother

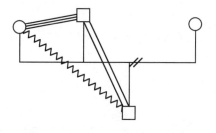

Genogram 4.8 Divorce and remarriage triangles

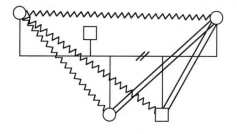

Genogram 4.9 Avoiding triangles in early remarried situation:
Stepmother in more distant position

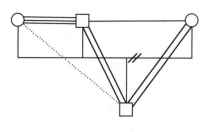

Genogram 4.10 Typical couple triangle in remarried situation

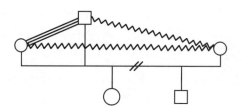

Genogram 4.11 Husband and conflicting new and ex-wives

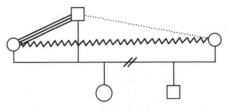

Eugene O'Neill, who had a poor relationship with his children by his second wife (Genogram 4.12). O'Neill separated from his first wife, Agnes, when their youngest child, Oona, was only three. In bitter disillusionment, he cut off not only Agnes, but the children as well, refusing even to mention their names (McGoldrick, 1995). This may have been due partly to continual resentment toward their mother for what he felt were exorbitant alimony payments, and in part due to his second wife's jealousy of his having any connections beyond her. When Oona married Charlie Chaplin, O'Neill refused to have anything to do with her ever again. Gelb and Gelb (1987) suggest that this triangle may have been part of a larger set of interlocking triangles, since Chaplin was apparently a very good friend of the ex-husband of O'Neill's wife, Carlotta. The triangles multiply quickly in remarried families.

Finally, the in-laws are not always neutral on the subject of remarriage. For example, there may be a great deal of tension between the husband's mother and his new wife. Thus, the grandparent generation often gets involved in remarried triangles, intensifying the process by joining with their adult child, especially against the ex-spouse, whom they may blame for the divorce.

Genogram 4.12 O'Neill remarried triangles

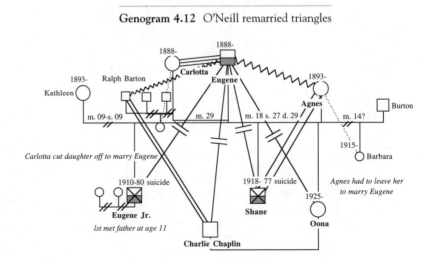

Genogram 4.13 Nuclear family triangle with adopted and biological children

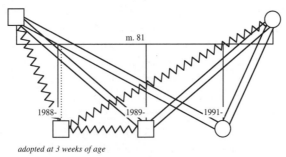

adopted at 3 weeks of age

Triangles in Families with Foster or Adopted Children

Parent-child triangles are particularly common when one or more of the children is a foster or adopted child. When there are also biological children in the family, the adopted child may have a unique position. In the family shown in Genogram 4.13, for example, tension between the parents—perhaps because of their failure to have their own children, perhaps for other reasons—was present. before the child was adopted. This led the couple to focus intensely and negatively on the adopted child, who was treated as an outsider, serving to distract the family from other concerns.

In many ways, families with foster or adopted children are like remarried families in that there are two families involved: the caretaking family and the biological family. This is true whether the biological parents are known or not, since people can triangulate a memory or idea as well as actual people. For example, consider the genogram shown in Genogram 4.14. Several triangles are possible here. The child may play one set of parents against the other. The caretaking parents may blame the biological parents for their difficulties (bad genes). Or, if there are also biological children, rivalry for the parents' attention and competition between the foster and biological children may occur.

Genogram 4.14 Triangle of adoptee with biological and adoptive parents

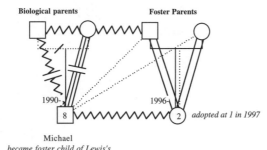

Michael
became foster child of Lewis's
at age 6 in 1996

Multigenerational Triangles

As mentioned earlier, triangles can cross many generations. Probably the most common three-generational triangle is one in which a grandparent and grandchild ally against the parents. In the Mead family genogram (Genogram 4.15) and the King family genogram (Genogram 4.16), we see that Margaret and Martin had very close relationships with their grandparents. Seeing this on a genogram suggests the hypothesis of a triangle where a parent is an ineffectual outsider to a cross-generational alliance. Such multigenerational triangles are likely to develop if the other parent dies or leaves because of separation or divorce. One of the most common patterns occurs when a single mother and her children share a household with her parents, as happened in Bill Clinton's family (Genogram 3.1). The mother may lose power as the grandparents take over child-rearing responsibilities or as a grandparent-grandchild alliance forms against her.

Genogram 4.15 Mead family

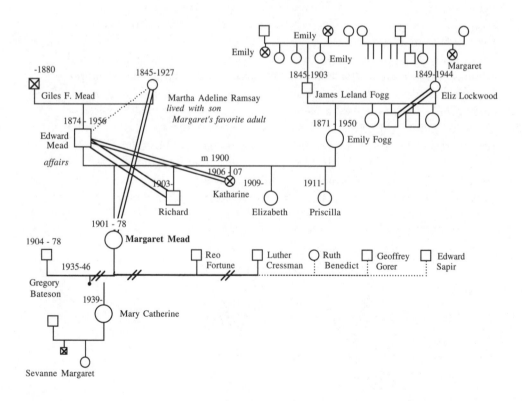

Genogram 4.16 Martin Luther King family

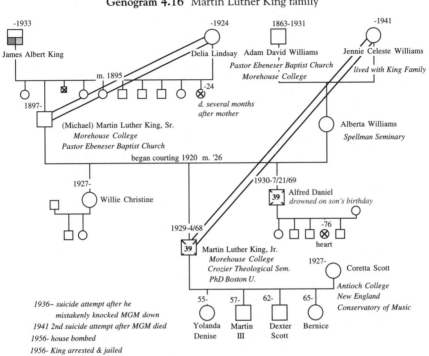

Relationships Outside the Family

There tends to be an inverse correlation between the intensity of relational patterns within a family and a family's relationships with outsiders, i.e., the more closed the system is to relationships outside the family, the greater the intensity of relationships within it. Thus, if one sees on the genogram patterns of fused relationships or intense triangles, one might then investigate the family's boundary with the outside world.

For example, in the Brontë family (Genogram 4.17), only Charlotte had any ongoing relationships outside the immediate family. The other three siblings who lived to adulthood all died within a nine-month period, one after another, almost as though their fusion made it impossible for them to live without each other. Such a genogram should suggest raising questions about the reason for the strong boundaries around the family. None of the siblings except Charlotte ever left home for more than a brief period. They became ill whenever they were away from home. The two sisters who died in childhood developed their fatal illnesses during their first period away from home and died within a short period of each other. Indeed, when Charlotte first told her father she wanted to marry he became enraged and fired her fiancé, who was his curate, later allowing the marriage only on the condition that they would never leave him (McGoldrick, 1995).

Genogram 4.17 Brontë family

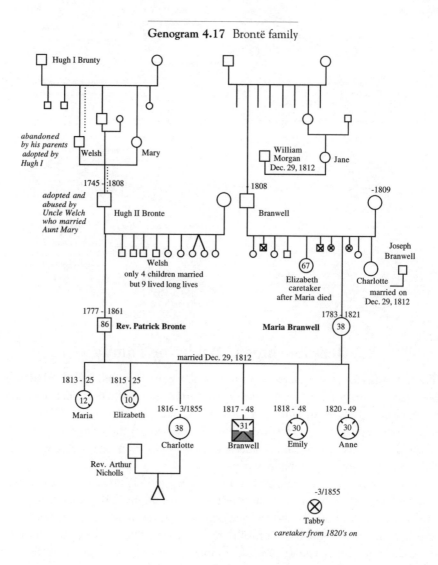

5
ASSESSING FAMILY ROLES, FUNCTIONING, BALANCE, RESILIENCE, AND RESOURCES

Reading the genogram for patterns of balance and imbalance in family structure, roles, functioning, and resources allows the clinician to derive hypotheses about how the family is adapting to stress. Balance and imbalance speak to the functional whole of a family system. Family systems are not homogenous, and contrasting characteristics are usually present in the same family. In well-functioning families, such characteristics usually balance out one another. We have already seen, for example, the complementary fit of oldest and youngest, where the oldest child's tendency to be caretaker balances the youngest's tendency to be taken care of by others.

The clinician detects patterns of balance and imbalance by looking for contrasts and characteristics that "stick out," and then asking: How do these contrasts and idiosyncrasies fit into the total functional whole? What balances have been achieved and what stresses are present in the system due to a lack of balance? For example, if one person is doing poorly in a family in which everyone else is doing well, one might ask what role the dysfunction plays in the total system.

The Family Structure

Sometimes, differences in family structure may be seen over a number of generations. For example, there may be a multigenerational contrast in the family structure for the two spouses, creating a graphically lopsided genogram. One spouse comes from a large family and has countless aunts and uncles, while the other is an only child of two only children. This could lead to both balance and imbalance. On the one hand, each spouse may be attracted to the experience of the other. One likes the privacy of a small family and the other the diversity of a large family. On the other hand, the imbalance between the large number of relatives on one side and the paucity on the other may create problems. One spouse may be used to playing to a crowd and engaging in multiple relationships, while the other needs a more exclusive, private relationship.

Another structural issue involving balance occurs when one spouse comes from a family where divorce and remarriage are common and the other comes from a long line of intact households. Seeing this structural contrast on the genogram might cue the clinician to explore the spouses' different expectations about marriage.

Roles

In well-functioning families, members take a variety of different roles: caretaker, dependent, provider, spokesperson, etc. Sometimes from the genogram it will be evident that there are too many people for one particular role. For example, Harry Stack Sullivan (Genogram 5.1) grew up as an only child in a household with many parental figures. In addition to his mother and father, his mother's mother, and, at times, his mother's sister were in the household. It is clear that there were many adults vying for the role of caretaker of the only child.

On the other hand, a single family member may be in the position of caring for an inordinate number of family members, as Ted Kennedy did after his brothers' deaths (see Genogram 2.25). Since Ted is the sole surviving male member

Genogram 5.1 Harry Stack Sullivan's family: Many figures for one role

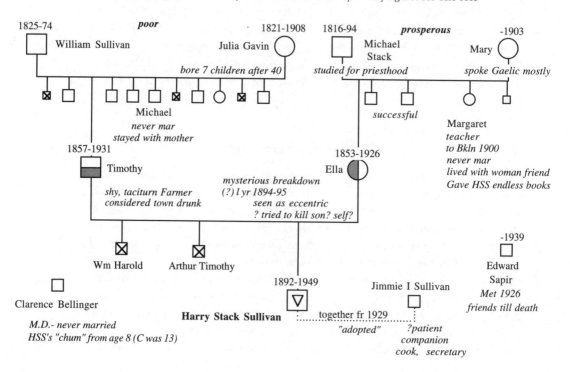

of his generation, he has had a special role in the three fatherless households, as well as responsibility for his own family. A clinician seeing this family would want to explore how a balance has been worked out and what other resources have been brought in to help take care of the many children involved.

In modern marriages role allocation is seldom based solely on gender and is often shared. Thus, both parents may be caretakers, providers, and spokespeople for the family. However, this balance is not achieved automatically or easily, and it may be an area of conflict, particularly for dual-career families.

Level and Style of Functioning

Family members operate with different styles and at different levels of functioning. Often these patterns are balanced, so that the functions of different family members all fit in a particular adaptive form. Again, we scan the genogram for contrasts and idiosyncrasies in functioning, which may help to explain how the system functions as a whole.

Any newly formed family needs to fit together different styles and ways of relating to the world. The result may be more or less complementary and growth-enhancing for the offspring. Virginia Woolf, for example (Genogram 5.2), felt she was the fortunate inheritor of two different, but complementary,

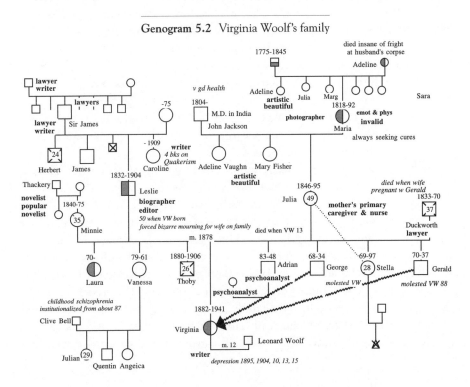

Genogram 5.2 Virginia Woolf's family

Genogram 5.3   Alcohol problems: Over- and underfunctioning

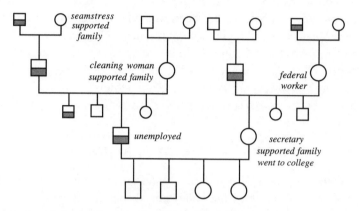

styles from the joining of her mother's and father's families. On her father's side, family members seemed to be bold, pragmatic, legalistic, and writers of persuasive political arguments. On her mother's side, family members tended to be beautiful, artistic, stylish, and somewhat unapproachable. Virginia tried to combine and balance these two styles in her own life and work.

Certain balances in families may also lead to or allow dysfunction in a family system. For example, we often see on a genogram a complementary pattern of alcoholics married to spouses who are overfunctioners (Bepko & Krestan, 1985; Steinglass, Bennett, Wolin, & Reiss, 1987), as in Genogram 5.3. The non-drinking spouse is pressed to become overresponsible, to balance an underresponsible alcoholic partner. Since alcoholic behavior by its nature leads to underresponsibility, the other partner takes up the slack; otherwise children must fill in, taking on adult roles. The willingness of the partner to be a caretaker and of the other to be taken care of may stabilize the relationship. At times the whole family may become organized in this complementary way around the dysfunction of one member.

Sometimes, when there is dysfunction in one area, the family will find ways to compensate for common difficulties. This seems to have been the case with the family of Alexander Graham Bell, the inventor of the telephone (Genogram 5.4). The difficulty in this family was deafness. Both Bell's mother and his wife were almost totally deaf. Three generations of males in the family—Bell himself, his father and uncle, and his grandfather—all specialized in speech projection and elocution. Bell's grandfather wrote a classic text on phonetic speech, and both Bell's father and his uncle devoted themselves to teaching their father's methods. The family was a highly inventive one. When Alexander was a young teenager, his father suggested that he and his brother develop a talking machine. They studied the mechanisms of speech so well that

Genogram 5.4 Alexander Graham Bell's family

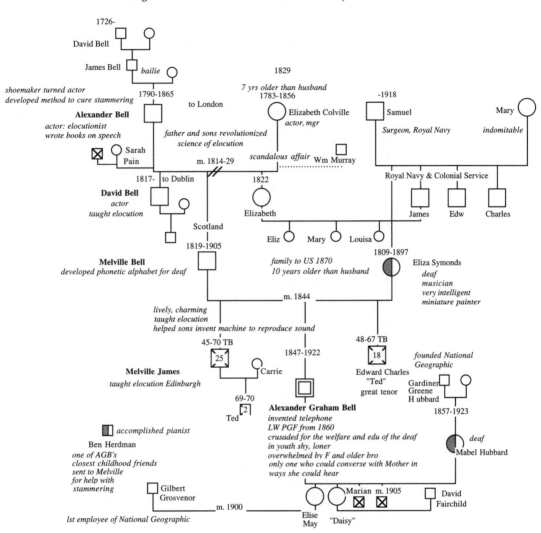

the instrument they developed annoyed a neighbor, who thought he heard a baby crying. Some members specialized in speech and hearing, compensating for those who spoke with difficulty because they could not hear at all.

In analyzing possible patterns of functioning in families, it is essential to determine whether there is a fit or a balance in the system. Do extreme contrasts between family members maintain the stability of the system or are they pushing the family toward a different equilibrium? At times a system breaks down not because of the dysfunction of one or two members but because of the burnout of caretakers who previously created a balanced fit in the system. In the case of chronic illness, family members are frequently able to mobilize themselves in the short term for support of the dysfunctional person, but are not able to maintain such behavior over the long term.

Tracking Resilience

Tracking families' resilience in the face of loss, trauma, and dysfunction is an extremely important aspect of genogram assessment because of its clinical relevance. All families need resilience in order to survive, and it is important to focus on such resourcefulness and to underline it. The Mexican artist Frida Kahlo (Genogram 5.5) provides a remarkable example of such resilience. Her very artwork reflected the tremendous inner resourcefulness she found to turn

Genogram 5.5. Frida Kahlo and Diego Rivera

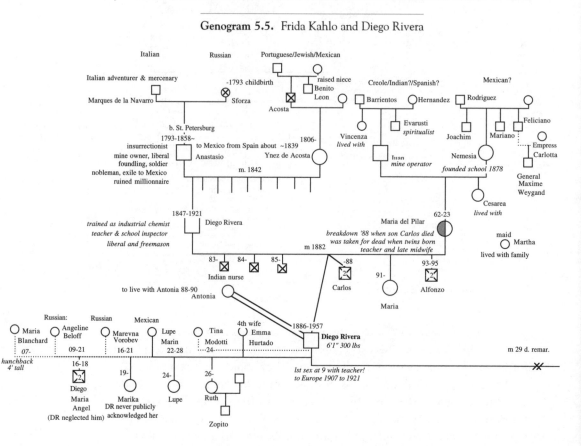

trauma and pain into something rich, complex and transformative. The resilience is evident in many aspects of the family history, such as her traumatic bus accident at age 18, which fractured her spine and left her in pain, in spite of numerous operations, for the rest of her life. Coincidentally, her father had suffered an accidental fall at the same age, which left him with brain damage and seizures, changing his life and becoming a factor in his emigration to Mexico the next year. Frida, who also experienced polio at age six, which led to her missing almost a year of school and left her with a weak leg, became her father's favorite child and discovered an outlet in art, as did her father and her maternal grandfather. Both Kahlo's parents experienced severe traumas early in life. Her mother, a brilliant and attractive woman of Spanish and Mexican background, had been in love with a German, who seems tragically to have committed suicide in her presence. All her life she kept a book of his letters and, though she married Guillermo Kahlo and had four daughters, she never

Genogram 5.5. Frida Kahlo and Diego Rivera

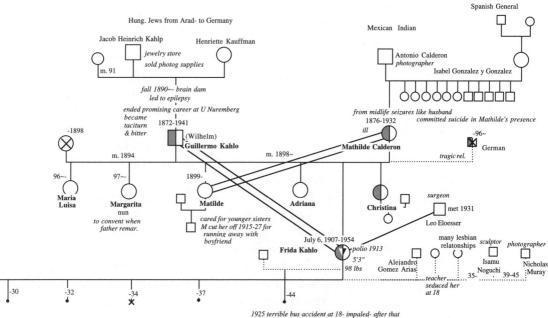

seems to have been able to live up to her potential. Kahlo himself, who had much promise when he began school at the University of Nuremberg, was unable to continue his studies after a severe fall at age 18, which caused brain damage and left him with seizures for the rest of his life. His mother died about the same time and Kahlo did not get along with the woman his father remarried the next year, so his father helped him emigrate to Mexico. There he married and had two children before his wife tragically died. It was his second wife, Frida's mother, who encouraged him to become a photographer, like her father. Unfortunately, the father never seems to have been able to master his young traumas and over the years he became bitter and withdrawn in spite of his obvious abilities and early efforts to reinvent himself with his second family and career. It was Frida who shows the most remarkable ability to transform traumatic experiences into hope and art.

Kahlo's husband, Diego Rivera, reflects a similar resilience in many aspects of his life, though not in his personal relationships with his partners or his children, where he showed much dysfunction. He had been a twin whose twin brother died at age two, after which his mother had a breakdown and Diego was sent away to the mountains for two years with his Indian caretaker. Three other babies had died previously, and a younger brother died also at age two. One strange story told is of Diego, age eight, and his sister, six, playing with the corpse of their two-year-old brother, whose coffin had been left open. Only Diego and this sister survived out of six children. In childhood he lived surrounded by women: his mother, his beloved nanny, Antonia, the maid, Martha, and two aunts Cesarea and Vincenza. This situation probably set the pattern he was always to follow of having many women around him. But his childhood was spent in the shadow of his parents' conflicts, his mother losing her grasp on reality, and his father suffering many failures and humiliations in work as he struggled to keep the family going. One of the paradoxes of Diego's life was that a grant from a patron who had been a slave trader enabled him to go to Europe to study when he was a struggling art student.

But his work and his life bridged many divergent worlds, beginning with his complex, mixed cultural heritage, which included Mexican, Indian, African, Italian, Russian, and Portuguese Jewish. He was proud of his exotic heritage, though he also tended to romanticize Mexico's Aztec past and his own, boasting of his African, Aztec, Spanish, and Chinese ancestors—he apparently had none of the latter! Though in his own life he frequently had to put up with crude racial abuse, he transformed the very concept of culture to something inclusive and creative. One college president claimed that his murals in Detroit soiled public walls and were the work of "an outside, half-breed, Mexican Bolshevist." Yet through his work he gave a whole nation pride in its history and its future, showing that Mexicans were not just the victims of the conquistadors or second-class citizens in relation to Europeans. His work and his life drew much from many cultures. His wives came from Russia, France, Italy, and Mexico, and he himself lived in France and Russia as well as in Mexico. He incorporated culture, class, and politics into his art, committing himself to art that went beyond the individual—large-scale public art, whose creation involved a team of workers and whose audience was the entire general population, who would see it on public walls and spaces.

Family Resources

Finally, family members often differ in resources such as money, health and vigor, skills, meaningful work, and support systems. When extreme differences in these areas appear on the genogram, it important to explore how the system handles the imbalance.

In the family shown in Genogram 5.6, the spouses differ in class and occupational background. Immediately questions arise:

- How do the spouses handle their differences in class and background?
- How do they handle their different levels of income and expectations about standards of living?
- Is there an important balance or imbalance in some other area? Is there a difference in values?
- What is the impact of spouses' coming into a marriage with very different financial resources? different educational and job status? different social class standing?
- What is the impact on siblings of having different financial resources? different educational and job status? different social class standing?

Genogram 5.6 Couple with different occupational backgrounds

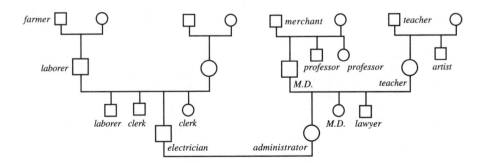

Of course, other family members come into play as well. How did the two different families feel about the marriage? Was there approval or disapproval for the match? The genogram alerts the clinician to these possible issues.

Differences in resources can also become problematic when one sibling becomes more successful than the others. For example, if one sibling in a family becomes highly successful and all others are less so in terms of finances or status, there may be an imbalance; the successful one may not be able to meet the needs of the siblings, and they in turn may resent the achiever, both for the success and the lack of support. When resources (emotional as well as financial) are lacking, one frequently sees siblings cutting off, particularly around the caretaking of a parent or an ill sibling. Families may get caught up in struggles over who did more for the person in need. In other families, where most siblings are doing well and only one sibling or one parent is in need, it may be easier to develop a satisfactory balance of resources without unduly taxing any one member. A very wealthy sibling may end up contributing financially but not with time or emotional caretaking, which also contributes to a sense of imbalance in the family. Geographic distance of siblings from each other or from parents may also create imbalances, especially if only one sibling lives close enough to do the caretaking for a needy parent. He, or more likely she, may burn out and become resentful. Daughters are much more likely to be saddled with family caretaking burdens. Siblings who are not married or who do not have children may also be inequitably expected to do the caretaking for parents (especially for a single parent). All such imbalances in sibling responsibility for parents should be explored and inequities challenged, because such imbalances can otherwise have far-reaching negative effects on family relationships.

6

USING GENOGRAMS TO TRACK FAMILIES THROUGH THE LIFE CYCLE

The genogram can be used to track the family pattern at each phase of the family life cycle. Different configurations on the genogram suggest possible triangles and issues that can be explored for each phase. Genograms and family chronologies are useful tools for assessing families in life cycle perspective, the spiral of family evolution as generations move through time in their development from birth to death (Carter & McGoldrick, 1998a; Gerson, 1995; Weber & Levine, 1995; see also bibliography section on the Family Life Cycle). Family evolution is like a musical composition, in which the meaning of individual notes depends on their rhythmic and harmonic relationship with each other and with the memories of past melodies, as well as with those anticipated but not yet written. Genograms can elucidate the family life cycle, which can in turn aid in interpretation of the genogram. Both the patterns that typically occur at various phases of the life cycle and the issues to be predicted when life events are "off schedule" are relevant to understanding family developmental process.

Families progress through a series of milestones, transitions, or nodal points in their development, which may include leaving home, forming a couple, the birth of children, child-rearing, launching, and retirement. At each nodal point in the life cycle the family must reorganize itself in order to move on successfully to the next phase. These transitions can be very difficult for some families, who have trouble adapting to new circumstances and who tend to rigidify at transition points.

Regardless of the presenting problem, clinicians should always assess whether the presenting problem might reflect difficulties the family is having handling life cycle transitions. The ages and dates on the genogram suggest what life cycle transitions the family is adapting to and whether life cycle events and ages occur within normative expectations. There are normative expectations for the timing of each phase of the family life cycle, i.e., the likely ages of family members at each transition point. While these norms are ever-changing and must not be regarded in any way as fixed, when events happen outside this range of expectations, the clinician should consider the possibility of some difficulty inhibiting the family in making the life cycle transition.

Thus, it is important to scan the genogram for family members whose ages differ greatly from the norm for their phase of the life cycle. The dates on the genogram of births, deaths, leaving home, marriage, separation, and divorce are all helpful in this regard. For example, the fact that three sons in a family married for the first time in their fifties might indicate some problems in leaving home and forming intimate relationships. It would be worth asking a couple in which the husband is 27 and the wife 47 how they happened to get together and how this pairing might fit with various patterns in their families of origin. A woman who has her first child at 43, a man who becomes a father at age 70, or a family in which all the sons died before middle age—all suggest systems where deviations in the normative pattern of the life cycle deserve further exploration.

In our culture, there appears to be a generally preferable time in the life cycle for couples to marry. Those who marry before the age of 20 or after the age of 30 are at greater risk for divorce, although the normative age at first marriage is dramatically higher in the past few years (see McGoldrick, 1998b). Couples are increasingly marrying in their mid to late twenties and many not until their mid thirties.

Also of interest is the period of time between meeting, engagement, and marriage, and between separation, divorce, and remarriage. A short interval between life events does not allow much time for family members to deal with the emotional shifts involved (McGoldrick & Carter, 1998b). For example, Henry Fonda's remarriage eight months after his second wife committed suicide (see Genogram 2.6) would suggest unresolved emotional issues and at least the possibility of an affair. In fact, Henry had begun a relationship with his future wife the year before. Rushing into the new marriage also suggests the importance to Henry of putting the previous marriage behind him. One would also wonder how the family, particularly the children, adjusted to such rapid family changes. In light of this, the fact that Henry never discussed Frances's suicide with his children makes it all the more apparent that he did not himself or with them process his grief or trauma before trying to move on.

The Life Cycle of Freud's Family

This chapter will use the Freud family to illustrate the use of genograms to track family process through the life cycle. Freud's genogram can help us to see him in context and put in perspective some of the history he did not want us to tell. Like Freud, many people would prefer to downplay their family history.

Courtship and Marriage of Freud's Parents: The Joining of Families

Since the life cycle is circular and repetitive, we can start at any point to tell the story of a family. With the Freud family, we might begin a few years before the birth of Sigmund, at the time of his parents' courtship.

At the marriage or remarriage phase, the genogram shows the coming together of two separate families, indicating where each spouse is in his or her own family life cycle. To start a new family, both partners must come to terms with their families of origin. The genogram gives clues to the roles and connectedness of the spouses to their own families. When one spouse competes with the other's family or when parents do not approve of their child's choice, in-law triangles may begin at this phase. The genogram also shows the previous relationships that may affect or interfere with current marital bonding. Unfortunately, we know virtually nothing of the in-law relationships in this generation of the Freud family.

As can be seen on the genogram of the Freud family in 1855 (Genogram 6.1) and Chronology 6.1, the marriage of Jacob Freud and Amalia Nathansohn had a number of atypical aspects. Jacob, who was 40, was marrying for the third time. Amalia was just 20. In fact, she was even younger than Jacob's sons from

---

Chronology 6.1 The Freud Family at Time of Jacob and Amalia's Marriage

1832	Jacob Freud, age 16, marries Sally Kanner.
1833	(April) Jacob and Sally's first child, Emanuel, is born.
1834	Jacob and Sally's second child, Philipp, is born.
1835?	Third child is born. Gender, date of birth and date and cause of death are unknown.
1837?	Fourth child is born. Gender, date of birth and date and cause of death are unknown.
1852	Jacob's first wife, Sally Kanner, is recorded as alive. Did they divorce? Did she die by end of year?
1852	Jacob's second marriage to Rebecca. Two entries list Jacob's wife as Rebecca that year, aged 31 and 32 (Krüll, 1986).
1852	(October–December) Rebecca dies (?)
1853	(December) Jacob hands over his business to son Emanuel.
1854	(or earlier) Emanuel marries Maria.
1854	(or slightly earlier) Amalia's father loses his fortune and is disgraced.
1855	(July 29) Jacob and Amalia are married. Jacob is listed as widower since 1852.
1855	(August 13) Emanuel's first son (later Sigmund's nephew) John is born.

Genogram 6.1 Freud/Nathansohn family, 1855

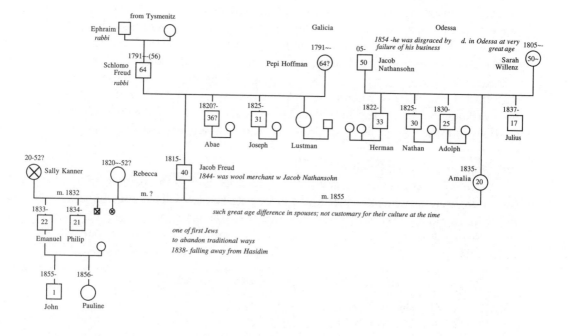

his first marriage. Virtually nothing is known about his first wife, Sally Kanner, or the two children from that family who died; even less is known about Jacob's second wife, Rebecca. We do not know what happened to either wife, whether the couple divorced or the wives died. In addition, Jacob's first marriage took place when he was only 16, suggesting the possibility of an unexpected pregnancy (Anzieu, 1986). The second marriage is even more mysterious. Rebecca was never mentioned by any family member and we know of her existence only from public records. She appears to have married Jacob in 1852. Jacob's sons Emanuel and Philipp were grown and would obviously have known her. Surely Amalia would at least have known of her existence, as they all lived in the same town; yet, if anyone ever did mention her to Freud, he never told anyone. Was there something about her of which the family was ashamed? In any case, Jacob and Amalia obviously began their new family in the shadow of Jacob's earlier marriages.

When examining a genogram, it is particularly important to note the ages of family members as they move through the life cycle. With any newly married couple, it is important to note the spouses' positions within the life cycles of their respective families. Jacob was already a grandfather, whereas Amalia,

20 years younger and a peer of his sons, was at the young adult phase. How did these two happen to marry? We know that such age differences were not the custom at this time and place (Krüll, 1986). One wonders what led Amalia to agree to marry a man so much older, with grown sons and two previous marriages. It seems that her father had recently lost his fortune and been disgraced, which may explain the situation (Swales, 1986). In any case, Amalia was a vivacious young woman, one of the youngest in her family. Jacob, for his part, had experienced many ups and downs. Having done fairly well in his thirties as a traveling salesman with his maternal grandfather, he seemingly came to a standstill in midlife. One would predict, upon seeing these differences in experience and expectation on a genogram, that this may be a problematic life cycle transition. Unresolved issues in earlier phases of the life cycle tend to lead to more difficult transitions and complexities in later life cycle stages. Thus, it is likely that with Jacob's previous marriages, his mysterious past, the discrepancies in their ages and expectations, as well as their financial precariousness, Jacob and Amalia entered their marriage with many complex issues unresolved.

There are at least two predictable triangles in the genogram of a remarried family: (1) that involving the two new spouses and the previous spouse (or the memory of the previous spouse), and (2) that involving the two new spouses and the children of the previous marriage. We know nothing of Amalia's relationship with Jacob's previous wives. Nor do we know details of her relationship with Emanuel and Philipp. We do know from comments Freud made in his adult life that in his fantasy his mother and Philipp were lovers, and that within three years of the marriage Jacob helped to arrange for his sons to emigrate to England, which he may have done partly to have them at a safe distance from his wife.

The Transition to Parenthood and Family with Young Children

A genogram of the early parent years often reveals stressors that make this phase especially difficult. By providing a quick map of the sibling constellation, the genogram may reveal the particular circumstances surrounding the birth of a child and how those circumstances may have contributed to the child's having a special position in that family. Finally, the genogram will show the typical mother-father-child triangles of this period.

Sigmund was born in 1856 in Freiberg, Moravia. As can be seen from the genogram of the Freud family for 1859 (Genogram 6.2) and Chronology 6.2, much was going on in the family around the time of his birth. His specialness for his father may have been intensified by the fact that Jacob's own father died less than three months before Sigmund was born and Sigmund was named for this grandfather, Schlomo, a rabbi. Sigmund was, perhaps, raised to follow in

---

Chronology 6.2 The Freud Family, 1856–59

1856   (Feb. 21) Schlomo Freud, Jacob's father dies. (Jacob is 40.)

1856   (May 6) Sigmund is born to Jacob and Amalia in Freiberg, Moravia (now Pribor, in the Czech Republic).

1857   (October) Sigmund's brother Julius is born.

1858   (March) Amalia's 20-year-old brother, Julius Nathansohn, dies of tuberculosis.

1858   (April 15) Sigmund's brother Julius dies.

1858   Wilhelm Fleiss is born. Sigmund identified Fleiss with his brother Julius.

1858   (December) Sigmund's sister Anna is born.

1859   (January) Sigmund's nursemaid leaves—jailed for theft, which had been reported by Sigmund's half-brother Philipp during Amalia's confinement with Anna.

1859   (August) Sigmund's half-brothers, Emanuel and Philipp, emigrate with their families, including Sigmund's nephew, John, to whom he is very attached.

1859   (August) Freud family moves from Freiberg to Leipzig, apparently because of economic reversals.

---

his footsteps by becoming a teacher and intellectual leader. Sigmund's family role was obviously also influenced by his innate brilliance. Another factor accounting for his special role was probably that he was born at the high point in the family's hopes. Shortly afterward they had to migrate twice and Jacob suffered significant business failures, from which he seems never to have entirely recovered. Sigmund's younger siblings, particularly Anna and Dolfi, may have borne the brunt of the negative effects of these changes on the family.

Equally important, Sigmund's brother Julius, born when Sigmund was 17 months old, lived for only seven months. The death of a child tends to intensify parental feelings about the surviving children. The child nearest in age, especially a child of the same sex, often becomes a replacement for the lost child. Thus, Sigmund may have become even more important to his mother after the death of her second son. The loss of this infant would itself have been intensified by the fact that, exactly one month before his death, Amalia's youngest brother, also named Julius, died at the age of 20 from pulmonary tuberculosis (Krüll, 1986). Undoubtedly she knew that her brother was dying when she named her son for him seven months earlier. The naming is especially interesting, since it goes against the Jewish custom of naming a baby in honor of someone who has already died. Is the emotional imperative somehow more

Genogram 6.2 Freud family, 1859

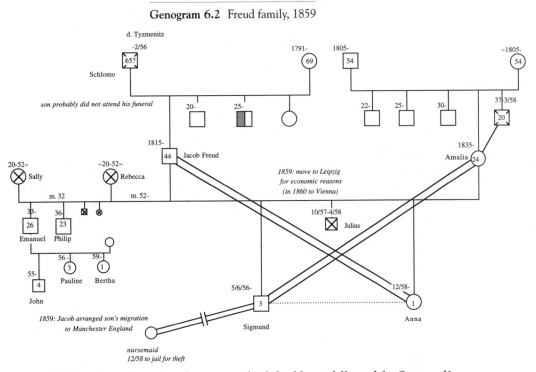

powerful here than the cultural custom, which had been followed for Sigmund? In later life Sigmund said that he had welcomed this brother with "ill wishes and real infantile jealousy, and his death left the germ of guilt in me" (cited in Krüll, 1986).

The oldest sometimes resents the later born, feeling threatened or displaced by the new arrival. From a very early age, Sigmund may have seen his sister Anna as an intrusion, and she may have resented his special position and privileges in the family. She was conceived the month before the death of the second child, Julius. Sigmund's sibling rivalry might have been compounded by family ambivalence about the first child born after a lost son. These feelings of rivalry can linger into adulthood. Sigmund's relationship with his sister Anna seems never to have been very close and they were alienated as adults.

Another complicating factor in terms of the broader family constellation can be seen on the genogram. For the first three years of his life, Sigmund was raised almost as a younger brother to his nephew John, who was a year or so older than he. Sigmund commented on the importance of this relationship to Ernest Jones:

> Until the end of my third year we had been inseparable; we had loved each other and fought each other and . . . his childish relationship has deter-

mined all my later feelings in intercourse with persons my own age. My
nephew, John, has since then had many incarnations, which have revived
first one and then another aspect of character and is ineradicably fixed in
my conscious memory. At times he must have treated me very badly and I
must have opposed my tyrant courageously. (1953, p. 8)

The first phase of this new family, of which Sigmund was the first child,
finally concluded with a splitting and emigration of the old family. We do not
know the details of why the Freud family left Freiberg. When Sigmund was
three, his stepbrothers and their families went to England to find their fortunes,
and Jacob moved his family first to Leipzig and then to Vienna, probably in part
because of the economic reversals or because they were involved in a counterfeiting scheme. Perhaps there were tensions between Amalia and her stepsons
Emanuel and Philipp, who may have been reminders to her of Jacob's earlier
loyalties. As mentioned, there is even a hint of a possible extramarital relationship. Also, Jacob and Amalia shared a nursemaid with Emanuel and his
wife and the children played well together. Another loss for Sigmund was the
nursemaid, who was dismissed from the household for stealing while Amalia
was confined for the birth of Anna. Thus, within a period of a few years,
Sigmund experienced a multitude of losses: the death of his brother, the dis-
missal of the nursemaid, the emigration of his stepbrothers and their children,
the birth of his sister which took his mother away, and finally the uprooting of
his whole family. The Freuds were never to be as financially stable again.

Sigmund was the first of eight children (Genogram 6.3 and Chronology
6.3). The genogram shows the family in the year Sigmund finished gymnasium
and began medical school.

It is the birth of the first child, more than the marriage itself, that most profoundly marks the transition to a new family. For the new spouse, the child
tends to signify greater legitimization and power of the current family in relation to the partner's previous family. Sigmund definitely seemed to have a special place in his mother's heart. He had an intense relationship with her and
she always referred to him as her "golden Sigi." By all accounts he was the center of the household. There is a well-known family story that when his sister
Anna wanted to play the piano, their mother bought one, but got rid of it
immediately when Sigmund complained that the noise bothered him. His sisters got no further piano lessons. Sigmund's special position is further indicated by the fact that the family gave him the privilege of naming his younger
brother, Alexander, born when Sigmund was ten. (In his own marriage,
Sigmund named every one of the six children, all for his male heroes or one of
their female family members!) The Freuds' cultural preference for sons further
exalted Sigmund's position in his family.

Chronology 6.3 Freud Family, 1860s and 1870s

1860	Freud family settles in Vienna.
1860	(March) Sigmund's sister Rosa is born.
1861	(March) Sigmund's sister Marie (Mitzi) is born.
1862	(July) Sigmund's sister Dolfi is born.
1863	(May) Sigmund's sister Paula is born.
1865	(July 20) Uncle Josef Freud arrested for counterfeiting.
1865	(October) Maternal grandfather (Jacob Nathansohn) dies.
1866	(February) Uncle Josef Freud sent to prison for 10 years.
1866	(April) Sigmund's brother Alexander, named by Sigmund, is born.
1868	Sigmund enters gymnasium.
1873	Sigmund enters medical school.

Genogram 6.3 Freud family, 1873

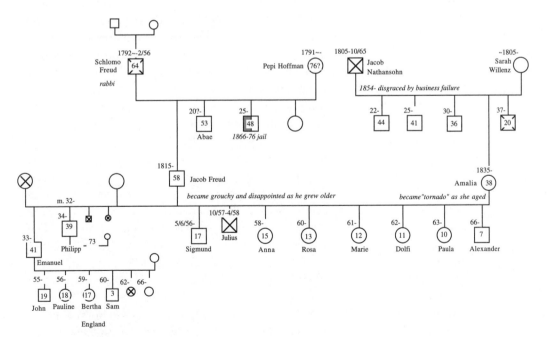

Family with Adolescents

Once children reach adolescence, the task is to prepare the family for a qualitative change in the relationships between the generations, as the children are no longer so dependent on their parents. During this period two common patterns of triangles are likely to develop, the first involving (a) the adolescents, (b) their peers, and (c) their parents, and the second involving (a) the adolescents, (b) their parents, and (c) their grandparents. As adolescents are seeking their identity and emerging into their sexual and creative potential, parents are often struggling with the realization of their own limitations both in terms of work and relationships, which may add to the intensity of intergenerational conflicts.

We have little specific information on family events during the years of Freud's adolescence, but the genogram suggests a family with many child-rearing burdens, since there were seven children, all still in the home. We may also wonder whether the discrepancy in age between Jacob and Amalia would be felt even more at this stage of the life cycle. Jacob, in his fifties, may have been feeling his age. Sigmund later described his father as having been rather grouchy and disappointed in his older sons, Emanuel and Philipp. In contrast, Amalia, 20 years younger, was still energetic, attractive, and youthful. We do not know whether these differences in age, energy level, and outlook led to tension or conflict between Jacob and Amalia, but, given her devotion to Sigmund and the demands of a large household, it is likely that her energies were more focused on her children than on her spouse. Sigmund later reported that he felt as though he had to make up for his father's absence. We also know that Jacob's brother was jailed during this period for counterfeiting, an experience that Sigmund later said turned his father's hair gray. It appears that Jacob was implicated in the scheme—or at least his sons were, which may have accounted for their earlier move to England (Krüll, 1986; Swales, 1986).

It is during adolescence that children begin to have interests outside the family, both in school and with friends. Sigmund did very well in school and was at the top of his gymnasium class for six of his eight years there. His success with his peers was less spectacular. By all accounts he was a shy, intense, serious young man who focused more on his studies than on socializing. The genogram will sometimes indicate important peers in a child's life and whether family boundaries easily expand to embrace outsiders (Gerson, 1995; McGoldrick & Carter, 1998b). We know of Sigmund having only one close friend at school, Eduard Silberstein, with whom he corresponded and formed a "secret society." At 16 he had a crush on a friend's sister, Gisela Fluss, but never expressed his feelings to her. Perhaps he was responding to a mandate from his family: to excel in school and to succeed in life, and so justify his special position in his family and to make up for their other disappointments—in the older sons and in Jacob, who never seems to have made a real living in Vienna.

Family at Midlife: Launching Children and Moving On

The launching phase, when children leave home to be on their own, in the past usually blended into marriage, since children often did not leave home until they married. Now most go through a period of being a single adult. This phase, the cornerstone of the modern family life cycle, is crucial for all the other phases that are to follow (Gerson, 1995; Carter & McGoldrick, 1998a). The short-circuiting of this phase, or its prolongation, may affect all future life cycle transitions. The genogram often reveals the duration of the launching phase, as well as factors that may contribute to a delay of launching.

The information that we have on the Freud family during the launching phase is quite scanty. As has already been mentioned, Sigmund held a favored, almost exalted position in his family. Sometimes this can lead to difficulties in launching, when a young adult is hesitant to leave such a favored position and the parents are unwilling to let their special child go. This was true for Sigmund, who lived with his parents until he was 30, when he married Martha Bernays and they moved to their own apartment. As was customary, one other daughter, Dolfi, never married and remained at home to be the parental caretaker, as Anna did in the next generation.

One interesting fact from the perspective of the life cycle is how long it took Sigmund to complete his medical studies (Chronology 6.4). He took eight years to get his degree, and did not practice for quite a few years after that. This was unusual in those days, particularly for students who were not independently wealthy. Perhaps he was hesitant to finish and move on to the next phase—supporting himself. Or perhaps he felt that he was needed by his mother at home. In any case, he, apparently, did not seriously think about supporting himself until he wanted to marry Martha. When a delay in moving on to the next phase is indicated by the genogram, as in Freud's case with his prolonged time as a student and his lengthy engagement, the clinician should explore the impediments to moving on in the life cycle.

Marriage, the Next Generation

Having gone through several transitions of the Freud family life cycle, we come to the next phase: the marriage of Sigmund Freud and Martha Bernays. A genogram of the time of marriage will often provide valuable clues to the difficulties and issues involved in the joining together of two family traditions in a new family.

Chronology 6.4 The Freud and Bernays Families in the 1880s

1865	Minna, youngest sister of Freud's wife, Martha, is born.
1867	Berman Bernays, Martha's father, goes bankrupt and is arrested for fraud.
1868	Berman goes to prison.
1865	Minna, youngest sister of Freud's wife, Martha, is born.
1868	Martha's oldest brother, Isaac, dies.
1873	Sigmund enters medical school.
1879	Berman dies, leaving the family in great debt.
1881	Sigmund completes medical school after eight years.
1882	(April) Sigmund meets future wife, Martha Bernays, and soon (June 17) becomes secretly engaged to her..
1882	Eli meets Anna.
1882	(April) Sigmund destroys his papers and letters.
1883	Minna, Martha's sister, becomes engaged to Ignaz Schonberg, close friend of Sigmund. Ignaz has TB.
1883	(June) Martha, Minna, and their mother move to Hamburg, a move arranged by Eli, probably because of the debts and embarrassment. Sigmund is very upset by the distance and blames Eli for it.
1883	(September) Sigmund's friend Nathan Weiss commits suicide.
1883	(October) Eli Bernays, Martha's brother, and Sigmund's sister Anna are married. Sigmund does not attend or even mention the wedding in letters to Martha (at least not in published correspondence).
1884	(July 18) Sigmund becomes involved with cocaine and recommends it to others. He publishes cocaine paper. Evidence suggests that Freud went on using and recommending the use of cocaine until the mid 1890s.
1884	Jacob Freud has business problems.
1885	(April) Sigmund destroys all of his papers again.
1885	(June) Schonberg breaks his engagement to Minna.
1886	Schonberg dies of tuberculosis.
1886	(September 14) Sigmund and Martha are married, enabled by a gift of money from Martha's aunt.
1887	(October) Sigmund and Martha's first child, Mathilde, is born (named for colleague Breuer's wife).
1887	Sigmund meets Wilhelm Fleiss, who becomes his most intimate friend until their break in 1904 over an accusation of plagarism.

If we look at the genogram of the family of Freud's wife, Martha Bernays (Genogram 6.4) and Chronology 6.4, we see certain striking parallels with the Freud family. Like the Freud family, the Bernays family had to deal with the death of young children. In 1867, when the children were not even teenagers, the father was arrested and then jailed briefly for fraud, surely bringing a sense of disgrace to the family, very similar to the shame for Sigmund and his siblings experienced when their uncle and perhaps father and half-brothers were involved in counterfeiting. There may also be a parallel in the previous generation with Freud's maternal grandfather, whose business failed, leaving the family with a sense of ruin and disgrace when Amalia was 18. When Martha was 18, her father died of a heart attack, leaving the family in great debt. Like the Freud family, with Jacob's apparent continued unemployment in his later years, it is not clear how the Bernays family survived. Eli, Martha's brother, who took over the running of the family, eventually fled Vienna to avoid bankruptcy and the payment of debts owed to friends. Martha's mother moved with her daughters to Hamburg, which seems to have infuriated Sigmund, who had met Martha in 1882 and was secretly engaged two months later. We might speculate that the similarities in background and experience of Sigmund and Martha may have been part of their attraction for one another.

What is immediately apparent from Genograms 6.4 and 6.5 is the unusual double connection between the Freuds and Bernays in Sigmund's generation. Such unusual configurations often suggest complicated relationships between

Genogram 6.4 Bernays family, 1883: Family at launching

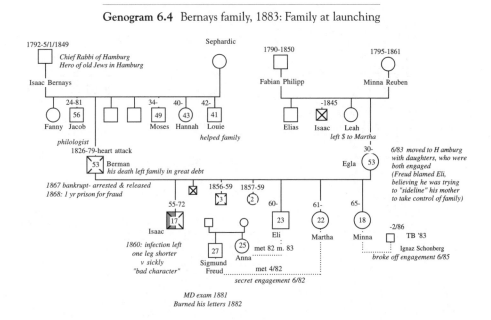

the two families, as well as possible triangles. The oldest son in each family married the oldest daughter of the other family. As mentioned earlier, Sigmund and his sister Anna never got along. Perhaps Sigmund felt the usual sibling rivalry of an oldest child with a younger sister. Or perhaps he associated Anna's birth with many losses (Chronology 6.2): their brother Julius, who was born and died between them, the family's financial troubles and forced migration, the loss of the nursemaid, and the emigration of his uncles and cousins. Whatever the reasons, Sigmund seemed to resent the marriage of Anna to Eli Bernays and did not attend their wedding. In fact, he did not even mention the event in his letters to Martha, although he wrote to her almost daily and shortly after the wedding discussed the possibility of attending the wedding of one of her cousins, certainly a much less important family event. Perhaps Sigmund resented Eli and Anna's being able to marry, when his own marriage seemed so far off. Indeed, it appears that Eli's control of a small legacy of Martha's from an aunt was at least part of the reason Sigmund and Martha could not marry sooner (Young-Bruehl, 1988).

Sigmund's negative feelings toward his sister and brother-in-law seemed to intensify later when the couple moved to New York and the less educated Eli became very wealthy, while the highly educated Sigmund had to struggle to support his family. Triangles were created around the polarization of Eli and

---

Genogram 6.5 Marriage: Freud/Bernays families, 1886

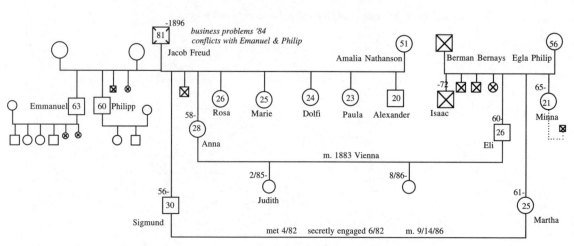

'85- destroys all papers

Anna's family having money but being materialistic and having bad values, while Freud and his side of the family eschewed money but thought of themselves as having intellectual superiority.

Typical triangles emerging at this life cycle stage involve one partner and the family of the other, and indeed, such triangling was prominent in this case. Even before their marriage there were difficulties between Sigmund and Martha regarding their families. Both came from families with financial problems, and financial concerns stood in the way of their marrying for more than five years. Sigmund blamed Eli for Martha's moving with her mother and sister to Hamburg the year after they were engaged, which made it extremely difficult for them to see each other for long periods of time. Freud felt threatened by Martha's relationship to her family of origin and was demanding and possessive about her loyalty to him. During their long courtship, he wrote to her:

> Are you already thinking of the day you are to leave, it is no more than a fortnight now, must not be more or else, yes, or else my egotism will rise up against Mama and Eli-Fritz and I will make such a din that everyone will hear and you understand, no matter how your filial feelings may rebel against it. From now on you are but a guest in your family like a jewel that I have pawned and that I am going to redeem as soon as I am rich. For has it not been laid down since time immemorial that the woman shall leave father and mother and follow the man she had chosen? (letter to Martha, 8/14/1882, Freud, 1960, p. 23)

Sigmund was overtly jealous of Martha's relationship with Eli, and even threatened to break off their engagement if she did not give up her loyalty to her brother. He later wrote to her:

> You have only an Either-Or. If you can't be fond enough of me to renounce your family for my sake, then you must lose me, wreck your life and not get much yourself out of your family. (cited in Appignanesi & Forrester, 1992, p. 31)

Nevertheless, throughout their marriage, Martha did maintain contact with other members of her family and remained true to their faith, Orthodox Judaism, despite her husband's rejection of religion. After many years of marriage she said that Sigmund's refusal to let her light the Sabbath lights from the first Friday night after her marriage was one of the most upsetting experiences of her life (Appignanesi & Forrester, 1992). As soon as Sigmund died, Martha, who was then 68 years old, began again to light the candles every Friday night.

Parenthood, the Next Generation

The early years of a family with young children are always eventful, though often difficult for marriages, with so much of the spouses' energy focused on their children and work. As can be seen on the Freud genogram for 1896 (Genogram 6.6) and Chronology 6.5, Sigmund and Martha married and had six children within eight years. While Martha handled virtually all parenting

---

Chronology 6.5 The Freud Family around 1896

1891   (February) Oliver, the third child, is born (named for Freud's hero, Oliver Cromwell).

1892   Beginning of Freud's estrangement from Breuer.

1892   (April) Ernst, the fourth child is born (named for Freud's teacher, Ernst Brucke).

1892   Eli Bernays, Martha's brother, goes to America.

1893   Eli returns to take his family to the U.S. with him. (Two daughters, Lucy and Hella, stay with Freud's family for a year.) Sigmund gives Eli some money for the trip.

1893   Sophie, the fifth child, is born and named for the niece of his teacher Hammerschlag.

1894   Sigmund is having heart problems, but does not tell his wife that he fears dying. He tries to give up smoking. He suffers depression, fatigue, and financial problems.

1895   (February) The "Emma Eckstein episode" begins. Freud has his friend Fleiss operate on his patient and Fleiss makes mistake, leaving gauze in the wound, which almost kills her.

1895   (March) Anna is conceived.

1895   Still depressed, having cardiac symptoms, Freud treats himself with cocaine. He starts smoking after giving it up for over a year. Decides to begin self-analysis. Fleiss performs a nasal operation on him.

1895   (December) Anna, the sixth and last child, is born, named for Freud's teacher Samuel Hammerschlag's daughter, a young widow and patient of Freud's (Anzieu, 1986). Freud connects the expansion of his practice with Anna's birth.

1895   (December) Martha's sister Minna comes to live with the Freud family.

1896   Outbreak of extremely negative feelings about Breuer.

1896   (April) Sigmund writes of migraines, nasal secretions, fears of dying.

responsibilities, Sigmund struggled to enlarge his medical practice and began some of his most creative intellectual work. When a family is in this phase, the clinician should be alert to child-rearing pressures and normative strains in the marriage (Shellenberger & Hoffman, 1995).

Chronology 6.5 The Freud Family around 1896 (continued)

1896   (May) Sigmund writes clearest account of seduction theory: belief that women's anxieties are based on childhood sexual abuse. His presentation scandalizes his audience.

1896   Sigmund writes of the medical community isolating him.

1896   Freud calls Emma Eckstein's hemorrhages "hysterical."

1896   (October 23) Jacob Freud dies. (Sigmund is 40 at the time.) Jacob had been very ill for a month or so. Because Martha is away on her first trip in 10 years to visit her mother, only Minna is there to console Sigmund over the loss of his father.

1897   (January) Sigmund is passed over for university promotion.

1897   (February) Freud is informed that he will finally be proposed for the title of professor. Martha's uncle Michael Bernays dies.

1897   (March) Sigmund's disgraced Uncle Joseph dies.

1897   (July) Freud takes a walking tour with Minna. (He will take at least 17 vacations with her over the next years.)

1897   (March) Daughter Mathilde has a very bad case of diptheria.

1897   (May) Sigmund is again passed over for promotion—becomes anxious.

1897   (May) Sigmund has incestuous dream about daughter Mathilde.

1897   (September) Sigmund renounces belief in seduction theory (he had thought that his father had inappropriate relationship with his sister). In despondence he feels need for self-analysis; outlines "Oedipal theory."

1897   (October 15) Freud develops ideas of Oedipus complex.

1899   Freud writes *The Interpretation of Dreams.*

1900   End of Sigmund's self-analysis.

1900   Trip with Fleiss ends in falling out that will turn out to be permanent.

1900   Trip with Minna in Italy. Did Minna become pregnant by Sigmund and have an abortion at a clinic? They traveled together extensively from September 12, 1900 through mid February 1901 (Swales, 1982). Jones said she was treated for TB, but there is no other mention of her having that illness.

Genogram 6.6   Freud family immediate household, 1896

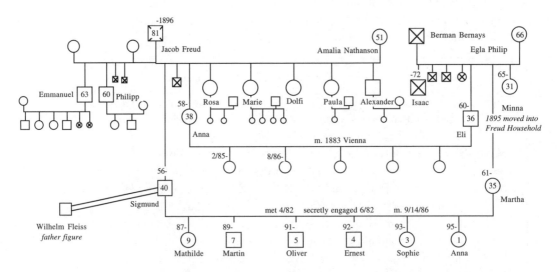

The birth of the last child may be an important turning point in family life. It seems that Martha became very preoccupied with raising her six children, while Sigmund, who was not very much involved with the children, moved closer intellectually and emotionally to his sister-in-law, Minna, whom he had described in May 1894 in a letter to his friend Fleiss as "otherwise my closest confidante" (Masson, 1985, p. 73). Minna moved into the Freud household in December 1895. Fourteen years earlier she had been engaged to Sigmund's best friend, Ignaz Schonberg, who had broken off the relationship shortly before his death from tuberculosis. According to Jones (1955), Sigmund's view in that early period was that he and Minna were alike because they were both wild, passionate people, who wanted their own way, whereas Ignaz and Martha were good-natured and adaptable.

Minna had never married. When other relatives appear as household members on a genogram, we should speculate about the possibility of triangles involving the spouses and the children. By all accounts Sigmund and Minna had an extremely close relationship. Minna's bedroom in the Freud household could be entered only through the master bedroom (Eissler, 1978). Minna and Sigmund took many vacations together (Swales, 1986), apparently because they both enjoyed traveling, whereas Martha did not, at least not at Sigmund's pace. Minna was much more interested than Martha in discussing Sigmund's ideas. Indeed, Martha said of psychoanalysis: "If I didn't realize how seriously my husband takes his treatments, I should think that psychoanalysis is a form of pornography" (Appignanesi & Forrester, 1992, p. 45). Recent research supports Jung's report that Minna told him that she and Sigmund had an affair. There is evidence that she became pregnant and had an abortion in 1901 (Swales, 1986). We know nothing about Martha's attitude toward her husband's relationship with her sister. Interestingly, as can be seen on the Freud genogram for 1939 (Genogram 6.7), Sigmund's oldest son, Martin, repeated this probable pattern and had an extramarital relationship with his wife's sister (Freud, 1988).

Repeating his own father's changes at midlife, Sigmund experienced a major life crisis during this phase of the life cycle. In Freud's case it led to his greatest intellectual discoveries and his major formulation of, and then recantation of, the seduction theory (Masson, 1992). It was also during these years that Sigmund showed symptoms of depression and "pseudo" cardiac problems. He complained of lethargy, migraines, and various other somatic and emotional concerns. He was clearly in a great deal of distress. It was during this period that he began his famous self-analysis and constructed the edifice of a new theory, which led to the publication of his most famous work, *The Interpretation of Dreams*.

Genogram 6.7　Freud family, 1939

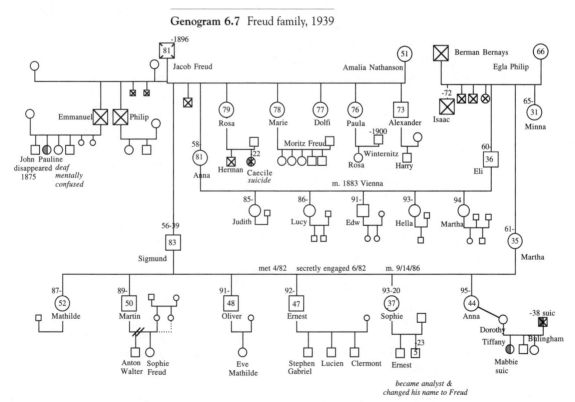

A look at the genogram may elucidate why this was such a turbulent, but productive, time in Sigmund's life. In December 1895, Anna, their last child, was born. Martha, worn out by five pregnancies in nine years, had been surprised and unhappy to learn that she was pregnant for the sixth time. It seems that after this last child Sigmund and Martha decided not to have another. Sex between the couple apparently began to diminish considerably at this point (Anzieu, 1986; Roazen, 1993). Anna was conceived exactly at the time of one of Freud's most explosive professional consultations. He referred his patient Emma Eckstein to his friend Wilhelm Fleiss, who believed in operating on people's noses to cure them of sexual problems, which Fleiss thought resulted from masturbation. Fleiss made a mistake during the operation and left gauze in the wound, which almost killed the woman. Freud, who had an extremely intense relationship with Fleiss, experienced a profound sense of disillusionment and distress over this situation.

Often the last child has a special position in the family. This was true of Anna, who was, by the way, named not for Freud's sister but for the daughter of his friend and beloved teacher, Samuel Hammerschlag. This young woman, Anna Hammerschlag Lichtheim, was herself a friend of the Freuds (Krüll, 1986). Anna Freud apparently felt that she was not the preferred child and spent an enormous amount of effort all her life trying to win her father's approval. She, rather than his wife, took care of him when he was ill. He became her analyst, beginning in 1918, when she was 23. She went in his stead to his own mother's funeral! She alone among his children never married, devoted herself to her father, and chose to carry on his work.

In 1896, less than a year after Anna was born, Sigmund's father died, a loss Sigmund said was the most significant and upsetting event in a man's life. At the time of his father's death, Martha was away visiting her mother for the first time in many years, and Minna was the only one there to console him, which may have contributed to the close tie they developed. The death of a parent marks a critical point in the life cycle. He wrote shortly after his father's death:

> By one of those obscure paths behind official consciousness, the death of the old man has affected me profoundly. . . . His life had been over a long time before he died, but his death seems to have aroused in me memories of all the early days. I now feel quite uprooted. (Masson, 1985, letter of November 2, 1886)

In addition to the loss, a parent's death is a painful reminder of one's mortality and of the passing of the mantle of tradition and responsibility to the next generation. Now Sigmund had his mother to support as well. In addition, his disgraced uncle Josef and an uncle of Martha's had died that year.

About this time Sigmund adopted Fleiss as a father figure in his self-analysis, which seems to have reflected his own midlife crisis, perhaps precipitated by a number of events in the family and his own life cycle (see McGoldrick & Carter, 1998a, for the intersection of the individual and the family life cycle). In addition to the loss of his father, the birth of his last child, his changing relationships with his wife and Minna, he was having career problems and he had just turned 40. He was struggling to support a large family. Just as the midlife period for Freud's father was marked by a new love relationship, occupational shift, and migration, Sigmund's crisis seemed to involve changing intimate relationships and career upheaval. He resolved it more positively than his father with the consolidation of his career: the publication of his book, his appointment as a professor, and his growing recognition as the founder of a new theory.

Family in Later Life

As members age, families must come to terms with the mortality of the older generation. As each generation moves up a level in the developmental hierarchy, all relationships must be reordered (Shields, King, & Wynne, 1995; Walsh, 1998). There are special problems for women, who are more often the caretakers (Dolfi and Anna) and who tend to outlive their spouses (Amalia and Martha). When the last parent dies, the relationships between siblings become independent for the first time. Often the genogram will reveal which child was delegated to become the caretaker of the aging parents, as well as common triangles among siblings over the management of these responsibilities. Sibling conflicts and cut-offs at this point usually reflect triangles with parents that have persisted from much earlier life cycle phases, especially with regard to who was the favored sibling in childhood.

Sigmund's father died in 1896, leaving Amalia to be cared for by her children for the next 35 years. Sigmund and his youngest brother, Alexander, took financial responsibility for their mother and sisters in later life, although it was the middle daughter, Dolfi, who remained at home, unmarried, with their mother. Sigmund also lived a long time, to the age of 83 (Genogram 6.7 and Chronology 6.6) and was cared for by his daughter Anna. Anna became her father's main follower and intellectual heir. Although Martha Freud was still alive (she lived until 1951), it was Anna who became his primary caretaker through his many operations for jaw cancer. For Anna, as for Dolfi in the previous generation, this meant that she was never able to leave home. She was 44 at the time of her father's death. He had been unwilling to function without her for many years. Though she had been briefly in love with her first cousin, Edward Bernays, in 1913, she later said it was good that the relationship had not worked out because, since he was her double cousin, it would have been

Chronology 6.6 The Freud Family after 1900

1902   (March 5) Sigmund becomes Professor Extraordinary.
****

1909   Daughter Mathilde marries.

1911   Death of half-brother Philipp.

1911   Cut-off with Alfred Adler. Freud called it "the disgraceful defec-
        tion of Adler, a gifted thinker but a malicious paranoiac" (letter
        of Aug 20, 1912, to James Jackson Putnam, quoted in Kerr, 1993,
        p. 416).

1912   Cut-off with follower William Stekel.

1913   Cut-off with Carl Jung.

1913   Daughter Sophie marries.

1914   First grandchild is born (Ernst Halberstadt, who later became an
        analyst and changed his name to Ernest Freud).

1914   Death of half-brother Emanuel.

1918   Freud begins analysis of his daughter Anna, which seems to have
        lasted at least until 1922.

1919   Martha has bad case of pneumonia and goes to sanitorium.

1919   Sigmund and Martha go to a spa for a "cure."
        Important follower, Victor Tausk, commits suicide.

1920   Daughter Sophie contracts pneumonia and dies.

1923   (May) Sigmund goes to friend Felix Deutsch for diagnosis of can-
        cer and first operation.

1923   (June 19) Favorite grandson, Sophie's son, dies of TB. Sigmund
        weeps for the first time. He never gets over the loss, which fol-
        lows so shortly on his own illness.

1923   (October 4) Sigmund has a second cancer operation.

1923   (October 11) Sigmund undergoes a third operation. Over next 16
        years he will undergo more than 33 operations.

1923   Eli dies in New York. Sigmund writes bitterly about his money
        and suggests that maybe now his sister Anna will do something
        for her four indigent sisters.

1924   Break with follower Otto Rank.
        Rift with Ferenczi.

1926   Theodore Reik is prosecuted for "quackery."

1930   Freud's mother, Amalia, dies.

1938   Family is finally able to emigrate.

1939   Sigmund Freud dies in London.

double incest. She had early dreamt that her father was the king and she the princess and people were trying to separate them by means of political intrigues. She resolved on becoming partners with Dorothy Burlingham, an American mother of four children, who was the youngest of eight daughters of the glass millionaire, Louis Comfort Tiffany. Though Dorothy never officially divorced, she and Anna lived and vacationed together for the rest of their lives. Together they ran a war nursery, a psychoanalytic training institute, and a world famous children's clinic. (Dorothy's husband committed suicide in 1938, having tried in vain to convince her to return to him.)

The genogram may be helpful for understanding or predicting the reactions of family members to key events at different stages of the cycle. For example, Sigmund had a very strong reaction to the death of his three-year-old grandson in 1923, shortly after he himself was diagnosed with cancer (Genogram 6.7):

> He was indeed an enchanting little fellow, and I myself was aware of never having loved a human being, certainly never a child, so much. . . . I find this loss very hard to bear. I don't think I have ever experienced such grief, perhaps my own sickness contributes to the shock. I worked out of sheer necessity; fundamentally everything has lost its meaning for me. (in E. Freud, 1960, June 11, 1923)

A month later he wrote that he was suffering from the first real depression of his life (Jones, 1955, p. 92). And three years later he wrote to his son-in-law that since this child's death he had not been able to enjoy life:

> I have spent some of the blackest days of my life in sorrowing about the child. At last I have taken hold of myself and can think of him quietly and talk of him without tears. But the comforts of reason have done nothing to help; the only consolation for me is that at my age I would not have seen much of him.

Sigmund's words suggest he was struggling to come to terms with his own mortality. This was particularly difficult, not only because his grandson's death was so untimely, but also because his daughter, Sophie, the child's mother, had died three years earlier at the age of 27.

Contrast this grandson's death with Sigmund's reaction to the death of his own mother seven years later, in 1930:

> I will not disguise the fact that my reaction to this event has, because of special circumstances, been a curious one. Assuredly, there is no saying what effects such an experience may produce in deeper layers, but on the surface I can detect only two things: an increase in personal freedom, since it was always a terrifying thought that she might come to hear of my death; and secondly the satisfaction that at least she has achieved the deliverance

for which she had earned a right after such a long life. No grief otherwise, such as my ten years younger brother is painfully experiencing. I was not at the funeral. Again Anna represented me as at Frankfort. Her value to me can hardly be heightened. This event has affected me in a curious manner. . . . No pain, no grief, which is probably to be explained by the circumstances, the great age, and the end of the pity we had felt at her helplessness. With that a feeling of liberation, of release, which I think I can understand. I was not allowed to die as long as she was alive, and now I may. Somehow the values of life have notably changed in the deeper layers. (quoted in Jones, 1955, p. 152)

In this case Sigmund, at 74, was more reconciled, through his years of struggling with cancer, with his own eventual death. He was relieved that the sequential order of the life cycle would be honored: first, the parents die and then the children. The untimely or traumatic loss of a family member is typically extremely difficult for families to mourn, and clinicians are urged to pay especially careful attention to untimely deaths on a genogram and to be alert to dysfunctional patterns that develop in response to such losses (Gerson, 1995; McGoldrick & Walsh, 1991; Shellenberger, 1997; Walsh & McGoldrick, 1998).

7
CLINICAL USES OF THE GENOGRAM

We have only begun to tap the clinical potential of the genogram. Genograms have been used in many different ways by different clinicians—to engage families, to reframe and detoxify family issues, unblock the system, clarify family patterns, connect families to their history and thus empower them and free them for their future. Over the past few years there has been a burgeoning of literature on clinical applications of the genogram. A wide range of uses and modifications have been proposed: family sculpting of genograms (Papp, Silverstein, & Carter, 1973; Satir, 1972), culturegrams (Congress, 1994; Hardy & Laszloffy, 1995), gendergrams (White & Tyson-Rawson, 1995), sexual genograms (Hof & Berman, 1986), genogrids emphasizing the social network developed to facilitate work with lesbians (Burke & Faber, 1997), family play genograms (Buurma, 1999; Gil & Sobol, 2000), and genograms with many age groups and different symptoms and life situations (see bibliography). This chapter offers a few suggestions to inspire readers about the rich potential of genograms in family therapy and family medicine.

The Genogram in Family Therapy

Engaging the Family

The genogram interview provides a practical way of engaging the whole family in a systemic approach to treatment (Alexander & Clark, 1998; Weber & Levine, 1995). We prefer to involve as many relevant family members as possible, so that both the clinician and the family members can see the problem in its familial context.

Genogram interviewing shows interest in the whole family system. The process of mapping family information on the genogram implies that a larger picture of the situation is needed to understand the problem. It conveys a major systemic assumption: that all family members are involved in whatever happens to any member. It also suggests the ongoing connectedness of the family, with both the past and the future.

Equally important, the genogram interview facilitates building rapport with family members by exploring their relationships around key family traditions and issues of specific concern to the family. Genogram questioning goes to the heart of family experiences: birth, love, illness and death, conflict and cut-off. Its structure provides an orienting framework for discussion of the full range of family experiences and for tracking and bringing into focus difficult issues such as illness, loss, and emotionally charged relationships.

Genograms may provide almost instant access to complex, emotionally loaded family material. However, the structure of the genogram interview allows the clinician to elicit such information in a relatively nonthreatening way (Shellenberger & Hoffman, in press). Also, the genogram framework helps both the clinician and the family to organize family experiences in ways that can lessen the toxicity of even the most painful experiences. Casual, matter-of-fact interviewing to complete a family genogram often leads to matter-of-fact giving of information. Even the most guarded person, quite unresponsive to open-ended questions, may be willing to discuss his or her family in such a structured format. There is also something impressive about not just gathering information but also displaying it to the family in an organized, graphic way. Cognitive understanding of symptomatic behavior as it relates to emotionally charged relationships can increase the family members' sense of mastery over their situation. Doing a family's genogram becomes a collaborative task that empowers family members, since they are the experts on their own history and the therapist is only the recorder and witness of it. On the other hand, creating a genogram offers the clinician the opportunity to give something back to the family, namely the graphic map of the family's story. For many families the richness of their history is an important affirmation, no matter what painful elements there may be.

Some clinicians display the genogram to the family either on the blackboard (Carter, 1982), on large note pads (Bradt, 1980), or on a computer. Genograms seem to possess a certain mystique and thus may become an important "hook" for some families. Wachtel (1982) has argued that their power is akin to that of psychological tests, which add weight and credibility to a clinician's inferences about family patterns. I (MM) often give to clients at the end of their first session a print-out of the computer-generated genogram that I make during the session. This invites clients' participation in the assessment, as I ask them to correct the genogram for me before the next meeting. They are often amazed and fascinated to see how much information about their history can be organized on a small page in this way.

Dealing with Resistance in the Genogram Interview

When people come in with a problem, they have often adopted their own views of what is wrong and what needs to be changed. This is often a rigid, nonsystemic view based on the belief that only one person, the symptomatic one, needs to change. Any effort to move directly to other problematic areas in the family will often be blocked by vehement denial of other family difficulties. One cannot simply set out to gather all the genogram information in the initial session and ignore the family's agenda for the appointment. Such a single-minded approach would surely alienate the family from treatment. Gathering information for the genogram should be part of a more general and gradual approach of joining with the family and seeking clues as to the current problem.

Resistance is often sparked as clinicians touch on painful memories and feelings related to the information being gathered. For instance, if it comes out that a brother died in a car accident, a grandparent committed suicide, or a child was born out of wedlock, various members may seek to redirect the focus of the session. "Why open up old wounds," they may ask, "when we know that Joe here is the problem?"

Sometimes, seemingly innocuous questions may provoke an intense reaction. For instance, one client burst into tears after being asked how many siblings he had. The question had stirred up memories of his favorite brother, who had died in a drowning accident. Ostensibly simple questions may also unearth family secrets (Imber Black, 1993, 1998). A question such as "How long have you been married?" may lead to embarrassment or concealment if the couple conceived their first child before marriage. Even questions of geography, such as "Where does your son live?" may be sensitive to a parent whose son is in jail or in a psychiatric hospital or totally out of contact with the parent.

The family's initial concealment of information may often be overcome by careful, sensitive exploration of the situation. Resistance can show up in various ways. It may be direct and vehement. Or it may be subterranean, with family members becoming bored, restless, or disruptive (Wachtel, 1982). When meeting repeated resistance to discussion of family history, the clinician may find that focusing on the resistant person for a while proves productive. Allow him or her to feel heard. Let him or her know you're still aware of and concerned with the presenting problem. Try to reassure him or her about where you're going. Let the family members know how doing a genogram will help you better understand their present situation and therefore be of assistance.

Sometimes family members are so resistant that you have to forego the genogram interview altogether for a bit. In these instances, as you refocus on the presenting problem, you should still seek to make connections between it and past events and patterns whenever possible. These connections help to remind people of their belonging to something larger than themselves. Constantly demonstrating the relevance of the larger family context to the family members' immediate concerns helps them realize they are not alone.

Eventually a family's resistance and concealment of information may be overcome as clients begin to see the connections between their concerns and historical family patterns. You can often return to organized questioning for the genogram in subsequent sessions.

The following case of the Rogers family (Genogram 7.1), edited segments of which are available on the videotape *The Legacy of Unresolved Loss* (available from Norton), offers an example of a family that began therapy with intense resistance to questioning about their genogram. Their reluctance is gradually overcome through linking the presenting problem to family history on the genogram. In the end, the family members themselves became "researchers" of their own genogram.

Kathleen Rogers, the second wife of David Rogers, made the initial appointment for the family in 1995. The guidance counselor of her 15-year-old stepdaughter, Michele, referred them for therapy because Michelle had been cutting high school classes and acting out. David, 49, was an attorney from a well-off family of British ancestry. He was resistant and distant although on the surface pleasant and outwardly cooperative. His first wife, Diane, of Puerto Rican background, had died in 1991 of leukemia after a two-year illness. In their 18-year marriage, they had had two children, Julian, now 21, and Michelle, 15, who was the identified patient. Ten months after Diane's death, David married Kathleen, 14 years his junior, a woman of Irish-German background who had never been married before. She was now a fulltime homemaker and mother of

---

Genogram 7.1 Rogers family

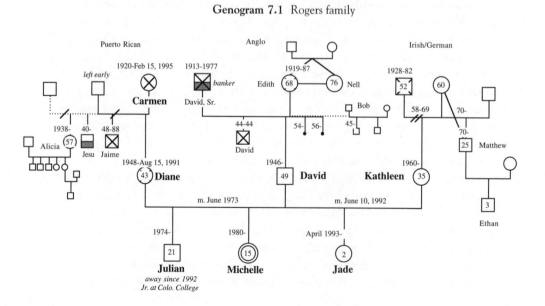

a two-year-old, Jade. Kathleen's parents had divorced in 1969, when she was nine, and her mother remarried the next year, and nine months later she had a son, Matthew, who became the favored child. Thus Kathleen, like her stepdaughter, had felt "on the outside" of a reconfigured family in her generation. Kathleen was basically out of contact with everyone in her family of origin at the start of therapy. She had never even seen her three-year-old nephew, Ethan. Her father, who had had a bar in Brooklyn, had died in 1982 of a heart attack.

Michelle had been the one in most contact with the Puerto Rican side of her family. She had gone with her mother and brother to Puerto Rico during the summers for many years and, when she was 11, she went alone for the summer to Puerto Rico, ostensibly to help her ailing maternal grandmother, Carmen, but really to protect her from the "sadness" of her mother's illness and death. Julian had been allowed to stay home because David thought that at age 17 he could better manage his mother's grave condition.

In the initial session the parents were clear that they wanted to solve Michelle's problem: her acting out in school, hanging out with the "wrong" friends, and having a "chip on her shoulder." Neither parent believed that the presenting problem had any connection to unresolved mourning for her mother or to the recent death of her maternal grandmother, Carmen, which had coincided with Michelle's behavioral change. Indeed, I learned in the course of therapy that Michelle had not even been brought home from Puerto Rico for her mother's funeral in 1991, nor had she been told about her grandmother's death until it was mentioned casually days later. When I (MM) tried to gather genogram information during the first session the father became actively hostile and said he felt I was wasting their time. He considered information about his own family completely irrelevant, including the fact that his father had died of cirrhosis of the liver (which he did not think was related to alcohol abuse) or that his name, David, had first been given to an older son who had died in infancy. Kathleen was even more negative about questions regarding her family, whose constellation had been almost identical to the current family pattern.

Gradually, I was able to help David listen to Michelle's feelings of closeness to both her mother and grandmother and to have him review the family genogram history with both his daughter and son, who returned from college for a session in which he expressed pain that the mother's death had never been discussed and that the father had remarried so quickly. David was asked to take his children to their mother's grave for the first time, and gradually he began to confront other losses in his own life, which he had also suppressed. Initially he had presented his own childhood as happy and uneventful, but eventually it came out that his parents had almost cut him off when he "married down" to a Puerto Rican. After months of therapy he finally agreed to try to learn more about his history from his only living relative, his Aunt Nell. He made a trip to his hometown to visit Aunt Nell, his mother's identical twin sister, whom he had not seen since his mother's funeral eight years earlier. He appeared at the next session more animated than ever before, carrying photograph albums and diaries his mother had kept, lent to him by his aunt. Through this information he was able to get in touch with his parents' difficulties and some of his own childhood pain for the first time. He uncovered two "secrets"—one about his father's drinking and the other about an affair his mother probably had with his father's best friend. When the affair came to light, relations between the two families, who had been very close for years, abruptly ended, resulting in the loss of David's best childhood friend as well as his father's only real friendship. As David learned about his history, he began to connect with his feelings on a deeper level and to become more responsive to both his daughter and his second wife, who had been having to bear all the feelings in the family without any of the power necessary to make things work out.

In this case it was possible to press on, in spite of the family's resistance, to get the basic genogram information, and then to proceed through the family member (Michelle) who most realized its relevance to make connections for others. Occasionally family members are so resistant to discussions of genogram information that we have to leave the subject until we find another way of engaging them. In those situations where we have eventually succeeded in building a relationship with the family, we have generally found that the resistance comes specifically from anxiety and fears about family experiences embedded in the genogram, for example, the stigma of a parent who committed suicide or was in a mental hospital.

Of course, there are times when people's discussion of their history becomes an avoidance of taking appropriate action in the present, and this must be challenged, as when a parent tries to sidestep the immediate needs of children or to avoid dealing with alcohol or drug abuse by sidetracking discussion to the genogram (or anything else, for that matter!).

The genogram can be useful in working with rigid systems. The genogram interview organizes questioning around key family life experiences: birth, marriage, life transitions, illness and death. Collecting information on these events can open up a rigid family system and help clients get in touch with paralyzing blocked emotional and interpersonal issues.

For example, the Carusos, an Italian family, were referred for consultation by their lawyer, who hoped the referral would influence the court case of the oldest of their three sons, John, who had been arrested for selling drugs (Genogram 7.2). Initially the family presented a united front: They were a close, loving family whose son had come under the influence of "bad friends."

Genogram 7.2 Caruso family

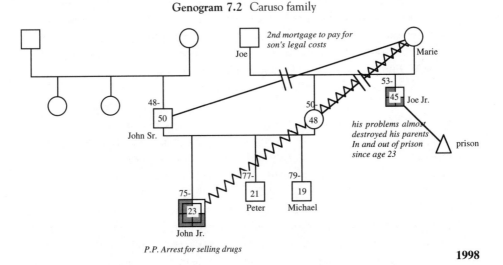

P.P. Arrest for selling drugs

1998

They denied the seriousness of his crime, offered little factual information, minimized any relationship problems, but said they were willing to do anything to help. Few connections were apparent in gathering the basic genogram information until we got to the question of the whereabouts of the maternal uncle. Mrs. Caruso said that she did not know where her brother was, but then admitted that he was in jail and had had many previous arrests. This led to questioning about the maternal grandmother's reaction to John's problem, at which point the family's united front began to break down. The parents reluctantly admitted that they had stopped talking to the maternal grandmother since John's arrest because of her "insensitive" response: "Let him rot in jail." Mr. and Mrs. Caruso had taken a second mortgage on their house to pay their son's bail and legal fees. Mrs. Caruso said she had always, until now, been very close to her mother, but now viewed her mother as "disloyal." Further detailed questioning about the family history led to the information that Mrs. Caruso's brother had first been arrested at age 23 (John's present age). The maternal grandfather had, against the grandmother's wishes, spent all the family savings repeatedly bailing his son out of trouble, and she was now very bitter that her son had brought almost total ruin on her family. It was only through discussing the details of the uncle's criminal behavior, a family secret that John and his brothers did not know, that the family's "cool" about their present situation was broken. Mrs. Caruso talked about her pain in watching her own mother's agony over the years, as well as her own fury at her brother for the shame he had brought on the family. She was desperately afraid of reliving her parents' experience, but feared that discussing the matter with her mother would confirm that the family was "doomed" to repeat the past; so she had stopped talking to her mother. As we spoke, John's brothers opened up for the first time in the interview, expressing their resentment of their brother for putting the family in the terrible position of having to decide whether to put their life savings on the line or let him go to jail. The father, who had been the most adamant in deny-ing any family difficulties, talked about his sense of betrayal and failure that his son had so cut him off. It was only through the leverage of the previous family experiences that the family's present conflicts became evident.

In their attempt to avoid dealing with painful past experiences and unre-solved emotional issues, families often rigidify their relationships and view of themselves. Calm, nonthreatening, "research" questions can often open up these matters, so that family members can begin to relate to one another in a different way around such issues. The genogram interview is especially useful for engaging obsessive, unresponsive, or uninvolved clients. Obsessive clients who may otherwise dwell on the endless details often come quickly to emo-tionally loaded and significant material during a genogram interview. Unresponsive family members may find themselves more engaged as their fam-ily story is revealed.

Probably the issue around which families become blocked more often than any other is loss (see bibliography section on Loss). Norman and Betty Paul (1986) led the way in the use of genograms to unblock the family system by focusing on losses in the multigenerational family. The meaning of symptoms is expanded by involving the clients in an explanation of deaths or life-threaten-ing experiences in either the immediate or extended family. In the Pauls' view, the "forgetting" and distortion in family members' perceptions that occur around loss are among the most important factors influencing symptom devel-opment. They routinely send genogram forms to prospective clients to be com-pleted before the first session; this information provides important information about how the clients orient themselves to their original family. In the first ses-sion the Pauls carefully track the dates of birth and death and the causes of death of family members for the past three generations. In their experience, clients usually indicate some degree of mystification about doing their genograms.

The Pauls' in-depth study of one such couple in A Marital Puzzle (1986) illustrated a case in which the husband was asked to bring genogram informa-tion to the first therapy session. He left off the chart the fact that both of his parents had died, although he had been specifically asked for it; when ques-tioned, he said he did not remember exactly when they had died. The Pauls' therapeutic model has focused attention on the importance of rediscovering such dissociated family experiences. Some years ago we developed family forms which asked for genogram information in multiple ways. The forms asked in three different sections for the dates of death of the grandparents. The respondents frequently gave different dates each time, indicating how charged the issue of death is.

Clarifying Family Patterns

Clarifying family patterns is at the heart of genogram usage. As we collect information to complete the genogram, we are constantly constructing and revising hypotheses based on our ongoing understanding of the family. We usually discuss our observations with the family and offer these observations as tentative hypotheses that the family may elaborate or revise as we jointly explore the family history.

The Caruso family discussed above illustrates how the genogram can become a guide for both family and therapist to patterns, clarifying the present dilemma in ways that open up possibilities for alternative behavior in the future. From the genogram, we could see a pattern of repetition of criminal behavior. Then, as the connection was made between the son's and the uncle's criminal behavior and the possibility of the family history being repeated was pointed out, the family began to look at the son's behavior within the family context and to explore the legacy and conflicts that were perpetuating the behavior. They could also concentrate their efforts on changing the pattern.

Clarifying genogram patterns serves an important educational function for family members, allowing them to see their lives and behavior as connected to the family history. In addition, dysfunctional behavior is often eliminated once the family patterns that underlie it are clarified.

Reframing and Detoxifying Family Issues

Families develop their own particular ways of viewing themselves. When there are many problems, family members' perspectives may often rigidify and become resistant to change. Genograms are an important tool for reframing behavior, relationships, and time connections in the family, and for "detoxifying" and normalizing the family's perception of itself. Suggesting alternative interpretations of the family's experience points the way to new possibilities in the future.

The genogram interview allows the clinician many opportunities to normalize the family members' understanding of their situation. Simply bringing up an issue or putting it in a more normative perspective can often "detoxify" it. Using information gathered on the genogram, the clinician can also actively reframe the meaning of behavior in the family system, enabling family members to see themselves in a different way (Bowen, 1978; Carter & McGoldrick, 1998b; Gerson, Hoffman, Sauls, & Ulrici, 1995; Shellenberger & Hoffman, in press). The family structure suggests normative expectations for behavior and relationships (e.g., "It's not surprising you're so responsible, since oldest children commonly are," or, "Usually two youngest who marry tend to wait for each other to take care of them. How did it go with you?"). Similarly, an understanding of life cycle fit can provide a normalizing experience (e.g., "People who marry as late as you did may be pretty set in their ways. Was that true for you?"). Pattern repetition and the coincidence of events show the larger context of problematic behavior (e.g., "Maybe your feelings had something to do with all the stressful events that were occurring at the time"). And relational patterns and family balance help demonstrate the interdependency of family members (e.g., "Most people react that way when they are the 'odd person out'," or, "Usually, when one person takes on more than her share of responsibility, the other person takes on less").

Bowen was a master at detoxifying reactive responses with genogram questioning. For example, below is an excerpt of an interview by Bowen of a man who felt intimidated by his "domineering, possessive mother":

> *Bowen:* What are the problems of being the only child of an only child mother?
>
> *Client:* My mother was a very domineering woman who never wanted to let go of anything she possessed, including me.
>
> *Bowen:* Well, if you're the only one, wouldn't that be sort of predictable? Often in a relationship like that people can with some accuracy know what the other thinks. . . . In other words, you're describing a sort of an intense relationship, and not too unusual with a mother and an only son, especially a mother who doesn't have a husband, and your mother was an only. How would you characterize your mother's relationship with her mother?

Here Bowen is using discussion of the family structure to normalize a mother's behavior and the special mother-child bond of an only child. Bowen's therapy is characterized throughout by such tracking, detoxifying, and reframing of multigenerational family patterns.

Using the Genogram to Design Interventions

Family therapists with a Bowen systemic approach have been using genograms for many years as the primary tool for assessment and for designing therapeutic interventions. More recently, therapists with different approaches have come to use the genogram for recordkeeping, family assessment, and designing strategic interventions.

Wachtel (1982) suggested using the genogram as a "quasi-projective technique" in family therapy, revealing unarticulated fears, wishes, and values of the individuals in the family. She described using about four one-hour sessions to complete a genogram on a marital couple. After getting the basic "factual data," she would ask the spouses for a list of adjectives to describe each family member, and then for stories to illustrate the adjectives used. Keeping track of the conceptions the spouses have about various family members and how these conceptions are passed down from one generation to another, she could then investigate the spouses' conception of the relationships between people, commenting throughout "on emerging family issues, patterns, and assumptions and their possible relevance to the current situation" (1982, p. 342). Differences of opinion become grist for the mill of therapy, and spouses are urged to seek missing genogram information between sessions.

Clinicians using a strategic approach have come to use the genogram not only for recordkeeping and family assessment, but as a map for designing strategic interventions. Pointing out why a family needs to be the way it is and what problems could arise through change sometimes paradoxically leads to change. Genogram patterns are used in this therapeutic model first to convey a positive understanding of the present dysfunctional situation, thus paradoxically challenging the rigidity of the present stabilization. As change does occur, genogram information is again used to reinforce emerging patterns and to underline the normative evolution of the family.

The use of the genogram in therapy can be an important way to counter the invalidation that recent immigrants and families of color often experience in most institutional settings, allowing families respectful acknowledgment of their history and helping them translate adaptive strategies they used in other contexts to solve current problems (Boyd-Franklin, 1989; Hines, 1998; McGoldrick et al., 1996). In general, in our "solution focused" society, their history is often invalidated, as they are pressed to adapt to U.S. culture and to suppress their own cultural and family experiences in order to accommodate to present needs.

For example, we worked with a Muslim family (Genogram 7.3), who had immigrated from Jordan to the U.S. in 1978. The father, Ahmed, was a steady worker as a machinist, but he had a history of abusing his wife and daughters. The family members were living separately, the daughters in a foster home, the mother in the family apartment, and the father with his brother, after several restraining orders had been placed on him.

The treatment program in which Ahmed was involved worked at multiple levels to support him as a person to take responsibility for his behavior (Almeida et al., 1998). To foster Ahmed's support system, we had to explore his

Genogram 7.3 Muslim family

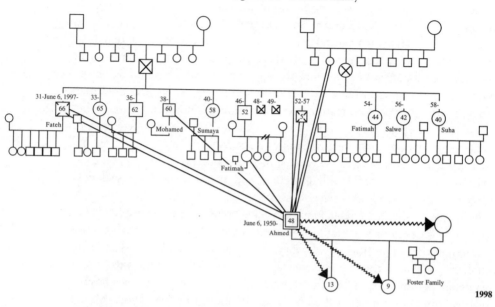

Fateh

Mohamed Sumaya

Fatimah

Fatimah Salwe Suha

June 6, 1950-
Ahmed

Foster Family

1998

history through his genogram, an exploration we did in part with his brother, Mohamed, with whom he had been staying. The discussion focused on his place within his family and his family's traumatic history. Initially both brothers seemed to experience the genogram questioning as a waste of time, in part because there was such a large family—13 siblings, 15 aunts and uncles, and 35 nieces and nephews to talk about. But as they got into the discussion of family members, the people on their genogram and their significance became "real," particularly for Ahmed, who had so many experiences of loss. Not only did it turn out that his birth was surrounded by the loss of three siblings, but the two brothers talked of their oldest brother, Fateh, who had died while visiting the previous year in Ahmed's home on his birthday "because his heart was so big from loving that it burst." Doing the genogram also brought Ahmed to tears when he remembered how he had loved the brother closest to him in age who had died in childhood of polio. These critical aspects of Ahmed's "belongingness" in his history became threads in his treatment, helping him to feel his own resourcefulness as he sought the inner strength to do the right thing for his wife and children, with the support of others in his treatment community (Almeida et al., 1998). Indeed, during that session we learned that one of their nieces, Fatimah, a practicing Muslim and a feminist, was living in a neighboring town. She became an important resource and ally in the therapy, bridging relationships between Ahmed, his wife, and his daughters.

Using Rituals Developed from the Genogram to Transform Loss

A major therapeutic task is to empower clients to bear witness to their own and each other's losses and to develop a sense of survivorship, meaning, mastery, and continuity. Families often need help in expanding their view of themselves and their loss in context—to see the continuity of their experience from the past into the future and their connections with each other, with their culture, and with other human beings. Many forces are at work in our society to deprive people of their sense of continuity. Reversing this puts not just the death, but their whole lives, in better perspective, strengthening them for their shared future.

We have found that relatively simple interventions aimed at connecting family members in the present and with their past losses may make a considerable difference in their sense of themselves and therefore in their resourcefulness in managing their future. Recently, a family brought this home to us in a striking way.

The Chen family (Genogram 7.4) was referred because Joe, the 14-year-old son, had been involved with drugs and was "acting out" at school. The school had previously referred the family to various drug treatment facilities several times. They described the parents as noncompliant with therapy and unable to set effective limits on their son, who was seen as a very bad influence in the school system.

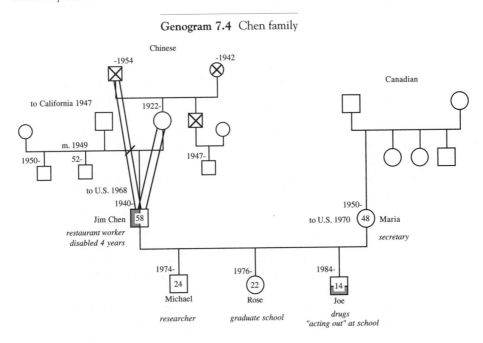

Genogram 7.4 Chen family

Mr. Chen, a 58-year-old restaurant worker who had been disabled for four years with a back injury, had immigrated from China at the age of 18. He met his wife, who immigrated from Canada at age 20, in the U.S. The couple had raised their two older children very successfully. The oldest, a son, finished college at age 19 and was doing professional research at a nearby university. Their daughter was in graduate school in another nearby city.

Inquiring about the family's history in relation to the son's drug abuse and acting out, we became convinced that the parents had indeed complied with all that had been requested of them, but had not felt connected to Al-Anon or to the school, probably in part because their cultural background was so different from that of the other families there. The parents had been taking the son, Joe, for regular drug screenings, and he had been clean for over a month, but the school was still bothered by his behavior and hoped to have him removed.

When we began to ask about the family's history, the father became very tearful about his father, who had died the year before he married. Taking this into consideration, we decided to construct a ritual based on the family's genogram history to empower the family in the present in relation to their survival history. We were not sure the father's pain over his father's death was connected to the present situation, but his obvious emotion about his father made clear that there was some connection. The father, mother, and Joe were all asked to write letters to the dead grandfather, hoping to bring into the present relationship patterns from the genogram. The following week all three read letters, excerpted below.

The father's letter:

> Dear Father:
>
> I think about writing to you all the time. I often think of you in the dim light of evening, which brings me back my memories of my childhood. Many kids have their golden childhood years. I never enjoyed what I experienced. Instead was war, hunger and loneliness. I didn't have a chance to attend school. Worst of all, no father to guide me. All these memories will remain forever in my heart and mind. They cause me such grief, all I can do is cry. My heart is bound by a rope that chokes it. I feel such heart ache. There are so many questions that I want to ask you. You are a husband and a father. Have you yet fulfilled your duty to your wife and your children? When I was in China we sent you many letters, but never once did we receive word from you. My mother took care of me, when I was a child. She worked hard and made little money, but she did the best she could to raise me. I heard from my uncle that she had a chance to remarry, but, because I was so young, she didn't want me to have a stepfather. My mother was bound by traditions, which would never allow her to remarry. So you ruined her whole life.

You had a farm in which you took special care of all the seedlings and vegetables and they grew. You want to take care that all the buds growing in the greenhouse are strong enough, before you take them out to the farmland to plant them. When you plant them out in the field, you make sure that there are no weeds, before you plant your vegetables. You fertilize, water and care for your vegetables very, very carefully. You worry that they will not grow. I also am your seed. How come you didn't take such good care of me? I wanted to go to school—to have a good education, just as you took care of vegetables, which need fertilizer and water. You make sure that vegetables grow with no weeds to block their growing. I too need this type of nourishment in the farm of education. Do you agree with me? You never gave me a chance to have a decent education. When I came to the United States, I told you all of this. But your heart is made of iron. You said to me: "You are 18 yrs old. I have brought you here so you can take care of your mother and your nephew." From such a young age I carried such a heavy burden to take care of my family alone. Do you believe that the way you treat your family is right? Do you feel ashamed of yourself? It's a quiet night. Please think about it. I have very little left to say, so I shall end here. I wish you good health. At last I can tell you that now I am married, with three children of my own. I am a good husband and a good father, not only to provide my family with food and shelter but I also to make sure that my children get as much from their education as they can. I love my children and there's nothing I would not do for any one of them.

Your son, Jim Chen

Joe then read his letter:

Dear grandfather,

How are you? All I can say is that you were pretty "beeped" up, but I can't really hate you for treating my father like that. I can't really say that I like you either, since I have never met you in my life. But from what I have heard of you, I guess you didn't care about my dad, your son. Well, I have to go.

Peace, your grandson.

The wife then read her letter:

Dear father-in-law:

I didn't meet you because you were dead before I married your son. But I know all about you and how you treated my husband and my mother-in-law. I feel hurt for them, especially for Jimmy. I can imagine how sad he felt through that period of time. Even though he did not have a normal childhood like the other kids had, because of you, he always told me that he forgives you. He has always believed in forgiveness, love and peace. You caused him and family much pain; he worked to help his mother, sister and nephew, so they could live well. He always told me that he never regretted that. He never was a burden. After we married he still sent her money for her needs as well as for our nephew. How could a good father treat his son like this? But Jimmy was lucky. He had wonderful uncles and a wonderful grandfather. Jimmy used his grandfather to learn the most from. Today Jimmy is not like you, but like his wonderful grandfather. He always remembers his grandfather with love—he was very firm, but at the same time treated him with affection and love. My husband treats his children just like his grandfather. I am proud of him and I tell my children how lucky they are. They have a wonderful father who is always there for them and any of their needs.

Prior to reading the letter, the son had been bored, turning in his chair, uninterested in the conversation. Following the letters, we were able to mobilize the family to work with us and the school to keep the son engaged, involved at home, and participating in school without further disruption.

In this case the genogram helped to empower a nuclear family in relation to their history, which had become disrupted and cut off. Rituals that enable family members to come together to bear witness to their history, however painful, can be a great resource and source of resilience.

Making Genograms Come Alive in Therapy

For years Virginia Satir, Peggy Papp, and others have used family sculpting to make genogram patterns come alive in therapy. In family sculpting, genogram patterns become visual, as group members form the triangles, fusion, and cut-off relationships of a family. Such visualizations, where people actually stand in for family members on a genogram, give genogram patterns an emotional immediacy. They also allow one to track the family constellation by moving the structure through time, depicting the addition and loss of family members, for example.

Another technique for making the genogram "live" is doing a family play genogram. Deborah Buurma (1999) has created a helpful guide for this use of family play genograms. Family members choose from an array of miniature people, animals, and objects to represent each family member. The exercise often brings out interesting information about family members' views of each other, as well as of long dead family members. The discussion they have about the miniatures each has chosen helps to clarify family history, expand a member's view of previous relationships and conflicts, and draw on their creativity, fantasy, and imagination as they use the miniatures as a jumping-off point for sharing understandings of family history. As with family sculpting, where participants are often asked to visualize how relationships would be different in the future if the family were to come to terms with its experiences, the family play genogram exercise may include setting up imaginary genograms that take family members into a hoped-for future when their relationships to each other and their history will be different. Introducing the element of play into the discussion of the actual facts of the genogram history often gives family members greater flexibility in imagining possibilities for change, even while acknowledging that the content of their history cannot be changed.

The Noguci family (Genogram 7.5) sought help for their 14-year-old son, Brandon, who was refusing to go to school, staying up or out all night and sleeping all day, and destroying furniture when confronted by his parents about his refusal to obey even the most minimal rules. The father, Koji, was a graphic designer who had come to the U.S. from Japan to study art. The mother, Terry, was an art teacher, from a working-class Irish background, who had met Koji in college.

Genogram 7.5 Noguci family

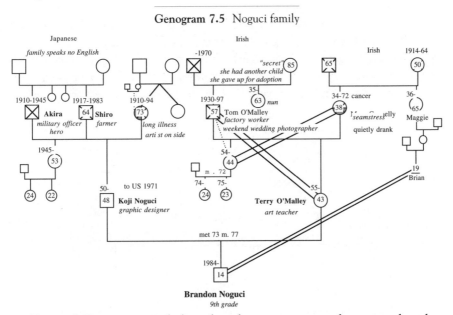

Koji and Terry came in feeling that they were not good parents, that they were being asked to do something they could not do and were therefore failures. They were angry at each other and at the school as well as at their son. They seemed unable to have any sustained conversation as a couple, their only attempts at conversation being about Brandon. They felt they had been told what to do, namely, to set firmer limits on the son and had not been able to do it.

Although the parents were compliant about giving genogram information, they were not engaged in the story of their history and were extremely defensive about being asked to participate in therapy. They strongly resisted thinking systemically, perhaps because they were deeply cut off from their families of origin and did not want to identify with them. This seemed to leave them totally lost about how to relate to their son. Brandon was also stuck between being a child and moving toward adulthood. He could not negotiate passage to adulthood because his parents never clarified boundaries, leaving it unclear which generation he belonged to. Whenever the therapist tried to focus on the parents' setting limits on Brandon or on their relationship with each other, they withdrew or got angry. Brandon was in general nonresponsive in the therapy with his parents or alone. In one session, in an attempt to engage Brandon in a nonverbal medium, the therapist asked him to make a sand tray world using miniatures. In an eloquent expression of his stuckness, Brandon was unable to make a single choice to include in the sand tray, until his parents joined the session to create a family sand tray. At that point, encouraged by his father, he reluctantly contributed a few figures.

The following week the therapist decided to do a family play genogram using the same miniatures, hoping to connect the family members to their history. The family's genogram was drawn on a large piece of paper. Starting with Brandon picking a figure for himself, each family member in turn picked a figure for each person on the genogram (Genogram 7.6). There was much discus-

Genogram 7.6 Noguci family play genogram

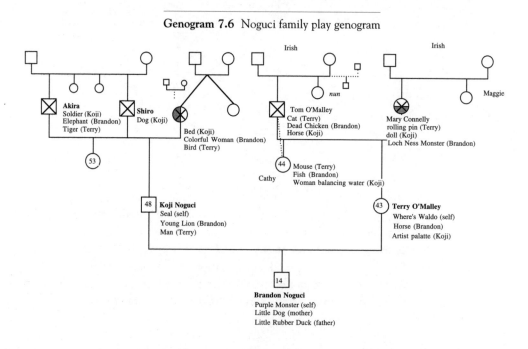

sion, inquiry, and laughter about the choices. Brandon insisted on including two of the same miniatures he had contributed to the family sand tray the previous week. This was the first indication of "belonging" and continuity since the therapy had begun. Terry's choices for her parents led to her first open exploration in therapy of the struggle she had in figuring out her place in her family. She chose a rolling pin for her mother and went on to talk about how she belonged to her father and her sister belonged to her mother, a "very boring housewife." It seemed apparent that her complex feelings for her parents and sister were compounded by her mother's death when she was just on the point of leaving home and her sister's marriage three months later. She had felt abandoned by her sister, even while she felt guilty that her father had always favored her. When Brandon asked her why she chose a cat for her father and a mouse for her sister, she said, with some feeling, that, though she had loved her father, he had always been cruel to her sister.

Koji's side of the genogram led to an interesting discussion of why he had also distanced from his family. Koji had chosen a soldier to play his uncle, Akira, his mother's first husband, a small dog to represent his father, Shiro, and a bed to represent his mother. Terry's mystification about these choices led Koji to explain several experiences he had hardly remembered himself until triggered by the play genogram. He had grown up not knowing his family history. At age eight he asked his older sister why their father's picture was kept on the altar with the pictures of all the dead relatives. The sister laughed and told the parents, who were also amused that he had confused his father, Shiro, with his uncle, who had died in the war. Koji felt humiliated by being laughed at and took the experience to mean he was an "outsider" in his family and could not ask the true history. Not until he was an adult and leaving for America did his mother, by then quite ill with arthritis and heart disease, tell him how grateful she had felt to his father, Shiro, who was seven years younger than she, for agreeing to marry her and take her little daughter from the first marriage. Otherwise, she had said, she would have had nowhere to go. She then told him that, as a twin, she had been given away by her parents to an older childless couple, while her twin sister had been raised by their parents. The older couple who took her in raised her, and she had cared for them, but both of them had been frail and died soon after her marriage to Akira.

Koji said he had chosen the bed for his mother because she was always ill. Brandon then chose an attractively decorated woman figure and placed her on the bed to be his grandmother. Koji said he had chosen the dog to be his father, because he always thought of his father as weak and, after what his mother told him, he felt perhaps his father could never replace his older brother Akira, the military hero who died in glory. Being only a farmer, with less education than his brother had had, he took the responsibility for his brother's wife, but could never really take the place of his brother, so he too felt an outsider.

Thus, Koji grew up feeling he did not belong in his family and did not understand his history. He was the child of two parents who both probably felt they were outsiders compared to their more desirable siblings. And perhaps when he formed a family with Terry, who herself had an impaired sense of belonging in her family, they complemented each other's difficulty being at the center of a family. Through the creation of the family play genogram, both parents were able to begin to tell their stories to each other and Brandon was able to participate and even give to his parents a newfound sense of connectedness. Brandon had chosen a small purple monster with arms outstretched to be himself, while Terry had chosen a "Where's Waldo" miniature to represent herself.

As the three of them shared the meaning of the figures they had chosen to represent themselves, each other and the extended family, they seemed to join for the first time in being a family who could surmount their difficult history and find a way of belonging with each other. Both parents laughed about the miniatures they had chosen for themselves. Terry's "Where's Waldo" was seen as someone who has an idea where he's going but is hard for others to find. The others agreed that this was true about her. Koji said he thought at times he was slippery like a seal but that he had also chosen the animal because of his power and ability to swim fast. We noticed that the parents had chosen more effective miniatures for the other parent than they had chosen for themselves. The symbols became a way of talking about the roles they were playing in relation to the roles they wanted to play. The parents had chosen symbols for Brandon (the duck and the little dog) that suggested someone who needs protection. Even Brandon's choice, the purple monster, seemed to be making a joke of intimidation.

In a follow-up discussion with Koji about his role, we wondered if he might not find some position that would be between the powerful, intimidating symbols of soldier or wolf that he had chosen to represent his father and his uncle, and the symbols he and his wife and son had offered (seal, lion cub, man). Their choices in the family play genogram seemed to make clear that the parents needed to take a stronger, more protective role with their son and had been hampered by their history in doing this. Both Brandon and Terry seemed in a way to be suggesting solutions to Koji's ineffective symbol of his mother (the bed). Brandon put a colorful woman in the bed and Terry had suggested the bird, who was both colorful and liked to sing. Koji was reminded that his mother had had a beautiful voice and loved to sing when she was young. There seemed a similar suggestion about Terry's mother. Terry had represented her with a rolling pin, reflecting for her a constrained role as housewife, while

Brandon's choice of the Loch Ness Monster might suggest a power that goes beyond death and beyond what can be seen.

This session became a key experience we could refer back to with a kind of shorthand to encourage Terry and Koji to take a stronger position in relation to their son, labeling him as a "play monster" rather than a real monster, who, like a little duck, needed to be taught to swim. Soon after this session both parents began to follow through on limits for Brandon, to the extent that they insisted he have consequences and go to court to appear before a judge for his truancy. When the judge gave a strong message that it was either school or jail until he was 16, Brandon began going to school.

Combining play, imagination, and creativity with the genogram history often appears to open families up to their history. Perhaps the element of play lowers their defenses and resistance; perhaps, as with Koji, the choice of miniatures can lead to making unconscious connections with deep childhood feelings one could not describe in words. In this case, the family play genogram provided a structure within which Brandon's parents could share stories of their experiences in their families of origin. Just as Brandon needed clear and definite limit-setting, the parents needed the concrete and nonthreatening structure of the play genogram to confront their history and change their present.

Genogram Applications in Family Practice

Families can be a source of both stress and support in times of medical illness. The genogram, as a primary tool for describing families and their functioning, is a crucial instrument in family health care. In the following brief discussion, we will focus on three areas: (1) systemic medical recordkeeping, (2) rapport-building, and (3) medical management and preventive medicine.

Systemic Medical Recordkeeping

Family physicians and other health care personnel with a commitment to continuing comprehensive care assume the responsibility of treating individuals not alone but in the context of their families. There is, moreover, growing research evidence of the relationship between the level of family functioning and the physical and emotional well-being of each family member (Lewis, Beavers, Gossett, & Phillips, 1976; Schmidt, 1978). The illness of an individual family member will disrupt the family's functioning; on the other hand, family dynamics may have a role in the development of illness in family members (Barth, 1993; McDaniel, Campbell, & Seaburn, 1990; McDaniel, Hepworth, & Doherty, 1992; Rolland, 1994, 1998). For example, family stresses have been related to the occurrence of a variety of illnesses and to the severity and duration of respiratory illnesses in children (Beautrais, Fergusson, & Shannon, 1982; Boyce et al., 1977; Meyer & Haggerty, 1962). In addition, the importance of family supports in counteracting such stresses and the role of family functioning in adherence and clinical response to treatment regimens have been demonstrated. In other words, the relationship between the family and the patient is a major factor in the development and outcome of an illness.

Thus, it makes sense for health care providers to gather family information relevant to understanding medical problems in their systemic family context (Alexander & Clark, 1998; Baird & Grant, 1998; Berolzheimer, Thrower, & Koch-Hatten, 1993; McDaniel et al., 1990). Unfortunately, however, most physicians do not pay systematic attention to family patterns, because they have no way to keep track of them and they have not been taught how to make use of family information in the limited time they have available. The genogram is perhaps the most clinically useful tool so far developed for assessing these connections between the family and illness. It is both efficient and economical, since it enables the physician to gather quickly specifically relevant information on the family and to record the information in a clear, easily readable format.

The major advantage of the genogram is its graphic format. When there is a genogram in the medical record, the clinician can glance at it and get an immediate picture of the family and medical situation without wading through a stack of notes. Critical medical information can be flagged on the genogram and the current medical problem can be seen immediately in its larger familial and historical context. Thus, the genogram in itself enhances a systemic perspective of illness.

Genograms can be gathered in a medical setting in a number of ways. Patients can complete a form before their first visit (see Appendix, Part 2), or a technician, nurse, secretary, or medical student can take a genogram before the patient sees the physician for the first visit, or patients may complete a computerized genogram interview (Gerson & Shellenberger, 1999b). Such genograms can be collected in 15-20 minutes even by a relatively unskilled interviewer. Or the physician can take the genogram, either at the first interview or as part of taking the patient's comprehensive medical history. Practically, however, due to time limitations, the physician may be able to gather only very basic information in the first interview; details can be added to the genogram as a relationship develops with the patient. Keeping charts of family members together further facilitates tracking of a family's medical symptoms and efforts toward wellness (Alexander & Clark, 1998; Baird & Grant, 1998; Berolzheimer et al., 1993; McDaniel et al., 1990).

Rapport-building

The process of gathering family information with the genogram may contribute to the establishment of rapport between the clinician and the patient. Interestingly, Rogers and Durkin (1984) found that most patients, after being given a 20-minute genogram interview, felt that such an interview could improve their medical care and their communication with their physician. In an increasingly complex, technological, fast-paced medical world, patients sometimes complain of impersonal medical technologists who show interest only in their disorders, rather than in them as people. Genogram interviewing shows an interest in the well-being of each family member. This is crucially important, because medical compliance is often related to the family's confidence and trust in the clinician.

Medical Management and Preventive Medicine

Finally, there is the application of the genogram in the management of medical treatment. Physicians can and sometimes do use their knowledge of patients' family relationships and patterns to develop diagnostic and therapeutic plans. The information on the genogram may be used directly in treatment planning or as a basis for referral. Smilkstein (1978) has argued that an assessment of family functioning is relevant to medical treatment, because (1) the physician may be able to "anticipate illness behavior, and in some instances to initiate preventive measures," (2) such an assessment "can be beneficial in anticipating compliance" and evaluating available resources for aiding in compliance, (3) documenting life events may pinpoint stressors that may affect treatment, and (4) critical psychosocial problems may call for active intervention and/or outside referral. He has suggested that it is particularly in "patient problem areas such as somatization, high utilization, multiple complaints, and chronic pain that assessment of family functioning and social support in general will be most rewarding" (pp. 266–67).

The genogram as an assessment and clinical instrument may serve all of the above functions. Indications on the genogram of previous illnesses or symptom patterns may lead to early detection of a problem and preventive treatment of family members at risk. The relational patterns on a genogram may suggest the likelihood of a family's complying with a given treatment recommendation and indicate what social supports will be available for managing an illness. The genogram shows the critical life events that may be stressing a patient, both currently and historically. Such events suggest a reorganization of the family to adapt to the change, particularly when life cycle transitions or role changes are involved. And finally, the genogram is an important record of the psychosocial functioning of the family that may indicate when intervention is necessary.

The following examples illustrate how a genogram may be used in medical treatment. The first illustrates the importance of gathering information in the initial interview.

A 28-year-old chemical engineer sought help at a local family practice center for stomach pains in August 1998. Because it was customary for the nurse to take a genogram on new patients prior to the doctor-patient encounter, Genogram 7.7 was drawn. Working from the genogram, the doctor began by trying to put the patient's stomach pain in context. She noted that this was a particularly difficult time for Mr. Anderson and hypothesized that recent critical family events might have had a stressful impact on him and his family. The patient and his wife of one and a half years were in the midst of several major transitions. They had moved six months earlier and they were expecting their first child in five months. In addition, the patient's sister and her husband had recently separated, an event whose impact might be reverberating throughout the family system.

Genogram 7.7 Mr. Anderson's family

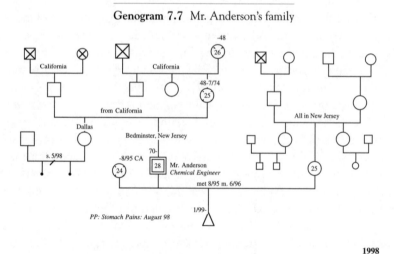

1998

The genogram reflects a number of temporal connections, anniversary reactions, and repetitive patterns that might be exacerbating the stressful nature of the upcoming events for Mr. Anderson. His first wife had died of cancer in August 1995, and thus he might be having an anniversary reaction. There is a repetitive pattern of early female death: His mother, his maternal grandmother, and his first wife all died in their twenties, which might make him acutely sensitive to the physical vulnerability of women in his family. It seemed likely that he would be particularly worried about his wife's up-coming childbirth, especially since his maternal grandmother had died in childbirth and his sister had had two miscarriages before her recent separation. Since Mr. Anderson and his mother occupied similar sibling positions on the genogram (both were youngests), the physician speculated that he might have identified with his mother and might now fear dying himself, since he was the same age as his mother when she died. The physician also noted the timing of the couple's marriage. Mr. Anderson met his current wife a week after his first wife's funeral and they were married within a year. Given the short transition period, the physician wondered whether Mr. Anderson had dealt with his grief related to his first wife's death and hypothesized a hidden triangle in which the present wife was in some ways the outsider to the unresolved relationship with his first wife.

And finally, looking at the level of support in the family, it was evident that Mr. Anderson had no family in the area, while his wife's parents and all her siblings were nearby, which, perhaps, left the couple with an imbalance in emotional resources. During a brief discussion of these family factors, Mr. Anderson was able to admit his fears about the pregnancy, as well as continuing thoughts of his first wife, about which he felt guilty. He accepted a referral for consultation with a family therapist. Physical examination did indicate that he was suffering from gastroesophageal reflux, probably exacerbated by his emotional state. Medication was prescribed. The patient was asked to bring his wife along to his follow-up visit two weeks later. By that time he had gone for the consultation with the family therapist and his symptoms had disappeared. He and his wife were apparently doing a good deal of talking about his past experiences and he was feeling much better psychologically as well as physically.

In this case the genogram interview identified a number of psychosocial stressors that needed to be dealt with and the referral began the process, easing the pressure on Mr. Anderson and his family. The genogram allowed the physician the opportunity to practice preventive health care.

The next example illustrates a more complex case, in which the response to genogram information was less immediate.

Dan Rogoski went to see his physician complaining of heart palpitations. The doctor learned that his father had died of a heart attack and his mother had suffered multiple heart attacks and strokes, but he could find no evidence of Mr. Rogoski having an organic dysfunction. The doctor decided he needed to find out more about Mr. Rogoski's family history and obtained a genogram (7.8). The doctor noted from the genogram a number of family events that might be affecting Mr. Rogoski. His son, John, who had had many behavioral and drug problems before joining the service, was due to return home shortly, and perhaps Mr. Rogoski was worried about the problems starting again. His ex-wife's mother had recently died, which might lead his ex-wife to put more pressure on him because of her own grief and anxiety. Mr. Rogoski's sister was deteriorating from multiple sclerosis. As the oldest in the family, and with his

Genogram 7.8 Mr. Rogoski's family

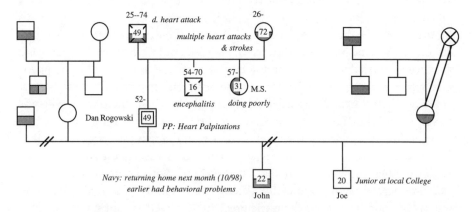

parents no longer alive, it was likely that he felt responsible for his sister's care, particularly as his brother had died of encephalitis. He might also fear his own vulnerability to disease.

Also of interest to the family physician was the fact that Mr. Rogoski was now the same age as his father when he had died of a heart attack, and his youngest son was now the age he had been at the time his father died. Perhaps he feared that history would repeat itself and the heart palpitations were an expression of this anxiety.

Finally, there was the pattern repetition of drinking in the family. Both of his parents had had drinking problems, as did his son, his first wife, and the families of both of his wives. Based on this history, it was possible that Mr. Rogoski had a drinking problem or that someone in his family thought he did.

From the genogram information, the physician was able to ask Mr. Rogoski about each of these areas of concern: his son coming home, his ex-wife, his sister's dysfunction, his being the same age as his father when he died, and his drinking. While Mr. Rogoski admitted to some general concern in each of these areas except drinking, he was sure they had no bearing on his physical state, saying he never let things like that get to him. As for the drinking, he admitted, when asked, that his wife thought he drank too much, but that was just because her father and her first husband were alcoholics and she was too sensitive. This answer, of course, raised more questions about the extent and nature of his drinking and about his relationship with his wife. Although physical findings were negative, the physician decided, on the basis of the information gathered here and the patient's response, to request a follow-up visit with both Mr. and Mrs. Rogoski two weeks later, "just to see how the heart was doing."

At the follow-up meeting the family stresses were reviewed and Mrs.

Rogoski confirmed her worries about her husband's anxiety and drinking. The doctor mentioned the possibility of their going to AA or Al-Anon or to therapy, but the idea was immediately rejected by both spouses. However, a month later Mrs. Rogoski called back, saying that she felt the tension had not diminished and she would now like the name of a therapist they could consult. The doctor again suggested that she could attend Al-Anon, but she refused, although she did take the name of a local therapist. At medical follow-up six months later, Mr. Rogoski proudly announced that he had celebrated his 50th birthday and felt very relieved and healthy. He said he had been trying to deal with his ex-wife about their son John, who seemed not to be getting on his feet after leaving the navy and was drinking too much.

Although neither Mr. Rogoski nor his wife responded immediately to the doctor's observations about the family situation, the genogram did help him to assess the family stress and relationship factors and gradually to become an important resource for the spouses at the point when they could respond. They will undoubtedly need to turn to him again in the future, and having the genogram in the chart will make it easier for him to keep track of ongoing changes as the children develop, as Mr. Rogoski's sister needs more support, as his conflicts with his ex-wife abate or continue, and if tension with his present wife over alcohol resurfaces.

There are indications that when one member of a family is in distress, others will react as well (Huygen, 1982). In this case, by recognizing the multiple stresses Mr. Rogoski was experiencing, the physician became aware of the need to bring in Mrs. Rogoski as well, to evaluate her response and ability to support her husband, and to at least plant the seed that other help was available for them if they should want to use it. This probably made it easier for Mrs. Rogoski to seek the referral when she did, since her doctor was already familiar with the situation and had himself suggested a source of help for them.

Genogram assessment in medical practice can suggest what family patterns are repeating themselves, so that preventive measures can be taken; what resources the patient has to help with an illness; what problems there may be in medical compliance; what family stresses may be intensifying the difficulty; and what type of further psychosocial intervention is needed, such as including others in follow-up medical visits or making outside referrals.

8

Using Genograms for Family Research

One of the most exciting possibilities of the genogram is the potential for further research on families. Since so many clinicians already collect family information on genograms, these everyday clinical genograms are too valuable a research resource to ignore. It is our view that the genogram has tremendous potential both clinically and in research on families and family process, because it is a relatively simple, non-intrusive, easily updated tool for collecting current and historical family information, already used routinely by many clinicians. The pooling and computerization of these genograms could provide an extensive database for family research. Since the genogram is relevant to clinical work, the clinician is motivated to gather accurate, meaningful data. Thus, the usual problem of obtaining cooperation from clinicians for research is partly avoided.

With regard to research, the multidimensional facets of the genogram gem have received only limited exploration. Although the genogram is almost as old as the fields of family therapy and family medicine, research on its clinical utility and validity, as well as its reliability, including standardization of the genogram interview, has been slow in coming. Much of the research examines the psychometric properties of the genogram. However, most clinicians want to know if the genogram enhances the systemic understanding of the clinician or family members.

The primary goal of this chapter is to encourage researchers and clinicians to identify gaps in the genogram research base and begin efforts to fill them. To move the development of this field forward, it is important to examine the three main areas of genogram research: (1) research on the genogram as a clinical tool; (2) research on families and family process; and (3) computer-generated genograms. In this chapter, we will review studies conducted in each of these areas and propose new areas for investigation.

Research on the Genogram as a Clinical Tool

This section includes background on issues related to genogram clinical research, as well as studies evaluating the usefulness and reliability of the genogram. First, attention will be drawn to the genogram interview and the research complexities inherent in this type of data collection and generation. Research complexities result from both the type and richness of the data available and the possible sources of error in collection of the data. Second, studies examining the clinical utility of the genogram in several settings will be analyzed.

Research Complexities

The genogram interview generates two types of material: The first includes family demographics and facts about the family; the second involves the nature of the relationships between the various family members and the systems dynamics evident in the family at the time of the interview and down through generations. Analogous to the musical composition described in Chapter 6, the genogram demographics and facts are like the notes written on a page of music. The notes provide the structure of the music but the composition only comes to life when played with its full richness. The richness is experienced when the orchestra and chorus perform. Then the rhythmic elements, harmonies, instrumentation, tone, direction by the conductor, venue for the performance, mood of the players or singers all interplay in the creative process. Clinical research using the genogram must attend to these two types of information collected, the data on which the inferences are drawn, like the notes on the page, and the inferences that are drawn, or the larger composition that is created. We would like to encourage research generating both kinds of information. For those using the tool for clinical work and research using the second type of material based on inferences about the data, we believe it is important for genogram interviewers to meet several requirements. They should have a firm grounding in the theoretical bases of the instrument, clinical experience in collecting this more sensitive type of information, and an interest in discovering the essence of the family being interviewed. Whenever research is conducted, reports of results should include a description of the level of theoretical and clinical background of those collecting the genogram information, along with a clear definition of the type of information collected.

To family clinicians, the strength of the genogram will be determined by whether families and/or practitioners benefit from its use. Family clinicians are interested in knowing if genogram interviews actually help family members or clinicians to "think systemically," to see their problems as "making sense" within a broader life context and as being more manageable. Clinicians want to know if the process of doing a genogram changes the nature of the relationship in the direction of increased openness with or trust in the clinician (i.e., process research). Clinicians also want to know if collection of genogram information enhances the care they provide (i.e., outcome research). For example, are clinicians who use genograms able to develop better predictions about individuals and families or better interventions than those who do not?

As with other clinical tools where the end goal is not only a set of facts, but also an inference such as a diagnosis, a prediction, or a clinical formulation, we have to think about reliability and validity as related to the data needed to draw the inference and the inferences to be drawn. Reliability studies examine whether the same information (e.g., demographic data; the nature of the relationships such as triangled, abusive, hostile, or close) collected in a genogram interview on more than one occasion or by different interviewers is consistent. Validity studies seek to determine if the information collected correlates with other family instruments and whether the information collected measures outcomes important for the clinician's formulations. While it would be much easier to evaluate the reliability and validity of the genogram if a structured protocol were used across all cases, much clinically useful information would be lost. It is important, instead, to maintain the integrity of the tool by preserving the capability of branching to different topics, hearing the impressions of different family members, exploring different themes and hypotheses, and dealing with whatever psychometric complexities this process presents. A brief overview of some of these complexities follows.

The first layer of complexity in conducting genogram research has to do with collecting the raw data such as facts, demographic information, and dates that are the foundation of the genogram or the music on the page. Sometimes interviewers are not careful or thorough about recording factual information. Also, clients, especially those dealing with stressful life events, may not remember or report information accurately. There is also the issue of completeness, as many people do not know about all of their family members or remember dates. That is why it is considered a dynamic document that can be updated over time. These factors may affect the reliability of the information collected. While lack of accuracy with the factual information collected on the genogram may affect reliability related to dates and names of people involved, it may be that accuracy of inferences drawn is not affected by occasional inaccuracies in dates or facts. The lack of information may also reflect family secrets that are not generally known to all family members (e. g., deaths, abortions).

Another layer of complexity in conducting genogram research occurs when we move beyond description of the facts, dates, and individuals to a higher level of inference about the family. This concerns the feature of primary importance to the genogram interview: the clinical picture, or composition, that is generated as inferences are drawn. In a musical composition, the development of and variations of themes, the director of the players, and the mood of the players and the audience all contribute to the richness of the composition that is played. So it is with a genogram that factors related to the clinician, the clients, and the dynamic between the client and clinician, the themes developed in the interview, the descriptions of current and past relationships all affect the clinical picture that is generated. Research related to clinical usefulness of the genogram must attend to all these complexities related to inferences drawn from family interviews. Five aspects within this layer of complexity will be described.

First, the creation of the clinical picture requires a higher order of inference than simple collection of data. Determining the presence of higher-order reasoning, tracking it, and determining the hypotheses or predictions generated from it is a research challenge. Second, there is a selection bias in the information collected, because of the theoretical leanings of different clinicians. For example, a medical clinician coming from a strictly biological orientation may focus on demographic and factual information and not attend to emotional or relationship dimensions, whereas a non-medically oriented family therapist may be very sensitive to relationship dynamics but fail to gather crucial medical information. Third, the genogram interview is a process; the nature, direction, and consequences of the process will be influenced by the dynamic between clinician and client or family. For example, the nature of the encounter will be influenced by the client's response to the clinician's questions, and one family member's presentation of information will affect another family member (Beck, 1987). Fourth, there is the phenomenon of different perspectives on the same event (the Rashomon effect). Clearly, members of the same family do not always agree in their reports of emotionally significant events. In fact, as mentioned in Chapter 2, forgetfulness and discrepancies in reporting of dates or events by different family members offer important clues to unacknowledged emotionally significant issues in the family. Fifth, the discussions that take place during a genogram interview may not change the behaviors or thinking of the participants at the moment, but may influence their interactions or behaviors in future encounters. These complexities are important to consider when designing or reviewing genogram research.

Efforts to address these two layers of complexities, the data collected and the inferences drawn, will lead to the collection of more reliable and valid data. These efforts include conducting proper training of interviewers to include the theoretical underpinnings for the process, delineating clear guidelines for interviews, maintaining flexibility in the interview process, and computerization of the process. When these procedures are in place, researchers may find, for example, that even though several clinicians have based their inferences about a family on very different genogram information, their hypotheses or predictions about the family are similar. Examples of the type of research that will lead to an enhanced understanding of the clinical usefulness of genograms include: assessing interactional behaviors before, immediately after, and several months after a genogram interview, investigating the clinician's or family's systemic understanding of the family (e.g., life cycle issues, family projection processes, and multigenerational legacies), and examining the comprehensiveness of predictions or treatment goals that are generated with genogram interviews.

We will present studies evaluating the clinical usefulness of the genogram and reliability studies. Most genogram research has emerged from the field of family medicine, with only one reliability study from the family therapy field. These findings are analyzed with particular attention to essential elements of genogram research—the backgrounds and training of the interviewers, the objectives of the study, the types of information collected and the inferences drawn.

Research on Clinical Usefulness

Much of the research on the clinical usefulness of the family genogram comes from the field of family medicine, where authors have promoted it as a way to make physicians more sensitive to psychosocial issues of their patients; to enhance evaluation, diagnosis, and care of patients; to provide a framework for assessment and interaction with someone in a specified population (e.g., the elderly) or at a certain time (e.g., diagnosis of a serious illness); and to prevent and intervene with family and medical problems (Alexander & Clark, 1998; Baird & Grant, 1998; Bannerman, 1986; Christie-Seely, 1986; Crouch & Davis, 1987; Dumas, Katerndahl, & Burge, 1995; Garrett, Klinkman, & Post, 1987; Like, Rogers, & McGoldrick, 1988; Mullins & Christie-Seely, 1984; Shellenberger, Shurden, & Treadwell, 1988; Sproul & Gallagher; 1982; Troncale, 1983). Let us look at some specific empirical studies from family medicine.

Haas-Cunningham (1994), a family therapist, conducted interviews of family medicine patients. She collected both medical and family relationship information and related the genogram information to health outcomes. She found that scores derived from a structured genogram interview were predictive of physical symptoms and health indicators, particularly in the first two to three years after the interview. Examining the connection between family emotional and physical health, she interviewed patients in a family practice center using genograms, along with health, life stress, and support indices. She sought to determine the relation of the genogram to health status and to physical symptoms at the time of the visit and two to three years later. She found that genogram information on the current family generation (Generation 1) was related to physical symptoms at intake and follow-up (i.e., two-three years later) and to physical function and symptom status at follow-up. The parent and sibling generation genogram information (Generation 2) was related to follow-up physical symptoms and physical symptom status, but even more strongly associated with emotional function. Haas-Cunningham's research is useful in several ways. The study structured a genogram interview to collect information relevant to specific research outcomes such as health status, integrated adjunctive assessment tools, and incorporated statistical methods for separately analyzing information from different generations of the family. At the same time, the robustness of the findings is limited by the small number of participants in her study and her choice of certain statistical methods (i.e., forward selection procedures for multiple regression analyses).

Rogers and his family medicine colleagues have conducted several studies based on genogram interviews. Their studies vary with regard to the type of information collected (usually limited to demographic data and facts, not family relationship information), the manner in which the data are generated (patients filling out a booklet requesting genogram-type information, ancillary personnel asking genogram information, or physicians themselves asking the genogram information), and the level of training in systems theory of the interviewers. Three types of studies are described: (1) those investigating patients' perceptions about providing their physicians with genogram information, (2) those assessing physicians' perspectives regarding the usefulness of collecting genogram information, and (3) studies assessing whether the presence of genogram information affected the predictions and referrals made by physicians.

Patient perceptions. Two studies by Rogers and colleagues investigated patients' perceptions as to the effect of giving genogram information on their health care and the quality of their doctor-patient relationship. The information collected in these studies was limited to factual information about illnesses and people in the family. In the first study, Rogers and Durkin (1984) found that family medicine patients who gave family history information in a brief genogram interview reported later that they felt the genogram would help their physician understand them better and thus provide improved health care. In a later study, however, Rogers and Rohrbaugh (1991) were unable to demonstrate that taking a brief genogram influenced patients' views of their encounters with their physicians. This was true whether physicians completed genograms on their patients or the patients themselves completed the genograms using a six-page booklet. Of course, the fact that taking a genogram limited to factual and not relationship information could not immediately be shown to impact a doctor-patient interaction is not an adequate measure of the value of genograms in family medicine. The real value for medicine is the fuller picture of the family and the ongoing understanding of family process through tracing genograms. Studies using more objective assessment techniques and collecting more complete genogram information are needed to examine whether the inclusion of genograms in medical history-taking influences the patients' perceptions of the quality of the doctor-patient relationship and usefulness of information provided.

Physician's perceptions. Physicians' perspectives regarding the usefulness of collecting genogram information were investigated by Rogers and Rohrbaugh (1991) in the study described above. The study was limited to the collection of factual information for a genogram, not relationship data. Rogers and Rohrbaugh found that physicians considered the genogram interview to be more relevant when they conducted the interview themselves rather than having the information entered in the chart by another health care professional. They found, however, that with this limited type of information present on the chart, there were no differences as to how physicians think about and deal with clinical problems. This was true whether the information was collected by the physician or given by patients themselves. The physicians in this study were volunteers for the study and had experience as teaching faculty. While the researchers document that the physicians participated in a one and a half-hour orientation session about genograms and the study, there is no description of the level of family systems training they had. This research highlights the importance of considering the professional using the tool in terms of his/her level of training in family systems and the type of information collected during the interview, whether factual or inference-generating material.

Effect on predictions and referral. Three studies by Rogers and colleagues sought to determine if the presence of genogram information helped in assessing family medicine patients, in making referrals, and in predicting who would seek medical care. In one, Rogers (1994) found that family information, such as that collected on genograms, can be used to identify family medicine patients at high risk for anxiety and depression. In another study, Rogers and Cohn (1987) found that completion of a screening genogram by an observer of a medical interview resulted in the recording of more information about family structure, major life events, repetitive illnesses, and family relationships than physicians recorded on their own. The researchers found, however, that physicians do not explore any more family issues or make any more referrals for emotional problems when genogram screening information is present on the medical chart than when it is not. Perhaps more exploration of family and emotional issues can be expected when physicians themselves collect the information and are trained in the theory underlying the interview, and when a fuller genogram interview is conducted. In another study, Rogers, Rohrbaugh, and McGoldrick (1992) asked a panel of physician experts to evaluate patient cases and predict the probability of the patient's experiencing an illness or making an unexpected physician visit over the subsequent three months based on genogram information. Predictions made by the experts were accurate when it came to the general health risk measure of total number of clinic visits patients made during the three-month follow-up period. However, the specific health risk predictions of the panel based on genogram information were no more accurate than those generated from other sources (i.e., demographic data and chart-review information). It is not surprising that specific predictions could not be made since there was no opportunity for formulation of inferences based on clinical contact.

The limitations of the studies in family medicine may explain the lack of consistent findings. First, there is an absence of documentation as to the training of research assistants or physicians in use of the genogram, their knowledge about the theoretical underpinnings, and their experience in managing family systems dynamics. These factors influence the understanding of the patient and family and the nature of the clinician-patient-family relationship. It is fundamental to outcome research, for example, to assess the process as well as the effects of an intervention. Second, these studies were conducted using a narrow scope of measurement instruments. Third, the type of information collected was usually limited to demographic information and facts. Fourth, the numbers of participants, patient encounters, and study sites were limited, and there was little diversity in the people participating in the studies.

The limitations of genogram research in family medicine are further highlighted in Berg's (1991) humorous comments about the nonsignificant results found by Rogers and Rohrbaugh. He reviews the specifics of their findings indicating no evidence that genograms influence how physicians think about and deal with clinical problems or the perceptions patients have about their doctor-patient encounter, saying, "Genograms recorded in a particular way in a specific teaching practice covering a single geographic area with a small group of English-speaking adults seen over a short period of time do not appear to make a difference during a single non-emergent patient visit in physician and patient perceptions of what occurred when quantified by a particular group of measurement instruments analyzed by an especially complex statistical technique."

Notwithstanding its limitations, the family medicine research is commendable. The results raise many interesting questions and allow us to see the complexity of empirically investigating the ways the genogram is useful in clinical settings.

Reliability Studies

Many of the reliability studies on the genogram have been conducted by family medicine researchers. Jolly, Froom, and Rosen (1980) found that family practice residents could elicit and record most of the "relevant" family information during a 16-minute genogram interview and that the information thus gathered could be read correctly from the genogram by different physicians with a high degree of accuracy. The sample was small and homogeneous, and the "relevant" data were limited to objective information sought by physicians; however, the results are suggestive of good inter-rater reliability of the measure. The test-retest reliability of the genogram data also has been assessed by Rogers and Holloway (1990), who investigated the completion rate and reliability of a self-administered genogram for family practice patients. They found a high degree of test-retest reliability with assessments completed two times, three months apart. The reliability of the tool in a family practice setting is likely to be enhanced further by the refinement of the categories used for data collection. These refinements can build upon the work of this book as well as research by Haas-Cunningham (1994) and Rohrbaugh, Rogers, and McGoldrick (1992). Further refinement of the categories used will likely enhance the reliability of the tool.

Less research on the reliability of the genogram has accumulated in the field of family therapy. Coupland, Serovich, and Glenn (1995) contend that the reliability of the genogram as an instrument per se cannot be assessed, arguing that the genogram is a heuristic tool rather than a measurement tool. They do assert, however, that the reliability of marriage and family therapists' use of the instrument can and should be assessed. In an effort to ascertain the reliability of family therapists' use of the instrument, they used fictitious scenarios, and asked 17 doctoral students in marriage and family therapy training programs to record genogram information. Students were found to be highly accurate in recording family members' names and symbols, moderately accurate in recording occupations, medical issues, and personal issues, and much less accurate in recording dates and ages. The authors suggest either that students find recording some information on a genogram to be irrelevant or that students are not trained in genogram construction. Ongoing supervision, including evaluation and critiques of genograms, is their recommended solution to the recording problem.

Research on Families and Family Process

A goal of family-centered research is to promote the understanding of the structure, function, patterns, and multigenerational legacies of families. Research on families using the genogram might involve examining the basic assumptions about family processes that guide the way genograms are used by clinicians. Many of these assumptions are based on Bowen's family systems theory and are quite testable. To give a flavor of this type of research, we use categories of interpretive principles as a framework for suggesting just a few of the many possible researchable questions. This information could be collected across a variety of families and in the context of a clinical setting where genograms are routinely used.

Family structure: Is symptomatology seen in some types of family structures more often than in other types? Is sibling position related to achievement motivation, responsibility, or symptomatology? Are couples with complementary sibling positions (oldest and youngest) more compatible than couples with noncomplementary sibling positions (both oldest or both youngest)?

Life cycle fit: Are families more likely to become symptomatic at points of life cycle transition? Is there disturbance in the system when life cycle transitions are unduly rushed or delayed? Do couples who marry early or late or who are at different points in their own life cycles have particular types of problems?

Pattern repetition across generations: What symptoms and problems, and what solutions, are likely to be passed down from one generation to the next? How common are alternating repetitive patterns of cut-off and fusion and high and low functioning? Can levels of "maturity" or differentiation be tracked from one generation to another?

Life events and family functioning: Do traumatic or critical family events occur around certain dates at a greater frequency than expected by chance? Is there a greater chance of symptomatology and/or "specialness" for children born around nodal events in families? What impact do untimely deaths have on other family members?

Relational patterns and triangles: Are there typical types of relational patterns that correspond to particular family structures (e.g., child-focused families, remarried families)? How do triangles in families change over time? How does a particular child get selected to be included in a parental-child triangle and thus become symptomatic?

Family balance and imbalance: Does there tend to be a balance in functioning in families across generations? (See Chapter 5.) What happens when there is an imbalance or lack of functional fit in a family? How does functional balance shift in families? Under what conditions do spouses or other family members become overfunctioners to compensate for a dysfunctional spouse? What happens when people from two different social classes or ethnic groups marry?

In addition to research based on Bowenian assumptions, authors espousing other theoretical orientations have contributed to the body of knowledge about families and family processes. For example, although not empirical in his methods, Sulloway (1996) provides extensive retrospective family research emerging from a historical and evolutionary psychology perspective. He focuses primarily on birth order, analyzing or reanalyzing previous birth order research, the historical roots of individuals and their personality characteristics as related to their families of origin, parental loss and the ways sibling respond to the losses, individual development as related to family structure, and the history of social and scientific revolutions. Sulloway demonstrates that individuals growing up in the same family show great interpersonal differences, hypothesized to be primarily related to their birth order. Beyond this, he proposes that many historical outcomes have depended on the birth order of the leaders involved in the events. This kind of extensive family research enhances our understanding of family functioning. The genogram is an excellent tool for conducting retrospective historical analyses, as well as prospective process and outcome research.

Many of the research directions we and other authors have identified could be undertaken by analyzing objective data across a large number of genograms. To do this, however, the data must be pooled together and organized, most likely through the use of computers.

Computer-generated Genograms

Imagine a clinician entering a therapy or examining room to see the client or patient, clicking on a button and presto, the individual's family genogram appears on the computer in the room. Or imagine the same clinician reviewing his or her previous caseload and wondering how effective he or she might be with families with small children. The computer is told to search for this type of family and the relevant family genograms appear one by one on the screen and are printed. Or finally, imagine the clinician wondering if there might be a pattern to a series of families he or she has seen. Again, the computer is consulted and asked to search for certain hypothesized features in each of the relevant families. With computer technology developing at an amazing pace, the computer is becoming an invaluable part of the clinician's armamentarium.

The computer facilitates the mechanical tasks of constructing the genogram. It takes the spatial guesswork out of drawing genograms and easily updates and redraws a genogram as new information on the family is gathered. The computer, however, is more helpful than simply a genogram drawer; it is an information manager. It organizes and retrieves information efficiently and quickly. Equally important, the computer can present information in a variety of forms and can be instructed to search for redundancies and patterns in data. All of these abilities are useful in assessing and studying families.

The value of the computer for large-scale genogram research is obvious. We already have mentioned the tremendous untapped data pool present in the thousands of genograms produced daily by clinicians. This information will become useful for research only if it becomes part of a computer database. Our hope is that as clinicians increasingly rely on computers to store and generate genograms, the pooling of individual clinicians' computer data on families (with identifying information omitted) will lead to a very large database for research purposes. Computers are extremely useful for pattern recognition; many genograms can be computer-analyzed simultaneously to generate patterns that will facilitate research and clinical use of the genogram.

Two software developers have created computerized versions of the genogram (Gerson & Shellenberger, 1999a, 1999b; WonderWare, 1998). These programs emphasize the systemic nature of family relationships. For example, the program allows the clinician to specify critical family relationships, such as fused, distant, abusive, triangled, etc., and the corresponding relationship lines appear on the genogram. In this manner, the higher order inferences about family relationships can be documented. In addition, two of the programs (Gerson & Shellenberger, 1999a; WonderWare, 1998) produce genograms for any date in the family's history. Thus, if the clinician chooses to show the family ten years earlier, the computer displays the corresponding age of each family member at that time and eliminates family members who were not yet born. Also, some computer programs compile a comprehensive chronology of important family events.

Gerson developed the first computerized genogram program in 1982. Windows, DOS, and Macintosh versions are available. Genogram-Maker Plus (Gerson & Shellenberger, 1999a) draws genograms based on family information entered into the computer, eliminating the usual design problems of creating a neat, well-spaced, readable genogram. When new information is entered, the program changes the genogram for the clinician automatically. From the computer-generated genogram, the clinician accesses information on each individual family member.

In another version of the computerized genogram called the AutoGenogram (Gerson & Shellenberger, 1999b), family members themselves sit at a computer and enter information about their families. A series of questions appears on the screen. After the questions are completed, the computer generates a genogram. Options in the program allow one to choose the level of detail desired in the interview (e.g., inclusion of family relationships or problems, inclusion of grandparents' families, parents' families, etc.). After completion of the genogram, the clinician makes desired adjustments using the standard computerized drawing program, the Genogram-Maker or Genogram-Maker Plus.

WonderWare (1998) developed a similar fill-in-the-blank type of software program called Relativity. The program asks for information to be entered on a set of screens. The strengths of this program are its attention to confidentiality issues and its mechanism for importing data from and exporting data to some other programs, such as genealogy programs. WonderWare does not, however, include a drawing feature to allow easy adjustments to the genogram by the use of drawing tools, or quick movement of the genogram on the page. For example, the symbols for individual people on the genogram cannot be moved using a click and drag method. Windows and DOS versions of this software are available.

Family genealogy programs (Broderbund, 1998; Palladium Interactive, Inc., 1998) are generally quite different from these clinical tools; typical genealogy programs do not offer a systematic way of illustrating family assessment information regarding relationships, family triangles, or the intergenerational transmission processes that Bowen describes. Instead they mainly record demographic information, family history, and family stories. Some programs incorporate family pictures and videos as part of the computer record.

A major trend toward the automation of clinical records has occurred in recent years. When such records are placed in a computer database, the information is more accessible and usable. Different clinicians can easily have access to the same files and information. In addition, automatic flags can be set up to warn the clinician of conditions applying in specific cases, e.g., the first anniversary of a child's death. The computer-generated genogram is an obvious application of family systems thinking to the collection of family information. As computer technology advances, the potential of the computer for the organization and display of data will change as well. For instance, using medical records system software, Chan and colleagues in Hong Kong (Chan, Donnan, Chan, & Chow, 1987) established a computerized medical records system that includes a three-generation family genogram in their general practice clinic.

The computer has become a part of the therapeutic process. For example, a clinician may display computer-generated genograms on a monitor to clients or to make systemic points. We do not fear that the technology will replace the clinician. Human judgment and intervention will always remain central to clinical work, but the machine may become an important partner in information management and organization.

The information-managing capabilities of the computer are too awesome to ignore. Our hope is to make those capabilities of direct use to the clinician and researcher. For the clinician, the computer-generated genogram is an example of such an application that organizes family information in a graphic form to emphasize the systemic, multigenerational nature of the family. For the researcher, the data entered into the computer program can be linked to medical or clinical data. For example, research can examine whether occurrence of critical events, such as serious illness, job loss, or untimely death in a family member, leads to exacerbation of mental or physical health problems, such as drinking, headaches, irritable bowel syndrome, or abuse.

In conclusion, we have attempted to show the usefulness of genograms in clinical work. Our hope is that our efforts will serve as a guide and stimulus to the further development of the genogram as both a clinical and research tool. In support of family research, a grant fund has been established in the memory of Randy Gerson to support practitioners, graduate students, and researchers in conducting family theory and genogram research (contact the American Psychological Foundation of the American Psychological Association for information, 750 First Street, Washington, DC 20002-4242).

We believe that the research potential of the genogram has barely been touched. We enthusiastically challenge both clinicians and academic researchers to define further the elements of the genogram that have clinical and research utility and to collect genogram information in an organized way so that the information can be pooled and analyzed across cases and tied to medical, psychological, and social outcomes. We see the development of the genogram as a research tool and the computerization of the genogram as going hand in hand, both leading to increased clinical proficiency and knowledge.

Appendix

For the convenience of teachers and clinicians, this appendix provides summaries of some important materials and skeletal formats for doing genograms. It includes:

1) a summary of the symbol standardization for doing genograms;
2) a skeletal genogram form for clinician use;
3) an outline for conducting a genogram interview;
4) an outline for genogram interpretation.

Part 1: Genogram Format

A. **Symbols** to describe basic family membership and structure (include on genogram significant others who lived with or cared for family members—place them on the side of the genogram with a notation about who they are).

B. **Family interaction patterns.** The relationship indicators are optional. The clinician may prefer to note them on a separate sheet. They are among the least precise information on the genogram, but may be key indicators of relationship patterns the clinician wants to remember.

C. **Medical history.** Since the genogram is meant to be an orienting map of the family, there is room to indicate only the most important factors. Thus, list only major or chronic illnesses and problems. Include dates in parentheses where feasible or applicable. Use DSM-IV categories or recognized abbreviations where available (e.g., cancer: CA; stroke: CVA).

D. **Other family information** of special importance may also be noted on the genogram:

1) Ethnic background and migration date
2) Religion or religious change
3) Education
4) Occupation or unemployment
5) Military service
6) Retirement

Standard Symbols for Genograms

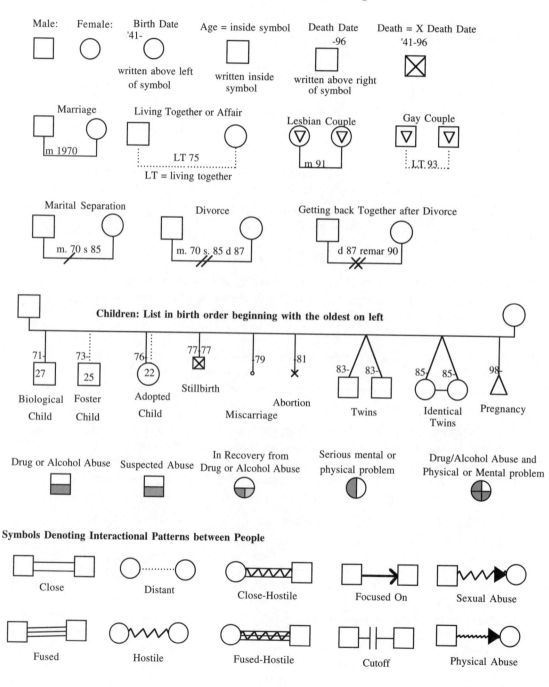

Male: Female: Birth Date   Age = inside symbol   Death Date   Death = X Death Date
'41-   -96   '41-96
written above left   written inside   written above right
of symbol   symbol   of symbol

Marriage   Living Together or Affair   Lesbian Couple   Gay Couple
m 1970   LT 75   m 91   LT 93
LT = living together

Marital Separation   Divorce   Getting back Together after Divorce
m. 70 s 85   m. 70 s. 85 d 87   d 87 remar 90

Children: List in birth order beginning with the oldest on left

71-   73-   76-   77-77   79   81   83- 83-   85- 85-   98-
27   25   22

Biological   Foster   Adopted   Stillbirth   Abortion   Twins   Identical   Pregnancy
Child   Child   Child   Miscarriage   Twins

Drug or Alcohol Abuse   Suspected Abuse   In Recovery from Drug or Alcohol Abuse   Serious mental or physical problem   Drug/Alcohol Abuse and Physical or Mental problem

Symbols Denoting Interactional Patterns between People

Close   Distant   Close-Hostile   Focused On   Sexual Abuse

Fused   Hostile   Fused-Hostile   Cutoff   Physical Abuse

7) Trouble with law

8) Physical or sexual abuse or incest

9) Obesity

10) Alcohol or drug abuse

11) Smoking

12) Dates when family members left home: LH '74.

13) Current location of family members

It is useful to have a space at the bottom of the genogram for notes on other key information: This would include critical events, changes in the family structure since the genogram was made, hypotheses and other notations of major family issues or changes. These notations should always be dated, and should be kept to a minimum, since every extra piece of information on a genogram complicates it and therefore diminishes its readability.

Part 2: Outline for a Brief Genogram Interview

I. Start with presenting problem
- Why are they coming for help now?
- When did the problem begin?
- Who noticed it?
- How does each person view it?
- How has each responded?
- What were relations like prior to the problem?
- Has the problem changed? How?
- What will happen if it continues?

II. Move to questions on household context
- Who lives in the household (name, age, gender)?
- How is each related?
- Where do other members live?
- Were there any similar problems in family before?
- What solutions were tried in the past (therapy, treatment, hospitalization, etc.)?
- What has been happening recently in the family?
- Have there been any recent changes or stressors?

III. Gather information on parents' birth families
- Number of siblings, names, dates of birth
- Place in birth order
- Parents' marriage (and separations, divorces, remarriages)

- Siblings' marriages (separations, divorces, remarriages, children)
- Cause of any deaths in the family

IV. Inquire about other generations
- Parents' parents (names, dates of birth and death, occupation, health)
- Causes of death
- Their siblings (names, dates and causes of death, occupation, health)

V. Probe ethnic/cultural variables
- Rituals within culture for handling death (attitude toward dying, body disposal, commemorative ceremonies)
- Beliefs about what happens after death
- Stigma or trauma associated with any death or loss
- Impact of ethnic-cultural variables on handling major life events, family relationships and roles, individual functioning, etc.

VI. Elicit attitudes about gender
- Impact of gender roles on household situation, on handling major life events, on individual functioning, etc.
- What are the gender rules within the family/culture regarding expressions of grief, funeral arrangements, or commemorative rituals?

VII. Ask about major life events
- Marriages
- Births
- Deaths, illnesses, disabilities
- Geographic moves
- Job changes
- Traumatic events such as natural disasters, wars

How did family adapt to these changes?

VIII. Inquire about family relationships
- Cut-offs
- Alliances
- Marital patterns
- Parent-child patterns
- Dominance/submission patterns

IX. Inquire about family roles
- Caretakers? "Sick" ones? "Problem" ones?
- "Good" ones? "Bad" ones?
- "Successful" ones? "Failures"?
- "Nice" ones? "Cold, distant" ones?

X. Inquire about family strengths

- Behaviors that indicate resilience
- Family members' character strengths: loyalty, courage, hope, humor, intelligence, and so forth.
- Family resources: ability to connect with outside resources, money, love, neighborhood community, religious community, work, and so forth

XI. Include questions on individual functioning

- Work (job, changes, unemployment, satisfaction)
- School (achievements, problems)
- Medical problems
- Psychiatric problems (depression, anxieties, phobias)
- Addictions (alcohol, drugs)
- Legal problems (arrests, lost professional license, current status of litigation)

Part 3: Genogram Interpretation

I. Family Structure and Composition

A. Marital Configurations

1) Single-parent households due to death or divorce or choice to form a single parent family can be stressful because of the obvious loss issues as well as loneliness, economic stress, child-rearing strain, etc.

2) Remarried households, where one or both parents have remarried following a death or divorce, bringing a stepparent into the household. Issues typically involve custody, visitation rights, jealousy, favoritism, loyalty, stepparent conflicts, stepsibling conflicts, etc.

B. Siblings

1) Birth order can have relevance for one's emotional and relational role in the family. For example, the oldest is more likely to be over-responsible, conscientious, and parental; the youngest childlike and carefree. Only children tend to be socially independent, less oriented toward peer relations, more adultlike earlier, more anxious at times, and like an oldest child, often the focus of parents' attention. All children after the oldest have to find some way to carve a niche for themselves.

2) Timing of sibling births vis-à-vis what else was happening in the family at the time. For example, was there a birth right after a loss? (Such a situation often indicates an attempt to replace or make up for the loss, etc.)

3) Family's expectations or "program" for the child.

4) Parental attitudes and biases re gender. Are males given preferred status? Or females? Are there alliances in the family by gender?

II. Family Place in the Life Cycle

In interpreting a genogram, you will also want to look at where individuals and the family as a whole are in the life cycle. Families progress through a series of stages or transitions, including leaving the home of origin, marriage, births, child-rearing, retirement. Upon reaching each milestone, the family must reorganize itself and move on successfully to the next phase. If patterns rigidify at transition points, families can have trouble in adapting to a later phase (Carter & McGoldrick, 1998a).

The clinician should note what life cycle transitions, if any, the family is adapting to, and how they have adapted to life cycle events in the past. When ages and dates do not add up in terms of how that family progressed through various stages, possible difficulties in managing that phase of the life cycle can be explored. For example, if adult children have not left home, one would want to explore any difficulties around beginning a new phase of the life cycle. Or, if a marriage occurred quickly after a loss, this may be a clue about issues of unresolved grief.

III. Pattern Repetition Across Generations

Since family patterns can be transmitted from one generation to the next, be alert in doing a genogram to any cross-generational patterns that reveal themselves in the following areas:

A. Patterns of Functioning

Are there things about how this family functions that you see in previous generations also? These patterns could be adaptive (creativity, resilience, strengths) or maladaptive (battering, child abuse, alcoholism, suicide, etc.)

B. Patterns of Relationships

Look for patterns of closeness, distance, cut-offs, or conflicts repeating over generations. For example, a family might have a pattern of forming relational "triangles" with mother and father allied against a child.

C. Patterns Related to Position in Family

People in similar positions as a previous generation member tend to repeat the same patterns. For example, the only son of a man who spent time in prison during his twenties may pattern himself after his father and end up going to prison during his twenties. Or a person may remarry and form a similar family constellation to the one he or she grew up in (as with the

Rogers family in Genogram 7.1). This factor may influence relationships with others in the same repetitive pattern.

IV. Balance in Family Roles and Functioning

In well-functioning families, members' characteristics tend to balance out one another. For example, a gregarious, social partner is balanced out by a more home-oriented spouse; a responsible older sibling is balanced out by an easygoing younger one. The roles and personalities of one provide a complementary fit with the other.

But some genograms show an imbalance in roles, with too many people vying for the same role of "caretaker," for example, or one person being responsible for too much. An alcoholic married to a caretaker, for instance, may seem a complementary fit, but ultimately this situation puts too much of a strain on the caretaker. Families may also show an imbalance in power between husbands and wives, brothers and sisters, darker and lighter skinned family members, or for some other reason depending on class, abilities, parental preferences, family values, etc. When imbalance appears, explore how the family handles it and what the implications would be of changing it to create a more equitable balance in family relationships.

BIBLIOGRAPHY

The bibliography has been divided into three sections. The first includes references to the professional literature cited in the text. The second is a bibliography arranged by topic. The third includes biographical sources and is arranged alphabetically by family name.

References

Ahrons, C. (1994). *The good divorce*. New York: Basic Books.

Alexander, D., & Clark, S. (1998). Keeping "the family" in focus during patient care. In P. D. Sloane, L. M. Slatt, P. Curtis, & M. H. Ebell (Eds.), *Essentials of family medicine* (3rd ed., pp. 25–39). Baltimore, MD: Williams & Wilkins.

Almeida, R., Messineo, T., Woods, R., & Font, R. (1998). The cultural context model. In M. McGoldrick (Ed.), *Revisioning family therapy: Race, culture and gender in clinical practice*. (pp. 414–431). New York: Guilford.

Baird, M. A., & Grant, W. D. (1998). Families and health. In R. B. Taylor, A. K. David, T. A. Johnson, Jr., D. M. Phillips, & J. E. Scherger (Eds.), *Family medicine principles and practice* (4th ed., pp. 10–15). New York: Springer-Verlag.

Bannerman, C. (1986). The genograms and elderly patients. *Journal of Family Practice, 23*, 426–427.

Barth, J. C. (1993). *It runs in my family: Overcoming the legacy of family illness*. New York: Brunner/Mazel.

Beautrais, A. L., Fergusson, D. M., & Shannon, F. T. (1982). Life events and childhood morbidity: A prospective study. *Pediatrics, 70*, 935–940.

Beck, R. L. (1987). The genogram as process. *American Journal of Family Therapy, 15*, 343–351.

Bepko, C. S., & Krestan, J. (1985). *The responsibility trap: Women and men in alcoholic families*. New York: Free Press.

Berg, A. O. (1991). Genograms, generalizability, quantities and qualities. *Journal of the American Board of Family Practice, 4*, 468–469.

Bernikow, L. (1980). *Among women*. New York: Harper & Row.

Berolzheimer, N., Thrower, S., & Koch-Hatten, A. (1993). Working with families. In P. D. Sloane, L. M. Slatt, & P. Curtis (Eds.), *Essentials of family medicine* (2nd ed., pp. 19–29). Baltimore, MD: Williams & Wilkins.

Bowen, M. (1978). *Family therapy in clinical practice*. New York: Jason Aronson.

Boyce, W. T., Jensen, E. W., Cassel, J. C., Collier, A. M., Smith, A. H., & Ramsey, C.T. (1977). Influence of life events and family routines on childhood respiratory illness. *Pediatrics, 60*, 609–615.

Boyd-Franklin, N. (1989). *Black families in therapy: A multisystems approach*. New York: Guilford.

Bradt, J. (1980). *The family diagram*. Washington. DC: Groome Center, 5225 Loughboro Road.

Broderbund Software, Inc. (1998). Family Tree Maker, Deluxe edition III [Computer software]. Novato, CA: Authors.

Burge, S. K. (1989). Violence against women as a health care issue. *Family Medicine, 2*, 368–373.

Burke, J. L., & Faber, P. (1997). A genogrid for couples. *Journal of Gay and Lesbian Social Services, 7*(1): 13–22.

Buurma, D. (1999). *The family play genogram: A guidebook*. 67 Valley View Ave., Summit, NJ 07901: Author.

Caplow, T. (1968). *Two against one. Coalitions in triads*. Englewood Cliffs, NJ: Prentice Hall.

Carter, E.A. (1978). Transgenerational scripts and nuclear family stress: Theory and clinical implications. In R. R. Sager (Ed.), *Georgetown family symposium* (Vol. III, 1975–77). Washington, DC: Georgetown University.

Carter, E. A. (1982). Supervisory discussion in the presence of the family. In R. Whiffen & J. Byng-Hall (Eds.), *Family therapy supervision*. London: Academic Press.

Carter, B., & McGoldrick, M. (Eds.), (1998a). *The expanded family life cycle: Individual, family and social perspectives* (3rd ed.). Boston: Allyn & Bacon.

Carter, B., & McGoldrick, M. (1998b) Overview of the family life cycle. In B. Carter & M. McGoldrick (Eds.), *The expanded family life cycle: Individual, family and social perspectives* (3rd ed.). Boston: Allyn & Bacon.

Carter, B., & McGoldrick, M. (1998c) Coaching at various stages of the life cycle. In B. Carter & M. McGoldrick (Eds.), *The expanded family life cycle: Individual, family and social perspectives* (3rd ed.). Boston: Allyn & Bacon.

Chan, D. H., Donnan, S. P. B., Chan, N., & Chow, G. (1987). A microcomputer-based computerized medical record system for a general practice teaching clinic. *Journal of Family Practice, 24*, 537–541.

Christie-Seely, J. (1986). A diagnostic problem and family assesment. *Journal of Family Practice, 22*, 329–339.

Cohler, B. A., Hosteler, J., & Boxer, A. (1998). In D. McAdams & E. de St. Aubin (Eds.), *Generativity and adult development. Psychosocial perspective on caring and contributing to the next generation*. Washington, DC: American Psychological Association Press.

Colon, F. (1973). In search of one's past: An identity trip. *Family Process, 12*(4), 429–38.

Colon, F (1998). The discovery of my multicultural identity. In M. McGoldrick (Ed.), *Revisioning family therapy: Race, culture and gender in clinical practice*. New York: Guilford.

Congress, E. P. (1994). The use of culturagrams to assess and empower culturally diverse families. *Families in Society*, November.

Coupland, S. K., Serovich, J., & Glenn, J. E. (1995). Reliability in constructing genograms: A study among marriage and family therapy doctoral students. *Journal of Marital and Family Therapy, 21*, 251–264.

Crouch, M. A. (1986). Working with one's own family: Another path for professional development. *Family Medicine, 18*, 93–98.

Crouch, M. A. (1989). A putative ancestry of family practice and family medicine: Genogram of a discipline. *Family Systems Medicine, 7*(2), 208–212.

Crouch, M., & Davis, T. (1987). Using the genogram (family tree) clinically. In M. Crouch & L. Roberts (Eds.), *The family in medical practice: A family systems primer* (pp. 174–192). New York: Springer-Verlag.

Darkenwald, G. G., & Silvestri, K. (1992). Analysis and assessment of the Newark literacy campaign: A report to the Ford Foundation. (Grant # 915-0298).

Dumas, C. A., Katerndahl, D. A., & Burge, S. K. (1995). Familial patterns in patients with infrequent panic attacks. *Archives of Family Medicine, 4*, 862–867.

Elder, G. H., Jr. (1977). Family history and the life course. *Journal of Family History, 22*, 279–304.

Elder, G. (1986). Military times and turning points in men's lives. *Developmental Psychology, 22,* 233–245.

Elder, G. (1992). Life course. In E. Borgatta & M. Borgatta (Eds.), *Encyclopedia of sociology* (Vol. 3, pp. 1120–1130), New York: Macmillan.

Ellenberger, H. F. (1970). *The discovery of the unconscious: The history and evolution of dynamic psychiatry.* New York: Basic Books.

Engel, G. (1975). The death of a twin: Mourning and anniversary reactions: Fragments of 10 years of self-analysis. *International Journal of Psychoanalysis, 56*(1), 23–40.

Fink, A. H., Kramer, L., Weaver, L. L., & Anderson, J. (1993). More on genograms: Modifications to a model. *Journal of Child and Adolescent Group Therapy, 3,* 203–206.

Fogarty, T. (1973). Triangles. *The Family.* New Rochelle, NY: Center for Family Learning.

Folwarski, J. (1998). No longer an orphan in history. In M. McGoldrick (Ed.), *Revisioning family therapy* (pp. 239–252). New York: Guilford.

Friedman, H., Rohrbaugh, M., & Krakauer, S. (1988). The timeline genogram: Highlighting temporal aspects of family relationships. *Family Process, 27,* 293–304.

Friesen, P., & Manitt, J. (1991). Nursing the remarried family in a palliative care setting. *Journal of Palliative Care, 6*(4), 32–39.

Garrett, R. E., Klinkman, M., & Post, L. (1987). If you meet Buddha on the road, take a genogram: Zen and the art of family medicine. *Family Medicine, 19,* 225–226.

Gerson, R. (1995). The family life cycle: Phases, stages and crises. In R. H. Mikesell, D. Lusterman, & S. McDaniel (Eds.), *Integrating family therapy: Handbook of family psychology and systems therapy* (pp. 91–111). Washington, DC: American Psychological Association.

Gerson, R., Hoffman, S., Sauls, S., & Ulrici, M. (1993). Family-of-origin frames in couple therapy. *Journal of Marital and Family Therapy, 12*(1), 59–47.

Gerson, R. P., & Shellenberger, S. (1999a). The Genogram-Maker Plus for Windows and Macintosh [Computer software]. Macon, GA: Humanware.

Gerson, R. P., & Shellenberger, S. (1999b). The AutoGenogram for Windows and Macintosh [Computer software]. Macon, GA: Humanware.

Gewirtzman, R. C. (1988). The genogram as a visual assessment of a family's fugue. *Australian Journal of Sex, Marriage and Family, 9,* 37–46.

Gil, E., & Sobol, B. (2000). Engaging families in therapeutic play. In Bailey, C. E. (Ed.), *Children in therapy: Using the family as a resource.* New York: Norton.

Guerin, P., Fogarty, T. F., Fay, L. F., & Kautto, J. G. (1996). *Working with relationship triangles.* New York: Guilford.

Haas-Cunningham, S. M. (1994). The genogram as a predictor of families at risk for physical illness (Doctoral dissertation, Syracuse University, 1993). *Dissertation Abstracts International, 54*(9-b), 4590.

Hamberger, L. K., Saundes, D. G., & Harvey, M. (1992). Prevalence of domestic violence in community practice and rate of physician inquiry. *Family Medicine, 24,* 256–260.

Hardy, K. V., & Laszloffy, T. A. (1995). The cultural genogram: Key to training culturally competent family therapists. *Journal of Marital and Family Therapy, 21*(3), 227–237.

Hines, P. M. (1998). The family life cycle of poor black families. In B. Carter & M. McGoldrick (Eds.), *The expanded family life cycle: Individual, family and social perspectives* (3rd ed.). Boston: Allyn & Bacon,

Hof, L., & Berman, E. (1986). The sexual genogram. *Journal of Marital and Family Therapy, 12*(1), 39–47.

Holmes, T. H., & Masuda, M. (1974). Life change and illness susceptibility. In B. S. Dohrenwend & B. Dohrenwend (Eds.), *Stressful life events: Their nature and effects.* New York: Wiley.

Holmes, T. H., & Rahe, T. H. (1967). The social adjustment rating scale. *Journal of Psychosomatic Research, 11,* 213–218.

Huygen, F. J. A. (1982). *Family medicine: The medical life history of families.* New York: Brunner/Mazel.

Imber Black, E. (Ed.). (1993). *Secrets in families and family therapy*. New York: Norton.

Imber Black, E. (1998). *The secret life of families*. New York: Bantam Books.

Ingersoll-Dayton, B., & Arndt, B. (1990). Uses of the genogram with the elderly and their families. *Journal of Gerontological Social Work, 15*(1–2), 105–120.

Jolly, W. M., Froom, J., & Rosen, M. G. (1980). The genogram. *Journal of Family Practice, 10*(2), 251–255.

Kerr, M. E., & Bowen, M. (1988). *Family evaluation*. New York: Norton.

Kuehl, B. P. (1995). The solution-oriented genogram: A collaborative approach. *Journal of Marital and Family Therapy, 21*(3), 239–250.

Laird, J. (1996). Family-centered practice with lesbian and gay families. *Families in Society: Journal of Contemporary Human Services, 77*(9), 559–572.

Lewis, K. G. (1989). The use of color-coded genograms in family therapy. *Journal of Marital and Family Therapy, 15*(2), 169–176.

Lewis, J. M., Beavers, W. R., Gossett, J. T., & Phillips, V. A. (1976). *No single thread: Psychological health in family systems*. New York: Brunner/Mazel.

Like, R. C., Rogers, J., & McGoldrick, M. (1988). Reading and interpreting genograms: A systematic approach. *Journal of Family Practice, 26*(4), 407–412.

Maccoby, E. E. (1990). Gender and relationships: A developmental account. *American Psychologist, 45*(4), 513–520.

McCowley, G., Kern, D. E., Kolodner, K., Dill, L., Schroeder, A. F., DeChant, H. K. Ryden, J., Bass, E. B., & Deregotes, L. R. (1995). The "battering syndrome": Prevalence and clinical characteristics of domestic violence in primary care and internal medicine practices. *Annals of Internal Medicine, 123*, 737–746.

McDaniel, S. H., Campbell, T. L., & Seaburn, D. B. (1990). *Family-oriented primary care: A manual for medical providers*. New York: Springer-Verlag.

McDaniel, S. H., Hepworth, J., & Doherty, W. J. (1992). *Medical family therapy: A biopsychosocial approach to families and health problems*. New York: Basic Books.

McGill, D. M. (1992). The cultural story in multicultural family therapy. *Families in Society: Journal of Contemporary Human Services, 73*, 339–349.

McGoldrick, M. (1989). Sisters. In M. McGoldrick, C. Anderson, & F. Walsh (Eds.), *Women in families* (pp. 244–266). New York: Norton.

McGoldrick, M. (1995). *You can go home again: Reconnecting with your family*. New York: Norton.

McGoldrick, M. (Ed.). (1998a). *Revisioning family therapy: Race, culture and gender in clinical practice*. New York: Guilford.

McGoldrick, M. (1998b). Becoming a couple. In B. Carter & M. McGoldrick (Eds.), *The expanded family life cycle: Individual, family and social perspectives* (3rd ed.). Boston: Allyn & Bacon.

McGoldrick, M., Broken Nose, M., & Potenza, M. (1998). Violence and the family life cycle. In B. Carter & M. McGoldrick (Eds.), *The expanded family life cycle: Individual, family and social perspectives* (3rd ed.). Boston: Allyn & Bacon.

McGoldrick, M., & Carter, B. (1998a). The individual life cycle in context. In B. Carter & M. McGoldrick (Eds.), *The expanded family life cycle: Individual, family and social perspectives* (3rd ed.). Boston: Allyn & Bacon.

McGoldrick, M., & Carter, B. (1998b). Remarried families. In B. Carter & M. McGoldrick (Eds.). *The expanded family life cycle: Individual, family and social perspectives*, (3rd ed.). Boston: Allyn & Bacon.

McGoldrick, M., Giordano, J., & Pearce, J. K. (Eds.). (1996). *Ethnicity and family therapy* (2nd ed.). New York: Guilford.

McGoldrick, M., & Walsh, F. (1991). Death and the family life cycle. In F. Walsh & M. McGoldrick (Eds.), *Living beyond loss*. New York: Norton.

McGoldrick, M., & Watson, M. (1998). Siblings through the life cycle. In B. Carter & M. McGoldrick (Eds.), *The expanded family life cycle: Individual, family and social perspectives* (3rd ed.). Boston: Allyn & Bacon.

McIlvain, H., Crabtree, B., Medder, J., Strange, K. C., & Miller, W. L. (1998). Using practice genograms to understand and describe practice configurations. *Family Medicine*, 30(7), 490–496.

McMillen, J. C., & Groze, V. (1994). Using placement genograms in child welfare practice. *Child Welfare*, 73(4), 307–318.

Medalie, J. H. (1978). *Family medicine: Principles and applications*. Baltimore: Williams & Wilkins.

Meyer, R. J., & Haggerty, R. J. (1962). Streptococcal infections in families: Factors altering individual susceptibility. *Pediatrics*, 29, 539–549.

Moon, S. M., Coleman, V. D., McCollum, E. E., Nelson, T. S., & Jensen-Scott, R. L. (1993). Using the genogram to facilitate career decisions: A case study. *Journal of Family Psychology*, 4, 45–56.

Mullins, M. C., & Christie-Seely, J. (1984). Collecting and recording family data—The genogram. In J. Christie-Seely (Ed.), *Working with the family in primary care* (pp. 179–191). New York: Praeger.

Palladium Interactive, Inc. (1998). Ultimate Family Tree Deluxe (version 2.0) [Computer software]. Spencer, IN: Authors.

Papp, P., Silverstein, O., & Carter, E. A. (1973). Family sculpting in preventive work with well families. *Family Process*, 12(25), 197–212.

Paul, N., & Paul B. B. (1986). *A marital puzzle*. New York: Gardner.

Pinderhughes, E. (1998). Black genealogy revisited: Restorying African American family. In M. McGoldrick (Ed.), *Revisioning family therapy: Race, culture, and gender in clinical practice* (pp. 179–199). New York: Guilford,

Rakel, R. E. (1977). *Principles of family medicine*. Philadelphia: W.B. Saunders.

Rogers, J. C. (1994). Can physicians use family genogram information to identify patients at risk of anxiety or depression? *Archives of Family Medicine*, 3, 1093–1098.

Rogers, J. C., & Cohn, P. (1987). Impact of a screening family genogram on first encounters in primary care. *Journal of Family Practice*, 4, 291–301.

Rogers, J. C., & Durkin, M. (1984). The semi-structured genogram interview: I. Protocol, II. Evaluation. *Family Systems Medicine*, 2(25), 176–187.

Rogers, J. C., Durkin, M., & Kelly, K. (1985). The family genogram: An underutilized clinical tool. *New Jersey Medicine*, 82(11), 887–892.

Rogers, J. C., & Holloway, R. (1990). Completion rate and reliability of the self-administered genogram (SAGE), *Family Practice*, 7, 149–51.

Rogers, J., C., & Rohrbaugh, M. (1991). The SAGE-PAGE trial: Do family genograms make a difference? *Journal of the American Board of Family Practice*, 4, 319–326.

Rogers, J. C., Rohrbaugh, M., & McGoldrick, M. (1992). Can experts predict health risk from family genograms? *Family Medicine*, 24, 209–215.

Rohrbaugh, M., Rogers, J. C., & McGoldrick, M. (1992). How do experts read family genograms? *Family Systems Medicine*, 10(1), 79–89.

Rolland, J. (1994). *Families, illness, and disability*. New York: Basic Books

Rolland, J. (1998). Chronic illness and the family life cycle. In B. Carter & M. McGoldrick (Eds.), *The expanded family life cycle: Individual, family and social perspectives* (3rd ed.). Boston: Allyn & Bacon.

Satir, V. (1972). *Peoplemaking*. Palo Alto: Science and Behavior Books.

Scharwiess, S. O. (1994). Step-sisters and half-brothers: A family therapist's view of German unification and other transitional processes. *Contemporary Family Therapy*, 16(3), 183–197.

Schmidt, D. D. (1978). The family as the unit of medical care. *Journal of Family Practice*, 7, 303.

Scrivner, R., & Eldridge, N. S. (1995) Lesbian and gay family psychology. In R. H. Mikesell, D. Lusterman, & S. McDaniel (Eds.), *Integrating family therapy: Handbook of family psychology and systems therapy* (pp. 327–345). Washington, DC: American Psychological Association.

Shellenberger, S. (1997). Losing one's match: A proposed model of Imago grief therapy. *Journal of Imago Relationship Therapy, 2*(2), 37–54.

Shellenberger, S., & Hoffman, S. (1995). The changing family-work system. In R. H. Mikesell, D. Lusterman, & S. McDaniel (Eds.), *Integrating family therapy: Handbook of family psychology and systems therapy* (pp. 461–479). Washington, DC: American Psychological Association.

Shellenberger, S., & Hoffman, S. (in press) Creating a safe emotional environment in systemic couples' therapy. In L. VandeCreek, S. Knapp, & T. L. Jackson (Eds.), *Innovations in clinical practice* (Vol. 17). Sarasota FL: Professional Resource Press.

Shellenberger, S., Shurden, K. W., & Treadwell, T. W. (1988). Faculty training seminars in family systems. *Family Medicine, 20,* 226–227.

Shellenberger, S., Watkins Couch, K., & Drake, M. (1989). Elderly family members and their caregivers: Characteristics and development of the relationship. *Family Systems and Health, 7,* 317–22.

Sherman, M. H. (1990). Family narratives: Internal representations of family relationships and affective themes. *Infant Mental Health Journal, 11,* 253–258.

Shernoff, M. J. (1984). Family therapy for lesbian and gay clients. *Social Work, 39,* 393–396.

Shields, C. G., King, D. A., & Wynne, L. C. (1995). Interventions with later life families. In R. H. Mikesell, D. Lusterman, & S. McDaniel (Eds.), *Integrating family therapy: Handbook of family psychology and systems therapy* (pp. 141–158). Washington, DC: American Psychological Association.

Slater, S. (1995). *The lesbian family life cycle.* New York: Free Press.

Sloane, P. D., Slatt, L. M., Curtis, P., & Ebell, M. (Eds.). (1998). *Essentials of family medicine* (3rd ed.). Baltimore, MD: Williams & Wilkins.

Smilkstein, G. (1978). The family APGAR: A proposal for a family function test and its use by physicians. *Journal of Family Practice, 6,* 1231.

Sproul, M. S., & Galagher, R. M. (1982). The genogram as an aid to crisis intervention. *Journal of Family Practice, 14*(55), 959–960.

Steinglass, P., Bennett, L., Wolin, S., & Reiss, D. (1987). *The alcoholic family.* New York: Basic Books.

Sulloway, F. J. (1996). *Born to rebel: Sibling relationships, family dynamics and creative lives.* New York: Pantheon.

Taylor, R. B., David, A. K., Johnson, T. A., Jr., Phillips, D. M., & Scherger, J. E. (Eds.) (1998). *Family medicine principles and practice* (5th ed.). Baltimore, MD: Williams & Wilkins.

Toman, W. (1976). *Family constellation* (3rd ed.). New York: Springer.

Tomson, P. (1985). Genograms in general practice. *Journal of the Royal Society of Medicine Supplement.* 78(8), 34–39.

Troncale, J. A. (1983). The genogram as an aid to diagnosis of distal renal tubular acidosis. *Journal of Family Practice, 17,* 707–708.

Wachtel, E. F. (1982). The family psyche over three generations: The genogram revisited. *Journal of Marital and Family Therapy, 8*(35), 335–343.

Wallechinsky, D., & Wallace, l. (1975). *The people's almanac.* New York: Harper & Row.

Walsh, F. (Ed.). (1994). *Normal family processes* (2nd ed.). New York: Guilford.

Walsh, F. (1995). From family damage to family challenge. In R. H. Mikesell, D. D. Lusterman, & S. McDaniel (Eds.), *Integrating family therapy: Handbook of family psychology and systems therapy* (pp. 587–606). Washington, DC: American Psychological Association.

Walsh, F. (1998). *Strengthening family resilience.* New York: Guilford.

Walsh, F., & McGoldrick, M. (1998). Death and the family life cycle. In B. Carter & M. McGoldrick (Eds.), *The expanded family life cycle: Individual, family and social perspectives* (3rd ed.). Boston: Allyn & Bacon.

Watson, M. (1998). African American siblings. In M. McGoldrick (Ed.), *Revisioning family therapy: Race, culture and gender in clinical practice*. New York: Guilford.

Watts Jones, D. (1998). Towards an African-American genogram. *Family Process, 36*(4), 373–383.

Weber, T., & Levine, F. (1995). Engaging the family: An integrative approach. In R. H. Mikesell, D. D. Lusterman, & S. McDaniel (Eds.), *Integrating family therapy: Handbook of family psychology and systems therapy* (pp. 45–71). Washington, DC: American Psychological Association.

White, M. B., & Tyson-Rawson, K. J. (1995). Assessing the dynamics of gender in couples and families: The gendergram. *Family Relations, 44*, 253–260.

White, M. (1995). Family therapy workshop, Family Institute of New Jersey.

WonderWare, Inc. (1998). Relativity [Computer Software]. Silver Spring, MD: Author.

Wright, L. (1995). Double mystery. *New Yorker*, August 7, pp. 45–62.

Bibliography by Topic

Assessment, Genograms, and Systems Theory

Bowen, M. (1978). *Family therapy in clinical practice*. New York: Jason Aronson.

Bowen, M. (1980). Key to the use of the genogram. In E. A. Carter & M. McGoldrick (Eds.), *The family life cycle: A framework for family therapy* (p. xxiii). New York: Gardner.

Bradt, J. (1980). *The family diagram*. Washington, DC: Groome Center, 5225 Loughboro Road.

Byng-Hall, J. (1995). *Rewriting family scripts*. New York: Guilford.

Caplow, T. (1968). *Two against one: Coalitions in triads*. Englewood Cliffs, NJ: Prentice Hall.

Carter, B., & McGoldrick, M. (Eds.). (1998a). *The expanded family life cycle: Individual, family and social perspectives* (3rd ed.). Boston: Allyn & Bacon.

Carter, E. A. (1978). Transgenerational scripts and nuclear family stress: Theory and clinical implications. In R. R. Sager (Ed.). *Georgetown family symposium* (Vol. III, 1975-77). Washington, DC: Georgetown University.

Christie-Seely, J. (1986). A diagnostic problem and family assesment. *Journal of Family Practice, 22*, 329–339.

Erdman, H. P., & Foster, S. W. (1986). Computer-assisted assessment with couples and families. *Family Therapy, 13*(1), 23–40.

Fleck, S. (1994). The family in health and disease. *New Trends in Experimental and Clinical Psychiatry, 10*(1), 41–51.

Fogarty, T. (1973). Triangles. *The Family*. New Rochelle, NY: Center for Family Learning.

Guerin, P. J. (Ed.). (1976). *Family therapy*. New York: Gardner.

Guerin, P. J., & Pendagast, E. G. (1976). Evaluation of family system and genogram. In P. Guerin (Ed.), *Family therapy*. New York: Gardner.

Guerin, P., Fogarty, T. F., Fay, L. F., & Kautto, J. G. (1996). *Working with relationship triangles*. New York: Guilford.

Haley, A. (1974). *Roots: The saga of an American family*. New York: Doubleday.

Hartman, A. (1995). Diagrammatic assessment of family relationships. *Families in Society, 76*(2), 111–122.

Karpel, M. A. (1994). *Evaluating couples: A handbook for practitioners*. New York: Norton.

Kerr, M. E., & Bowen, M. (1988). *Family evaluation*. New York: Norton.

Lewis, K. G. (1989). The use of color-coded genograms in family therapy. *Journal of Marital and Family Therapy, 15*(2), 169–176.

Lieberman, S. (1979). *Transgenerational family therapy*. London: Croom Helm.

Like, R. C., Rogers, J., & McGoldrick, M. (1988). Reading and interpreting genograms: A systematic approach. *Journal of Family Practice, 26*(4), 407–412.

Marlin, E. (1989). *Genograms*. Chicago: Contemporary Books.

McGoldrick, M. (1980). Problems with family genograms. *American Journal of Family Therapy, 7*, 74–76.

McGoldrick, M. (1995). *You can go home again: Reconnecting with your family*. New York: Norton.

McGoldrick, M. (Ed.). (1998a). *Revisioning family therapy: Race, culture and gender in clinical practice*. New York: Guilford.

Papadopoulos, L., Bor, R., & Stanion, P. (1997). Genograms in counselling practice: A review (Part I). *Counselling Psychology Quarterly, 10*(1), 17–28.

Pendagast, E. G., & Sherman, C. O. (1977). A guide to the genogram. *The Family, 5*, 3–14.

Richardson, R. W. (1987). *Family ties that bind: A self-help guide to change through family of origin therapy* (2nd ed.). Bellingham, WA: Self-Counsel Press.

Satir, V. (1968). *Conjoint family therapy*. Palo Alto: Science and Behavior Books.

Satir, V. (1972). *Peoplemaking*. Palo Alto: Science and Behavior Books.

Stanion, P., Papadopoulos, L., & Bor, R. (1997). Genograms in counselling practice: Constructing a genogram (Part II). *Counselling Psychology Quarterly, 10*(2), 139–148.

Starkey, P. J. (1981). Genograms: A guide to understanding one's own family system. *Perspectives in Psychiatric Care, 19*, 164–173.

Stone, E. (1988). *Black sheep & kissing cousins: How our family stories shape us*. New York: Times Books.

Tomson, P. (1985). Genograms in general practice. *Journal of the Royal Society of Medicine Supplement, 78*(8), 34–39.

Van Treuren, R. R. (1986). Self perception in family systems: A diagrammatic technique. *Social Casework, 67*(5), 299–305.

Wachtel, E. F. (1982). The family psyche over three generations: The genogram revisited. *Journal of Marital and Family Therapy, 8*(35), 335–343.

Walsh, F. (Ed.). (1994). *Normal family processes* (2nd ed.). New York: Guilford.

Career Counseling

Heppner, M. J., O'Brien, K. M., Hinkelman, J. M., & Humphrey, C. F. (1994). Shifting the paradigm: The use of creativity in career counseling. *Journal of Career Development, 21*(2), 77–86.

Moon, S. M., Coleman, V. D., McCollum, E. E., & Nelson, T. S. (1993). Using the genogram to facilitate career decisions: A case study. *Journal of Family Psychotherapy, 4*(1), 45–56.

Okiishi, R. W. (1987). The genogram as a tool in career counseling. *Journal of Counseling and Development, 66*(3), 139–143.

Splete, H., & Freeman-George, A. (1985). Family influences on the career development of young adults. *Journal of Career Development, 12*(1), 55–64.

Chronologies, Time, and Time Lines

Elder, G. H., Jr. (1977). Family history and the life course. *Journal of Family History, 22*, 279–304.

Elder, G. (1986). Military times and turning points in men's lives. *Developmental Psychology, 22*, 233–245.

Elder, G. (1992). Life course. In E. Borgatta & M. Borgatta (Eds.), *Encyclopedia of sociology* (Vol. 3, pp. 1120–1130). New York: Macmillan.

Jewett, C. (1982). *Helping children cope with separation and loss*. Harvard, MA: Harvard Common Press.

Stanton, M. D. (1992). The time line and the "Why now?" question: A techniquue and rationale for therapy, training, organizational consultation and research. *Journal of Marital and Family Therapy, 18*(4), 331–343.

Walsh, F. (1983). The timing of symptoms and critical events in the family life cycle. ln H. Liddle (Ed.), *Clinical implications of the family life cycle*. Rockville, MD: Aspen.

Coaching: Family of Origin Work

Bowen, M. (1978). On the differentiation of self. In *Family therapy in clinical practice*. New York: Jason Aronson.

Carter, B., & McGoldrick, M. (1998). Coaching through the life cycle. In B. Carter & M. McGoldrick (Eds.), *The expanded family life cycle: Individual, family, and social perspectives* (3rd ed.). Boston: Allyn & Bacon.

Carter, B. (1991). Death in the therapist's own family. In M. McGoldrick, C. Anderson, & F. Walsh (Eds.), *Living beyond loss: Death in the family* (pp. 273–283). New York: Norton.

Carter, E. A., & McGoldrick Orfanidis, M. (1976). Family therapy with one person and the family therapist's own family. In P. Guerin (Ed.), *Family therapy*. New York: Gardner.

Colon, F. (1973). In search of one's past: An identity trip. *Family Process, 12*(4), 429–38.

Colon, F. (1998). The discovery of my multicultural identity. In M. McGoldrick. (Ed.). *Revisioning family therapy: Race, culture and gender in clinical practice* (pp. 200–214). New York: Guilford.

Crouch, M.A. (1986). Working with one's own family: Another path for professional development. *Family Medicine, 18*, 93–98.

Folwarski, J. (1998). No longer an orphan in history. In M. McGoldrick (Ed.), *Revisioning family therapy* (pp. 239–252). New York: Guilford.

Friedman, E.H. (1971). The birthday party: An experiment in obtaining change in one's own extended family. *Family Process, 10*(2).

Friedman, E. H. (1987). The birthday party revisited: Family therapy and the problem of change. In P. Titelman (Ed.), *The therapist's own family* (pp. 113–188). New York: Jason Aronson.

Guerin, P., & Fogarty, T. (1972). The family therapist's own family. *International Journal of Psychiatry, 10*.

Hall, C. M. (1987). Efforts to differentiate a self in my family of origin. In P. Titelman (Ed.), *The therapist's own family* (pp. 209–222). New York: Jason Aronson.

Herz, F. (Ed.). (1994). *Reweaving the family tapestry*. New York: Norton.

Lerner, H. G. (1984). The cosmic countermove. *Family Therapy Networker*, Sept-Oct.

Lerner, H. (1985). *The dance of anger*. New York: Harper Collins.

Lerner, H. (1989). *The dance of intimacy*. New York: Harper Collins.

Lerner, H. (1993). *The dance of deception*. New York: Harper Collins.

Mahboubi, J., & Searcy, A. (1998). Racial unity from the perspective of personal family history: Where Black or White entered our families. In M. McGoldrick (Ed.). *Revisioning family therapy: Race, culture, and gender in clinical practice* (pp. 229–238). New York: Guilford,

McGoldrick, M. (1998). Belonging and liberation: Finding a place called "home." In M. McGoldrick (Ed.), *Revisioning family therapy: Race, culture, and gender in clinical practice* (pp. 215–228). New York: Guilford.

Pinderhughes, E. (1998). Black genealogy revisited: Restorying African American family. In M. McGoldrick (Ed.), *Revisioning family therapy: Race, culture, and gender in clinical practice* (pp. 179–199). New York: Guilford.

We became family therapists. (1972). In A. Ferber et al. (Eds.), *The book of family therapy*. New York: Science House.

Computerized Genograms

Chan, D. H., Donnan, S. P. B., Chan, N., & Chow, G. (1987). A microcomputer-based computerized medical record system for a general practice teaching clinic. *Journal of Family Practice, 24*, 537–541.

Ebell, M., & Heaton, C. (1988). Development and evaluation of a computer genogram. *Journal of Family Practice, 27*, 536–538.

Gerson, R., & McGoldrick, M. (1985). The computerized genogram. *Primary Care, 12*, 535–545.

Couples

Carter, B. (1996). *Love, honor and negotiate: Making your marriage work*. New York: Pocket Books.

Gerson, R., Hoffman, S., Sauls, S., & Ulrici, M. (1993). Family-of-origin frames in couples therapy. *Journal of Marital and Family Therapy, 19*, 341–354.

Hof, L., & Berman, E. (1986). The sexual genogram. *Journal of Marital and Family Therapy, 12*(1), 39–47.

McGoldrick, M., & Garcia Preto, N. (1984). Ethnic intermarriage: Implications for therapy. *Family Process, 23*(3), 347–64.

Paul, N., & Paul, B. B. (1986). *A marital puzzle*. New York: Gardner.

Scarf, M. (1987). *Intimate partners: Patterns in love and marriage*. New York: Random House.

Wood, N. S., & Stroup, H. W. (1990). Family systems in premarital counseling. *Pastoral Psychology, 39*(2), 111–119.

Culture and Race

Boyd-Franklin, N. (1989). *Black families in therapy: A multisystems approach*. New York: Guilford.

Boyd-Franklin, N. (1995). Therapy with African American inner city families. In R. H. Mikesell, D. Lusterman, & S. McDaniel (Eds.), *Integrating family therapy: Handbook of family psychology and systems therapy* (pp. 357–371). Washington, DC: American Psychological Association.

Congress, E. P. (1994). The use of culturagrams to assess and empower culturally diverse families. *Families in Society*. November.

Eddington, A. (1998). Moving beyond white guilt. *Transformation, 13*(3), 2–7.

Estrada, A. U., & Haney, P. (1998). Genograms in a multicultural perspective. *Journal of Family Psychotherapy, 9*(2), 55–62.

Hardy, K. V., & Laszloffy, T. A. (1992). Training racially sensitive family therapists: Context, content and contact. *Families in Society, 73*(6), 363–370.

Hardy, K. V., & Laszloffy, T. A. (1995). The cultural genogram: Key to training culturally competent family therapists. *Journal of Marital and Family Therapy, 21*(3), 227–237.

Kaslow, F. (1995). Descendants of holocaust victims and perpetrators: Legacies and dialogue. *Contemporary Family Therapy*, September, 275–290.

Kelly, G. D. (1990). The cultural family of origin: A description of a training strategy. *Counselor Education and Supervision, 30*(1), 77–84.

Lappin, J. (1983). On becoming a culturally conscious family therapist. *Family Therapy Collections*, Vol 6., pp. 122–136.

McIntosh, P. (1998). Unpacking the invisible knapsack of white privilege. In M. McGoldrick (Ed.), *Revisioning family therapy: Race, culture and gender in clinical practice* (pp. 147–152). New York: Guilford.

McGoldrick, M., Giordano, J., & Pearce, J. K. (Eds.). (1996). *Ethnicity and family therapy* (2nd ed.). New York: Guilford.

McGoldrick, M., Garcia-Preto, N., Moore Hines, P., & Lee, E. (1989). Ethnicity and women. In M. McGoldrick, C. Anderson, & F. Walsh, (Eds.), *Women in families* (pp. 169–199). New York: Norton.

Odell, M., Shelling, G., Young, K. S., Hewett, D. H.,& L'Abate, L. (1994). The skills of the marriage and family therapist in straddling multicultural issues. *American Journal of Family Therapy, 22*(2), 145–155.

Parnell, M., & Vanderkloot, J. (1992). Mental health services—2001: Serving a new America. *Journal of Independent Social Work, 5*(3–4), 183–203.

Preli, R., & Bernard, J. M. (1993). Making multiculturalism relevant for majority culture graduate students. *Journal of Marital and Family Therapy, 19*(1), 5–16.

Salgado de Bernal, C., & Alvarez-Schwarz, M. (1990). The genogram as a training instrument for family therapists. *Revista Latinoamericana de Psicologia, 22*(3), 385–420.

Scharwiess, S. O. (1994). Step-sisters and half-brothers: A family therapist's view of German unification and other transitional processes. *Contemporary Family Therapy, 16*(3), 183–197.

Watts Jones, D. (1998). Towards an African-American genogram. *Family Process, 36*(4), 373–383.

Woodcock, J. (1995). Healing rituals with families in exile. *Journal of Family Therapy, 17*(4), 397–409.

Divorce and Remarriage

Friesen, P., & Manitt, J. (1991). Nursing the remarried family in a palliative care setting. *Journal of Palliative Care, 6*(4), 32–39.

McGoldrick, M., & Carter, B. (1998b). Remarried families. In B. Carter & M. McGoldrick (Eds.), *The expanded family life cycle: Individual, family and social perspectives* (3rd ed.). Boston: Allyn & Bacon.

Peck, J. S. (1988). The impact of divorce on children at various stages of the family life cycle. *Journal of Divorce, 12*(2–3), 81–106.

Sager, C. J., Brown, H. S., Crohn, H., Engel, T., Rodstein, E., & Walker, L. (1983). *Treating the remarried family.* New York: Brunner/Mazel.

Drug and Alcohol Abuse

Barthwell, A. G. (1995). Alcoholism in the family: A multicultural exploration. In M. Galanter (Ed.), *Recent developments in alcoholism: Vol. 12: Alcoholism and women.* New York: Plenum Press.

Bepko, C. S., & Krestan, J. (1985). *The responsibility trap: Women and men in alcoholic families.* New York: Free Press.

Dardia, T. (1989). *The thirsty muse: Alcohol and the American writer.* New York: Tichnor & Fields.

Darmsted, N., & Cassell, J. L. (1983). Counseling the deaf substance abuser. Readings in Deafness. *Mono. No. 7,* 40–51.

Hutchinson, W. S., Jr. (1988). Family assessment and treatment methods. In F. Dickman, B. R. Challenger, W. G. Emener, & W. Hutchinson, Jr. (Eds.), *Employee assistance programs: A basic text* (pp. 204–209). Springfield, IL: Charles C Thomas.

Lawson, A., & Lawson, G. (1998) *Alcoholism and the family: A guide to treatment and prevention* (2nd ed.). Gaithersburg, MD: Aspen.

Nowinski, J., & Baker, S. (1998). *The twelve-step facilitation handbook: A systematic approach to early recovery from alcoholism and addiction.* San Francisco: Jossey-Bass.

Stanton, M. D., & Heath, A. W. (1995). Family treatment of alcohol and drug abuse. In R. H. Mikesell, D. D. Lusterman, & S. McDaniel (Eds.), *Integrating family therapy: Handbook of family psychology and systems therapy* (pp. 529–541). Washington, DC: American Psychological Association.

Steinglass, P., Bennett, L., Wolin, S., & Reiss, D. (1987). *The alcoholic family.* New York: Basic Books.

Vukov, M. G., & Eljdupovic, G. (1991). The Yugoslavian drug addict's family structure. *International Journal of the Addictions, 26*(4), 415–422.

Wolin, S. J., Bennett, L. A., & Jacobs, J. S. (1988). Assessing family rituals in alcoholic families. In E. Imber-Black, J. Roberts, & R. Whiting (Eds.), *Rituals in families and family therapy* (pp. 230–256). New York: Norton.

Family Life Cycle

Cohler, B., Hosteler, A. J., & Boxer, A. (1998). In D. McAdams & E. de St. Aubin (Eds.), *Generativity and adult development. Psychosocial perspectives on caring and contributing to the next generation*. Washington, DC: American Psychological Association Press.

Erlanger, M. A. (1997). Changing roles and life cycle transitions. In T. D. Hargrave & C. Midori Hanna (Eds.), *The aging family: New visions in theory, practice, and reality* (pp. 163–177). New York: Brunner/Mazel.

Gerson, R. (1995). The family life cycle: Phases, stages and crises. In R. H. Mikesell, D. D. Lusterman, & S. McDaniel (Eds). *Integrating family therapy: Handbook of family psychology and systems therapy* (pp. 91–111). Washington, DC: American Psychological Association.

Hadley, T., Jacob, T., Miliones, J., Caplan, J., & Spitz., D. (1974). The relationship between family developmental crises and the appearance of symptoms in a family member. *Family Process, 13*, 207–14.

McGoldrick, M. (1998). History, genograms and the family life cycle: Freud in context. In B. Carter & M. McGoldrick (Eds.), *The expanded family life cycle: Individual, family and social perspectives* (3rd ed.). Boston: Allyn & Bacon.

Norris, J. E., & Tindale, J. A. (1994). *Among generations: The cycle of adult relationships*. New York: W. H. Freeman & Company.

With Children

Buurma, D. (1999). *The family play genogram: A guidebook*. 67 Valley View Ave., Summit, NJ 07901: Author.

Carr, A. (1997). Involving children in family therapy and systemic consultation. *Journal of Family Psychotherapy, 5*(1), 41–59.

Fink, A. H., Kramer, L., Weaver, L. L., & Anderson, J. (1993). More on genograms: Modifications to a model. *Journal of Child & Adolescent Group Therapy, 3*(4), 203–206.

Gil, E., & Sobol, B. (2000). Engaging families in therapeutic play. In Bailey, C. E. (Ed.), *Children in therapy: Using the family as a resource*. New York: Norton.

With Adolescents

Cole-Kelly, K., & Kaye, D. (1993). Assessing the family. In M. I. Singer, L. T. Singer, & T. M. Anglin (Eds.), *Handbook for screening adolescents at psychosocial risk* (pp. 1–40). New York: Macmillan.

With Young Adults

Santa Rita, E., & Adejanju, M. G. (1993). The genogram: Plotting the roots of academic success. *Family Therapy, 20*(1), 17–28.

Splete, H., & Freeman-George, A. (1985). Family influences on the career development of young adults. *Journal of Career Development, 12*(1), 55–64.

Vinson, M. L. (1995). Employing family therapy in group counseling with college students: Similarities and a technique employed in both. *Journal for Specialists in Group Work, 20*(4), 240–252.

With Expectant Families

Condon, J. J. (1985). Therapy of the expectant family: The foetus as a force to be reckoned with. *Australian & New Zealand Journal of Family Therapy, 6*(2), 77–81.

With Aging

Bannerman, C. (1986). The genogram and elderly patients. *Journal of Family Practice, 23*(5), 426–428.

Erlanger, M. A. (1990). Using the genogram with the older client. *Journal of Mental Health Counselling, 12*(3), 321–331.

Gwyther, L. (1986). Family therapy with older adults. *Generations, 10*(3), 42–45.

Ingersoll-Dayton, B., & Arndt, B. (1990). Uses of the genogram with the elderly and their families. *Journal of Gerontological Social Work, 15*(1–2), 105–120.

Shellenberger, S., Watkins Couch, K., & Drake, M. A. (1989). Elderly family members and their caregivers: Characteristics and development of the relationship. *Family Systems Medicine, 7*(3), 317–322.

Shields, C. G., King, D. A., & Wynne, L. C. (1995). Interventions with later life families. In R. H. Mikesell, D. D. Lusterman, & S. McDaniel (Eds.), *Integrating family therapy: Handbook of family psychology and systems therapy* (pp. 141–158). Washington, DC: American Psychological Association.

Foster Care, Adoption, and Child Welfare

Allen, M. (1990). *Training materials for post adoption family therapy.* Iowa City, IA: National Center on Family Based Resources.

Colon, F. (1978). Family ties and child placement. *Family Process, 17,* 289–312.

Finch, R., & Jaques, P. (1985). Use of the geneogram with adoptive families. *Adoption and Fostering, 9*(3), 35–41.

Flashman, M. (1991). Training social workers in public welfare: Some useful family concepts. *Journal of Independent Social Work, 5*(3–4), 53–68.

Groze, V., Young, J., & Corcbran-Rumppe, K. (1991). *Post adoption resources for training, networking and evaluation services (PARTNERS): Working with special needs adoptive families in stress.* Washington DC: Department of Health and Human Services.

Hoyle, S.G. (1995). Long-term treatment of emotionally disturbed adoptees and their families. *Clinical Social Work Journal, 23*(4), 429–440.

McMillen, J. C., & Groze, V. (1994). Using placement genograms in child welfare practice. *Child Welfare, 73*(4), 307–318.

Pinderhughes, E. E., & Rosenberg, K. (1990). Family-bonding with high-risk placements: A therapy model that promotes the process of becoming a family. In L. M. Glidden (Ed.), *Informed families: Adoption of children with handicaps.* New York: Haworth Press.

Sandmeier, M. (1988). *When love is not enough: How mental health professionals can help special needs adoptive families.* Washington, DC: Child Welfare League of America.

Young, J., Corcoran-Rumppe, K., & Groze, V. K. (1992). Integrating special needs adoption with residential treatment. *Child Welfare, 71,*(6), 527–535.

Gender and Gendergrams

Holmes, S. E., & Anderson, S. A. (1994). Gender differences in the relationship between differentiation experienced in one's family of origin and adult adjustment. *Journal of Feminist Family Therapy, 6*(1), 27–48.

Howe, K. (1990). Daughters discover their mothers through biographies and genograms: Educational and clinical parallels. *Women and Therapy, 10*(1–2), 31–40.

McGoldrick, M. (1998). Women through the family life cycle. In B. Carter & M. McGoldrick (Eds.), *The expanded family life cycle: Individual, family, and social perspectives* (2nd ed.). Boston: Allyn & Bacon.

McGoldrick, M., Anderson, C., & Walsh, F. (1989). *Women in families: A framework for family therapy.* New York: Norton.

Rekers, G. A. (1985). The genogram: Her story of a woman. *Women & Therapy, 4*(2), Summer.

White, M. B., & Tyson-Rawson, K. J. (1995). Assessing the dynamics of gender in couples and families: The gendergram. *Family Relations, 44,* 253–260.

Genogram Variations and Sociograms

Burke, J. L., & Faber, P. (1997). A genogrid for couples. *Journal of Gay and Lesbian Social Services, 7*(1), 13–22.

Friedman, H., Rohrbaugh, M., & Krakauer, S. (1988). The timeline genogram: Highlighting temporal aspects of family relationships. *Family Process, 27,* 293–304.

Friesen, P., & Manitt, J. (1991). Nursing the remarried family in a palliative care setting. *Journal of Palliative Care, 6*(4), 32–39.

Gwatkin, S., & Kraus, M. A. (manuscript in preparation). Technicolor genograms.

Hardy, K. V., & Laszloffy, T. A. (1995). The cultural genogram: Key to training culturally competent family therapists. *Journal of Marital and Family Therapy, 21*(3), 227–237.

Hartman, A. (1995). Diagrammatic assessment of family relationships. *Families in Society, 76*(2), 111–122.

Hof, L., & Berman, E. (1986). The sexual genogram. *Journal of Marital and Family Therapy, 12,* 39–47.

Lewis, K. G. (1989). The use of color-coded genograms in family therapy. *Journal of Marital and Family Therapy, 15*(2), 169–176.

McIlvain, H., Crabtree, B., Medder, J., Strange, K. C., & Miller, W. L. (1998). Using practice genograms to understand and describe practice configurations. *Family Medicine, 30*(7), 490–496.

Sherman, R., & Fredman, N. (1986). *Handbook of structural techniques in marriage and family therapy.* New York: Brunner/Mazel.

Watts Jones, D. (1998). Towards an African-American genogram. *Family Process, 36*(4), 373–383.

White, M. B., & Tyson-Rawson, K. J. (1995). Assessing the dynamics of gender in couples and families: The gendergram. *Family Relations, 44*(3), 253–260.

Health Care, Medicine, Nursing, Stress, Illness

Alexander, D., & Clark, S. (1998). Keeping "the family" in focus during patient care. In P. D. Sloane, L. M. Slatt, P. Curtis, & M. H. Ebell (Eds.), *Essentials of family medicine* (3rd ed., pp. 25–39). Baltimore, MD: Williams & Wilkins.

Baird, M. A., & Grant, W. D. (1998). Families and health. In R. B. Taylor, A. K. David, T. A. Johnson, Jr., D. M. Phillips, & J. E. Scherger (Eds.), *Family medicine principles and practice* (5th ed., pp. 26–31). Baltimore, MD: Williams & Wilkins.

Barth, J. C. (1993). *It runs in my family: Overcoming the legacy of family illness.* New York: Brunner/Mazel.

Berolzheimer, N., Thrower, S. M., & Koch-Hatten, A. (1993). Working with families. In P. D. Sloane, L. M. Slatt, & P. Curtis (Eds.), *Essentials of family medicine* (2nd ed., pp. 19–29). Baltimore, MD: Williams & Wilkins.

Blossom, H. J. (1991). The personal genogram: An interview technique for selecting family practice residents. *Family Systems Medicine, 9*(2), 151–158.

Christie-Seely, J. (1981). Teaching the family system concept in family medicine. *Journal of Family Practice, 13,* 391.

Craddock, N., McGuffin, P., & Owen, M. (1994). Darier's disease cosegregating with affective disorder. *British Journal of Psychiatry, 165*(2), 272.

Crouch, M. A., & Davis, J. (1987). Using the genogram (family tree) clinically. In M.A. Crouch & L. Roberts (Eds.), *The family in medical practice: A family systems primer* (pp. 174–192). New York: Springer-Verlag.

Crouch, M. A. (1989). A putative ancestry of family practice and family medicine: Genogram of a discipline. *Family Systems Medicine, 7*(2), 208–212.

Cutillo-Schmitter, T. A. (1993). Family asessment. In C. S. Faucett (Ed.), *Family psychiatric nursing*. St. Louis, MO: Mosby.

Doherty, W. J., & Baird, M. A. (1983). *Family therapy and family medicine*. New York: Guilford.

Engelman, S. R. (1988). Use of the family genogram technique with spinal cord injured patients. *Clinical Rehabilitation, 2*(1), 7–15.

Fohs, M. W. (1991). Family systems assessment: Interventions with individuals having a chronic disability. *Career Development Quarterly, 39*(4), 304–311.

Fossum, A. R., Elam, C. L., & Broaddus, D. A. (1982). Family therapy in family practice: A solution to psychosocial problems? *Journal of Family Practice, 15*, 461.

Garrett, R. E., Klinkman, M., & Post, L., (1987). If you meet the Buddha on the road, take a genogram: Zen and the art of family medicine. *Family Medicine, 19*, 225–226.

Glimelius, B., Bilgegard, G., Hoffman, K., Hagnebo, C., et al. (1993). A comprehensive cancer care project to improve the overall situation of patients receiving intensive chemotherapy. *Journal of Psychosocial Oncology, 11*(1), 17–40.

Haas-Cunningham, S. M. (1994). The genogram as a predictor of families at risk for physical illness (Doctoral dissertation, Syracuse University, 1993). *Dissertation Abstracts International, 54*(9-b), 4590.

Holmes, T. H., & Rahe, T. H. (1967). The social adjustment rating scale. *Journal of Psychosomatic Research, 11*, 213–218.

Holmes, T. H., & Masuda, M. (1974). Life change and illness susceptibility. In B. S. Dohrenwend & B. Dohrenwend (Eds.), *Stressful life events: Their nature and effects*. New York: Wiley.

Howkins, E., & Allison, A. (1996). Shared learning for primary health care teams: A success story. *Nurse Education Today, 17*(3), 225–231.

Huygen, F. J. A. (1982). *Family medicine*. New York: Brunner/Mazel.

Huygen, F. J. A., van den Hoogen, H. J. M., van Eijk, J. T. M., & Smits, A. J. A. (1989). Death and dying: A longitudinal study of their medical impact on the family. *Family Systems Medicine, 7*, 374–384.

Jolly, W. M., Froom, J., & Rosen, M. G. (1980). The genogram. *Journal of Family Practice, 10*(2), 251–255.

Josse, J. (1993). The use of family trees in general practice. *Postgraduate Update*. May 1, 775–780.

Levine, F. B. (1997). The girl who went on strike: A case of childhood diabetes. In S. H. McDaniel, J. Hepworth, & W. J. Doherty (Eds.), *The shared experience of illness: Stories of patients, families, and their therapists* (pp. 58–72). New York: Basic Books.

Liossi, C., Hattira, P., & Mystakidou, K. (1997). The use of the genogram in palliative care. *Palliative Medicine, 11*(6), 455–61.

Massad, R. J. (1980). *In sickness and in health: A family physician explores the impact of illness on the family*. Philadelphia: Smith, Kline & French.

McDaniel, S. (1997). Trapped inside a body without a voice: Two cases of somatic fixation. In S. H. McDaniel, J. Hepworth, & W. J. Doherty (Eds.), *The shared experience of illness: Stories of patients, families, and their therapists* (pp. 274–290). New York: Basic Books.

McDaniel, S. H., Hepworth, J., & Doherty, W. J. (1992). *Medical family therapy*. New York: Basic Books.

McWhinney, I. R. (1981). *An introduction to family medicine*. New York: Oxford University Press.

Medalie, J. H. (1978). *Family medicine: Principles and applications*. Baltimore, MD: Williams & Wilkins.

Milhorn, H. T. (1981). The genogram: A structured approach to the family history. *Journal of the Mississippi State Medical Association, 22*(10), 250–52.

Mullins, M. C., & Christie-Seely, J. (1984). Collecting and recording family data—The genogram. In J. Christie-Seely (Ed.), *Working with the family in primary care* (pp. 179–191). New York: Praeger.

Norwood, W. (1993). An initial exploration through the use of the genogram of the pre-morbid functioning of families with a person with a head injury. *Dissertation Abstracts International, 54*(3-A), 870.

Penn, P. (1983). Coalitions and binding interactions in families with chronic illness. *Family Systems Medicine, 1*(2), 16–25.

Rakel, R. E. (1977). *Principles of family medicine*. Philadelphia: W. B. Saunders.

Richardson, H. B. (1945). *Patients have families*. New York: Commonwealth Fund.

Rolland, J. (1994). *Families, illness, and disability*. New York: Basic Books

Rosen, G., Kleinman, A., & Katon, W. (1982). Somatization in family practice: A biopsy-cho-social approach. *Journal of Family Practice, 14*, 493.

Schilson, E., Barun, K., & Hudson, A. (1993). Use of genograms in family medicine: A family physician/family therapist collaboration. *Family Systems Medicine, 11*(2), 201–208.

Schmidt, D. D. (1978). The family as the unit of medical care. *Journal of Family Practice, 7*, 303.

Shellenberger, S., & Phelps, G. (1997). When it never stops hurting: A case of chronic pain. In S. H. McDaniel, J. Hepworth, & W. J. Doherty (Eds.), *The shared experience of illness: Stories of patients, families, and their therapists* (pp. 231–241). New York: Basic Books.

Sloane, P. D., Slatt, L. M., Curtis, P., & Ebell, M. (Eds.). (1998). *Essentials of family medicine* (3rd ed.). Baltimore, MD: Williams & Wilkins.

Smilkstein, G. (1984). The physician and family function assessment. *Family Systems Medicine, 2*(3), 263–278.

Smoyak, S. (1982). Family systems: Use of genograms as an assessment tool. In I. Clements & D. Buchanan (Eds.), *Family therapy in perspective*. New York: Wiley.

Stavros, M. K. (1991). Family systems approach to sexual dysfunction in neurologic disability. *Sexuality and Disability, 9*(1), 69–85.

Taylor, R. B., David, A. K., Johnson, T. A., Jr., Phillips, D. M., & Scherger, J. E. (Eds.). (1998). *Family medicine principles and practice* (5th ed.). Baltimore, MD: Williams & Wilkins.

Wright, L. M., & Leahey, M. (1984). *Nurses and families: A guide to family assessment and intervention*. Philadelphia: F. A. Davis.

Lesbian and Gay Families and Networks

Burke, J. L., & Faber, P. (1997). A genogrid for couples. *Journal of Gay and Lesbian Social Services, 7*(1), 13–22.

Feinberg, J., & Bakerman, R. (1994). Sexual orientation and three generational family patterns in a clinical sample of heterosexual and homosexual men. *Journal of Gay and Lesbian Psychotherapy, 2*(2), 65–76.

Laird, J. (1996). Family-centered practice with lesbian and gay families. *Families in Society: Journal of Contemporary Human Services, 77*(9), 559–572.

Laird, J. (1996). Invisible ties: Lesbians and their families of origin. In J. Laird & R. J. Green (Eds.), *Lesbians and gays in couples and families* (pp. 89–122). San Francisco: Jossey-Bass.

Magnuson, S., Norem, K., & Skinner, C. H. (1995). Constructing genograms with lesbian clients. *The Family Journal: Counseling and Therapy for Couples and Families*, 110–115.

Scrivner, R., & Eldridge, N. S. (1995). Lesbian and gay family psychology. In R. H. Mikesell, D. D. Lusterman, & S. McDaniel (Eds.), *Integrating family therapy: Handbook of family pychology and systems therapy* (pp. 327–345). Washington, DC: American Psychological Association.

Shernoff, M. J. (1984). Family therapy for lesbian and gay clients. *Social Work, 39*, 393–396.

Slater, S. (1995). *The lesbian family life cycle*. New York: Free Press.

Weinstein, D. L. (1993). Application of family therapy concepts in the treatment of lesbians and gay men. *Journal of Chemical Dependency Treatment, 5*(1), 141–155.

Loss

Boss, P. (1991). Ambiguous loss. In F. Walsh & M. McGoldrick (Eds.), *Living beyond loss* (pp. 161–175). New York: Norton.

Bowen, M. (1991). Family reaction to death. In F. Walsh & M. McGoldrick (Eds.), *Living beyond loss* (pp. 79–92). New York: Norton.

Crosby, J. F. (1989). Museum tours in genogram construction: A technique for facilitating recall of negative affect. *Contemporary Family Therapy, 11*(4), 247–258.

Engel, G. (1975). The death of a twin: Mourning and anniversary reactions: Fragments of 10 years of self-analysis. *International Journal of Psychoanalysis, 56*(l), 23–40.

Ferra Bucher, J. S. (1991). Family interaction and suicide: Case studies from a transgenerational perspective. *PSICO, 21*(1), 41–64.

Kuhn, J. (1981). Realignment of emotional forces following loss. *The Family, 5*(1), 19–24.

McDaniel, S. H., Hepworth, J., & Doherty, W. J. (1992). *Medical family therapy*. New York: Basic Books.

McGoldrick, M. (1991). The legacy of loss. In F. Walsh & M. McGoldrick (Eds.), *Living beyond loss* (pp. 104–129). New York: Norton.

McGoldrick, M. (1991). Echoes from the past: Helping families mourn their losses. In F. Walsh & M. McGoldrick (Eds.), *Living beyond loss* (pp. 50–78). New York: Norton.

McGoldrick, M., Almeida, R., Moore Hines, P., Garcia Preto, N., Rosen, E., & Lee, E. (1991). Mourning in different cultures. In F. Walsh & M. McGoldrick (Eds.), *Living beyond loss* (pp. 176–206). New York: Norton.

McGoldrick, M., & Walsh, F. (1983). A systemic view of family history and loss. In L. R. Wolberg & M. L. Aronson (Eds.), *Group and family therapy: 1983*. New York: Brunner/Mazel.

McGoldrick, M., & Walsh, F. (1991). Death and the family life cycle. In F. Walsh & M. McGoldrick (Eds.), *Living beyond loss* (pp. 30–49). New York: Norton.

Mikesell, S. G., & Stohner, M. (1995). Infertility and pregnancy loss: The role of the family consultant. In R. H. Mikesell, D. D. Lusterman, & S. McDaniel (Eds.), *Integrating family therapy: Handbook of family psychology and systems therapy* (pp. 421–436). Washington, DC: American Psychological Association.

Paul, N., & Paul, B. B. (1982). Death and changes in sexual behavior. In F. Walsh (Ed.), *Normal family processes* (pp. 229–250). New York: Guilford.

Seaburn, D. B. (1990). The time that binds: Loyalty and widowhood. *Psychotherapy Patient, 6*(3–4), 139–146.

Walsh, F. (1978). Concurrent grandparent death and birth of schizophrenic offspring: An intriguing finding. *Family Process, 17*, 457–63.

Walsh, F., & McGoldrick, M. (1998). Death and the family life cycle. In B. Carter & M. McGoldrick (Eds.), *The expanded family life cycle: Individual, family and social perspectives* (3rd ed.). Boston: Allyn & Bacon.

Walsh, F., & McGoldrick, M. (Eds.). (1991). *Living beyond loss: Death and the family*. New York: Norton.

Walsh, F., & McGoldrick, M. (1991). Loss and the family: A systemic perspective. In F. Walsh & M. McGoldrick (Eds.), *Living beyond loss* (pp. 1–29). New York: Norton.

Whitman-Raymond, R. (1988). Pathological gambling as a defense against loss. *Journal of Gambling Behavior, 4*(2), 99–109.

Wortman, C., & Silver, R. (1989). The myths of coping with loss. *Journal of Counseling and Clinical Psychology, 57*, 349–357.

Migration

Hernandez, M., & McGoldrick, M. (1998). Migration and the family life cycle. In B. Carter & M. McGoldrick (Eds.), *The expanded family life cycle: Individual, family and social perspectives* (3rd ed.). Boston: Allyn & Bacon.

Mock, M. (1998). Forced to flee: Clinical work with refugee families. In M. McGoldrick (Ed.), *Revisioning family therapy: Race, culture and gender in clinical practice* (pp. 347–359). New York: Guilford.

Mirkin, M. (1998). The impact of multiple contexts on recent immigrant families. In M. McGoldrick (Ed.), *Revisioning family therapy: Race, culture and gender in clinical practice* (pp. 370–383). New York: Guilford.

Sluzki, C. (1998). Migration and the disruption of the social network. In M. McGoldrick (Ed.), *Revisioning family therapy: Race, culture and gender in clinical practice* (pp. 360–369). New York: Guilford.

Research on Genograms

Coupland, S. K., Serovich, J., & Glenn, J. E. (1995). Reliability in constructing genograms: A study among marriage and family therapy doctoral students. *Journal of Marital and Family Therapy, 21*(3), 251–263.

Friedman, H. L., & Krakauer, S. (1992). Learning to draw and interpret standard and time-line genograms: An experimental comparison. *Journal of Family Psychology, 6*(1), 77–83.

Hurst, N. C., Sawatzky, D. D., & Pare, D. P. (1996). Families with multiple problems through a Bowenian lens. *Child Welfare, 75*(6), 693–708.

Perfetti, L. J. C. (1990). The base 32 method: An improved method for coding sibling constellations. *Journal of Marital and Family Therapy, 16*(2), 201–204.

Rogers, J. C. (1994). Can physicians use family genogram information to identify patients at risk of anxiety or depression? *Archives of Family Medicine, 3,* 1093–1098.

Rogers, J. C., & Cohn, P. (1987). Impact of a screening family genogram on first encounters in primary care. *Journal of Family Practice, 4,* 291–301.

Rogers, J. C., & Durkin, M. (1984). The semi-structured genogram interview: I. Protocol, II. Evaluation. *Family Systems Medicine, 2*(25), 176–187.

Rogers, J. C., Durkin, M., & Kelly, K. (1985). The family genogram: An underutilized clinical tool. *New Jersey Medicine, 82*(11), 887–892.

Rogers, J. C., & Holloway, R. (1990). Completion rate and reliability of the self-administered genogram (SAGE), *Family Practice, 7,* 149–51.

Rogers, J. C., & Rohrbaugh, M. (1991). The SAGE-PAGE trial: Do family genograms make a difference? *Journal of the American Board of Family Practice, 4,* 319–326.

Rogers, J. C., Rohrbaugh, M., & McGoldrick, M. (1992). Can experts predict health risk from family genograms? *Family Medicine, 24,* 209–215.

Rohrbaugh, M., Rogers, J. C., & McGoldrick, M. (1992). How do experts read family genograms? *Family Systems Medicine, 10*(1), 79–89.

Schools, Job Settings, and other Larger Systems

Darkenwald, G. G., & Silvestri, K. (1992). Analysis and assessment of the Newark literacy campaign: A report to the Ford Foundation. (Grant # 915-0298).

Friedman, E. H. (1985). *Generation to generation: Family process in church and synagogue.* New York: Guilford.

Okum, B. F. (1984) *Family therapy with school-related problems.* Rockville, MD: Aspen.

Santa Rita, E., & Adejanju, M. G. (1997). The genogram: Plotting the roots of academic success. *Schools and Family Therapy,* pp. 89–100.

Shellenberger, S., & Hoffman, S. (1995). The changing family-work system. In R. H. Mikesell, D. D. Lusterman, & S. McDaniel (Eds). *Integrating family therapy: Handbook of family psychology and systems therapy* (pp. 461–479). Washington, DC: American Psychological Association.

Willan, S., & Hugman, Y. (1988). Family therapy within a school's psychological service. In W. M. Walsh & N. J. Giblin (Eds.), *Family therapy in school settings* (pp. 7–14). Springfield IL: Charles C Thomas.

Siblings

Adler, A. (1959). *The practice and theory of individual psychology*. Paterson, NJ: Littlefield, Adams.

Bank, S. P., & Kahn, M. D. (1997). *The sibling bond*. New York: Basic Books.

Bass, D. M., & Bowman, K. (1990). Transition from caregiving to bereavement: The relationship of care-related strain and adjustment to death. *The Gerontologist, 30,* 135–142.

Bernikow, L. (1980). *Among women*. New York : Harper & Row.

Bowerman, C. E., & Dobash, R. M. (1974). Structural variations in inter-sibling affect. *Journal of Marriage and the Family, 36,* 48–54.

Brody, G. H., Stoneman, Z., & Burke, M. (1987). Child temperaments, maternal differential behavior, and sibling relationships. *Developmental Psychology, 23*(3), 354–362.

Carroll, R. (1988). Siblings and the family business. In M. D. Kahn & K. G. Lewis (Eds.), *Siblings in therapy: Life span and clinical issues* (pp. 379–398). New York: Norton.

Chappell, N. L. (1991). *Social supports and aging*. Toronto: Butterworths.

Cicirelli, V. G. (1982). Sibling influence throughout the life span. In M. E. Lamb & B. Sutton-Smith (Eds.), *Sibling relationships: Their nature and significance across the lifespan* (pp. 267–284). Hillsdale, NJ: Erlbaum.

Cicirelli, V. G. (1985). Sibling relationships throughout the life cycle. In L. L'Abate (Ed.), *The handbook of family psychology and therapy*. Homewood, IL: The Dorsey Press.

Cicirelli, V. G. (1989). Feelings of attachment to siblings and well-being in later life. *Psychology and Aging, 4,* 211–216.

Cicirelli, V. G. (1995). *Sibling relationships across the life span*. New York: Plenum.

Connidis, I., & Davies, L. (1990). Confidants and companions in later life. The place of family and friends. *Journal of Gerontology, 45,* S141–149.

Connidis, I. A. (1989). Contact between siblings in later life. *Canadian Journal of Sociology, 14,* 429–442.

Connidis, I. A. (1989). *Family ties and aging*. Toronto: Butterworths.

Connidis, I. A. (1989). Siblings as friends in later life. *American Behavioral Scientist, 33,* 81–93.

Elder, G. H., Jr. (1962). Structural variations in child rearing relationship. *Sociometry, 25,* 241–262.

Falbo, T. (Ed.). (1984). *The single-child family*. New York: Guilford.

Fishel, E. (1979). *Sisters: Love and rivalry inside the family and beyond*. New York: Morrow.

Freudenberg, B. E. (1982). The effect of sisters on feminine development. *DAI, 43*(03), Sec A, PO 672.

Gaddis, V., & Gaddis, M. (1973). *The curious world of twins*. New York: Warner.

Gold, D. T. (1987). Siblings in old age. Something special. *Canadian Journal on Aging, 6,* 199–215.

Gold, D. T. (1989). Sibling relationships in old age: A typology. *International Journal of Aging and Human Development, 28,* 37–51.

Holden, C. E. (1986). Being a sister: Constructions of the sibling experience. University of Michigan (0127), *Dissertation Abstracts International*, V47(10), SECB, PP4301.

Hoopes, M. H., & Harper, J. M. (1987). *Birth order roles and sibling patterns in individual and family therapy*. Rockville, MD: Aspen.

Jalongo, M. R., & Renck, M.A. (1985). Sibling relationships: A recurrent developmental and literary theme. *Childhood Education, 61*(5), 346–351.

Johnson, C. L. (1982). Sibling solidarity: Its origin and functioning in Italian-American families. *Journal of Marriage and the Family, 44,* 155–67.

Krell, R., & Rabkin, L. The effects of sibling death on the surviving child: A family perspective. *Family Process, 18*(4), 471–8.

Lamb, M. E., & Sutton-Smith, B. (1982). *Sibling relationships: Their nature and significance across the lifespan.* Hillsdale, NJ: Erlbaum.

Leder, J. M. (1993). *Brothers and sisters: How they stage our lives.* New York: Ballantine.

Marcil-Gratton, N., & Legare, J. (1992). Will reduced fertility lead to greater isolation in old age for tomorrow's elderly? *Canadian Journal on Aging, 11,* 54–71.

Mathias, B. (1992). *Between sisters: Secret rivals, intimate friends.* New York: Delacorte Press.

McGhee, J. L. (1985). The effects of siblings on the life satisfaction of the rural elderly. *Journal of Marriage and the Family, 41,* 703–714.

McGoldrick, M. (1989). Sisters. In M. McGoldrick, C. Anderson, & F. Walsh (Eds.), *Women in families* (pp. 24–266). New York: Norton.

McGoldrick, M., & Watson, M. (1998). Siblings through the life cycle. In B. Carter & M. McGoldrick (Eds.), *The expanded family life cycle: Individual, family and social perspectives* (3rd ed.). Boston: Allyn & Bacon.

McKeever, P. (1983). Siblings of chronically ill children: A literature review with implications for research and practice. *American Journal of Orthopsychiatry, 53*(2), 209–218.

McNaron, T. A. H. (Ed.). (1985). *The sister bond: A feminist view of a timeless connection.* New York: Pergamon Press.

Merrell, S. S. (1995). *The accidental bond: The power of sibling relationships.* New York: Times Books.

Miller, N. B., & Cantwell, D. P. (1978). Siblings as therapists: A behavioral approach. *American Journal of Psychiatry, 133*(4), 447–50.

Norris, J. E., & Tindale, J. A. (1994). *Among generations: The cycle of adult relationships.* New York: W. H. Freeman.

Notar, M., & McDaniel, S. A. (1986). Feminist attitudes and mother-daughter relationships in adolescence. *Adolescence, 21*(81), 11–21.

Nuckolls, C. W. (1993). *Siblings in South Asia: Brothers and sisters in cultural context.* New York: Guilford.

Rosenberg, B. G., & Sutton-Smith, B. (1969). Sibling age spacing effects on cognition. *Developmental Psychology, 1,* 661–669.

Rosenberg, B. G., & Sutton-Smith, B. (1964). Ordinal position and sex role identification. *Psychological Monographs, 70,* 297–328.

Sandmaier, M. (1994). *Original kin: Intimacy, choices and change in adult sibling relationships.* New York: Dutton.

Schmuck, R. (1963). Sex of sibling, birth order position, and female dispositions to conform in two-child families. *Child Development, 34,* 913–8.

Shanas, E., & Streib, G. F. (1965). *Social structure and the family.* Englewood Cliffs, NJ: Prentice Hall.

Skrtic, T. M., Summers, J. A., Brotherson, M. J., & Turnbull, A. P. (1983). Severely handicapped children and their brothers and sisters. In J. Blacher (Ed.), *Severely handicapped young children and their families. Research in review.* New York: Academic Press.

Stoneman, Z. et al. (1986). Same-sex and cross-sex siblings: Activity choices, roles, behavior and gender stereotypes. *Sex Roles, 15*(9–10), 495–511.

Sulloway, F. J. (1996). *Born to rebel: Sibling relationships, family dynamics and creative lives.* New York: Pantheon.

Sutton-Smith, B., & Rosenberg, B. G. (1970). *The sibling.* New York: Holt, Rinehart & Winston.

Toman, W. (1976). *Family constellation* (3rd ed.). New York: Springer.

Troll, L. E. (1994). Family connectedness of old women. Attachments in later life. In B. F. Turner & L. E. Troll (Eds.), *Women growing older* (pp.169–201). Thousand Oaks, CA: Sage.

Ulanov, A., & Ulanov, B. (1983). *Cinderella and her sisters: The envied and the envying.* Philadelphia: Westminster Press.

Vadasy, P. F., Fewell, R. R., Meyer, D. J., & Schell, G. (1984). Siblings of handicapped children: A developmental perspective on family interactions. *Family Relations, 33*(1), 155–67.

Valliant, G. (1977). *Adaptation to life*. Boston: Little, Brown.

Welts, E. P. H. (1988). Ethnic patterns and sibling relationships. In M. D. Kahn & K. G. Lewis (Eds.), *Siblings in therapy: Life span and clinical issues* (pp. 66–87). New York: Norton.

Wright, L. (1995). Double mystery: Recent research into the nature of twins and reversing many of our most fundamental convictions about why we are who we are. *New Yorker*, August 7, pp. 45–62.

Zukow, P. G. (Ed.). (1989). *Sibling interaction across cultures*. New York: Springer-Verlag.

Supervision and Training

Bahr, K. S. (1990). Student responses to genogram and family chronology. *Family Relations, 39*, 243–249.

Canzoneri, K. W. (1993). The development of systemic thinking in counselors-in-training: A descriptive analysis. *Dissertation Abstracts International, 53*(10-A), 3475–3476.

Carter, E. A. (1982). Supervisory discussion in the presence of the family. In R. Whiffen & J. Byng-Hall (Eds.), *Family therapy supervision*. London: Academic Press.

Deveaux, F., & Lubell, I. (1994). Training the supervisor: Integrating a family of origin approach. *Contemporary Family Therapy 16*(4), 291–299.

Getz, H. G., & Protinsky, H. O. (1994). Training marriage and family counselors: A Family of origin approach. *Counselor Education and Supervision, 33*, 183–190.

Haber, R. (1997). *Dimensions of family therapy supervision: Maps and means*. New York: Norton.

McGoldrick, M. (1982). Through the looking glass: Supervision of a trainee's trigger family. In J. Byng-Hall & R. Whiffen (Eds.), *Family therapy supervision*. London: Academic Press.

Pistole, M. C. (1995). The genogram in group supervision of novice counselors: Draw them a picture. *Clinical Supervisor 13*(1), 133–143.

Shore, W., Wilkmie, H., & Croughan-Minihane, M. (1994). Family of origin genograms: Evaluation of a teaching program for medical students. *Family Medicine, 26*, 238–243.

Thomas, V. K., & Striegel, P. (1994). Family of origin work for the family counselor. In C. H. Huber (Ed.), *Transitioning from individual to family counseling: The family psychology and counseling series, no. 2* (pp. 21–30). Alexandria, VA: American Counseling Association.

Wells, V. K., Scott, R. G., Schmeller, L. J., & Hilmann, J. A. (1990). The family-of-origin framework: A model for clinical training. *Journal of Contemporary Psychotherapy, 20*(4), 223–235.

Therapy from Multiple Orientations

Anderson, W. T., Anderson, R. A., Hovestadt, A. J. (1988). Intergenerational family therapy: A practical primer. In P. A. Keller & S. R. Heyman (Eds.). *Innovations in clinical practice: A source book, 7* (pp. 175–188). Sarasota, FL: Professional Resource Press.

Arrington, D. (1991). Thinking systems—seeing systems: An integrative model for systematically oriented art therapy. *Arts in Psychotherapy, 18*(3), 201–211.

Beck, R L. (1987). The genogram as process. *American Journal of Family Therapy, 15*(4), 343–351.

Kuehl, B. P. (1995). The solution-oriented genogram: A collaborative approach. *Journal of Marital and Family Therapy, 21*(3), 239–250.

Kuehl, B. P. (1996). The use of genograms with solution-based and narrative therapies. *The Family Journal: Counseling and Therapy for Couples and Families, 4*, 5–11.

Massey, R. F., Comey, S., & Just, R. L. (1988). Integrating genograms and script matrices. *Transactional Analysis Journal, 18*(4), 325–335.

Mauzey, E., & Erdman, P. (1995). Let the genogram speak: Curiosity, circularity and creativity in family history. *Journal of Family Psychotherapy, 6*(2), 1–11.

Nicholl, W. G., & Hawes, E. C. (1985). Family lifestyle assessment: The role of family myths and values in the client's presenting issues. *Individual Psychology: Journal of Adlerian Theory, Research and Practice, 41*(2), 147–160.

Sherman, R. (1993). Marital issues of intimacy and techniques for change: An Adlerian systems perspective. *Journal of Adlerian Therapy, Research and Practice, 49*(3–4), 318–329.

Sproul, M. S., & Gallagher, R. M. (1982). The genogram as an aid to crisis intervention. *Journal of Family Practice, 14*(55), 959–60.

Woolf, V. V. (1983). Family network systems in transgenerational psychotherapy: The theory, advantages and expanded applications of genograms. *Family Therapy, 10*(35), 119–137.

Videotape on Genograms

McGoldrick, M. (1996). *The legacy of unresolved loss: A family systems approach.* New York: Norton.

Violence: Physical and Sexual abuse

Gewirtzman, R. C. (1988). The genogram as a visual asessment of a family's fugue. *Australian Journal of Sex, Marriage and Family, 9*(1), 37–46.

Nichols, W. C. (1986). Understanding family violence: An orientation for family therapists. *Contemporary Family Therapy, 8*(3), 188–207.

Biographical References

Adams Family

Levin, P. L. (1987). *Abigail Adams.* New York: St. Martin's Press.

Musto, D. (1981). The Adams family. *Proceedings of the Massachusetts Historical Society, 93*, 40–58.

Nagel, P C. (1983). *Descent from glory: Four generations of the John Adams family.* New York: Oxford University Press.

Nagel, P. C. (1987). *The Adams women.* New York: Oxford University Press.

Shepherd, J. (1975). *The Adams chronicles: Four generations of greatness.* Boston: Little, Brown.

Adler Sources

Adler, Alexandra. (March 1984, August 1984) Personal interviews.

Adler, Kurt. (Alfred's son) (August 1984). Personal interview.

Adler, Kurt. (Sigmund's son) (August, 1984). Personal communication.

Ansbacher, H. (1984). Personal communication.

Ansbacher, H. L. (1970). Alfred Adler: A historical perspective. *American Journal of Psychiatry, 127,* 777–782.

Ellenberger, H. F. (1970). *The discovery of the unconscious. The history and evolution of dynamic psychiatry.* New York: Basic Books.

Furtmuller, C. (1979). Alfred Adler: A biographical essay. In H. L. Ansbacher & R. R. Ansbacher (Eds.), *Superiority and social interest: A collection of later writings.* New York: Norton.

Hoffman, E. (1994). *The drive for self: Alfred adler and the founding of individual psychology.* New York: Addison-Wesley.

Rattner, J. (1983). *Alfred Adler.* New York: Frederick Ungar.

Sperber, M. (1974). *Masks of loneliness: Alfred Adler in perspective.* New York: Macmillan.

Stepansky, P. E. (1983). *In Freud's shadow: Adler in context.* Hillsdale, NJ: The Analytic Press.

Allen, Woody

Adler, J. (1992). Unhappily ever after. *Newsweek,* August 31.

Corless, R. (1992). Scenes from a breakup. *Time Magazine*, August 31.

Grimes, W. (1992). A chronology of a film's making and a relationship's unmaking. *New York Times*, August 31, pp. c14–15.

Lax, E. (1991). *Woody Allen: A life*. New York: Simon & Schuster.

Bateson/Mead Sources

Bateson, M. C. (1984). *With a daughter's eye*. New York: Morrow.

Bateson, M. C. (1988). *Peripheral visions*. New York: Morrow.

Bateson, M. C. (1990). *Composing a life*. New York: Atlantic Monthly Press.

Cassidy, R. (1982). *Margaret Mead: A voice for the century*. New York: Universe Books.

Grosskurth, P. (1988). *Margaret Mead: A life of controversy*. London: Penguin Books.

Howard, J. (1984). *Margaret Mead: A life*. New York: Ballantine Books.

Lipset, D. (1980). *Gregory Bateson: The legacy of a scientist*. Englewood Cliffs, NJ: Prentice Hall.

Mead, M. (1972). *Blackberry winter, my earlier years*. New York: Simon & Schuster.

Rice, E. (1979). *Margaret Mead: A portrait*. New York: Harper & Row.

Bell Family

Bruce, R. V. (1973). *Bell: Alexander Graham Bell and the conquest of solitude*. Boston: Little, Brown.

Eber, D. H. (1982). *Genius at work: Images of Alexander Graham Bell*. New York: Viking.

Grosvenor, E. S., & Wesson, M. (1997). *Alexander Graham Bell*. New York: Abrams.

Mackay, J. (1997). *Alexander Graham Bell: A life*. New York: Wiley.

Blackwell/Stone/Brown Sources

Cazden, E. (1983). *Antoinette Brown Blackwell: A biography*. Old Westbury, NY: The Feminist Press.

Hays, E. R. (1967). *Those extraordinary Blackwells*. New York: Harcourt Brace.

Horn, M. (1980). *Family ties: The Blackwells, a study of the dynamics of family life in nineteenth century America*. Ph.D. Dissertation, Tufts University.

Horn, M. (1983). Sisters worthy of respect: Family dynamics and women's roles in the Blackwell family. *Journal of Family History*, 8(4), 367–382.

Wheeler, L. (Ed.). (1981). *Loving warriers: Selected letters of Lucy Stone and Henry B. Blackwell*, 1853 to 1893. New York: Dial Press.

British Royal Family

Bradford, S. (1996). *Elizabeth*. New York: Riverhead Books.

Campbell, C. (1998). *The real Diana*. New York: St. Martin's Press.

Davies, N. (1998). *Queen Elizabeth II: A woman who is not amused*. New York: Carol Publishing Group.

Delderfield, E. R. (1998). *Kings and queens of England and Great Britain* (3rd Ed.) Devon, England: David & Charles.

Fearon, P. (1996). *Behind the palace walls: The rise and fall of Britain's royal family*. Seacacus, NJ: Carol Publishing Group.

Kelley, K. (1997). *The royals*. New York: Warner.

Morton, A. (1997). *Diana: Her true story*. New York: Simon & Schuster.

Brontë Sources

Barker, J. (1995). *The Brontës*. London: Weidenveld & Nicolson.

Cannon, J. (1980).*The road to Haworth: The story of the Brontës' Irish Ancestry*. London: Weidenfeld and Nicolson.

Chitham, E. (1986). *The Brontës' Irish background*. New York: St. Martin's Press.

Frazer, R. (1988). *The Brontës: Charlotte Brontë and her family*. New York: Crown.

Gaskell, E. (1975). *The life of Charlotte Brontë*. London: Penguin.

Lock, J. & Dixon, W. T. (1965). *A man of sorrow: The life, letters, and times of Reverend Patrick Brontë*. Westport, CT: Meckler Books.

Peters, M. (1975). *Unquiet soul: A biography of Charlotte Brontë*. New York: Atheneum.

Wilks, B. (1986). *The Brontës: An illustrated biography*. New York: Peter Bedrick Books.

Burton/Taylor

Bragg, M. (1990). *Richard Burton: A life*. New York: Warner Books.

Ferris, P. (1981). *Richard Burton*. New York: Coward, McCann & Geoghegan.

Kelley, K. (1981). *Elizabeth Taylor: The last star*. New York: Simon & Schuster.

Morley, S. (1988). *Elizabeth Taylor*. New York: Applause Books.

Callas Family

Allegri, R., & Allegri, R. (1997). *Callas by Callas*. New York: Universe.

Callas, J. (1989). *Sisters*. New York: St. Martin's.

Moutsatos, K. F. (1998). *The Onassis women*. New York: Putnam.

Stassinopoulos, A. (1981). *Maria Callas: The woman behind the legend*. New York: Simon & Schuster.

Clinton Family

Brock, D. (1996). *The seduction of Hillary Rodham*. New York: The Free Press.

Clinton Kelly, V., with J. Morgan (1994). *My life: Leading with my heart*. New York: Pocket Books.

Clinton, R. (1995). *Growing up Clinton*. Arlington, TX: Summit Publishing Group.

King, N. (1996). *The woman in the White House*. New York: Carol Publishing.

Maraniss, D. (1995). *First in his class: The biography of Bill Clinton*. New York: Touchstone.

Maraniss, D. (1988). *The Clinton enigma*. New York: Simon & Schuster.

Morris, R. (1996). *Partners in power*. New York: Henry Holt.

Warner, J. (1993). *Hillary Clinton: The inside story*. New York: Signet.

Einstein Family

Clark, R. W. (1971). *Einstein. The life and times*. New York: Avon.

Highfield, R., & Carter, P. (1993). *The private life of Albert Einstein*. New York: St. Martin's.

Pais, A. (1994). *Einstein lived here*. New York: Oxford University Press.

Renn, J., & Schulmann, R. (1995). *Albert Einstein/Mileva Maric: The love letters*. Princeton: Princeton University Press.

Specter, M. (1994). Einstein's Son? It's a question of relativity. *New York Times*, July 22, p. 1.

Sullivan, W. (1987). Einstein letters tell of anguished love affair. *New York Times*, May 3, p. 1.

Farrow Family

Farrow, M. (1997). *What falls away: A memoir*. New York: Bantam.

Fonda Family Sources

Fonda, A. (1986). *Never before dawn: An autobiography*. New York: Weidenfeld & Nicolson.

Collier, P. (1992). *The Fondas*. New York: Putnam.

Fonda, P. (1998). *Don't tell dad*. New York: Hyperion.

Guiles, F. L. (1981). *Jane Fonda: The actress in her time*. New York: Pinnacle.

Hayward, B. (1977). *Haywire*. New York: Alfred Knopf.

Teichman, H. (1981). *Fonda: My life*. New York: New American Library.

Foster Family

Foster, B., & Wagener, L. (1998). *Foster child*. New York: Signet.
Chunovic, L. (1995). *Jodie: A biography*. New York: Contemporary Books.

Freud Family

Anzieu, D. (1986). *Freud's self analysis*. Madison, CT: International Universities Press.
Appignanesi, L., & Forrester, J. (1992). *Freud's women*. New York: Basic Books.
Bernays, A. F. (Nov. 1940). My brother Sigmund Freud. *The American Mercury*, 336–340.
Bernays, Edward. Personal interview.
Bernays, Hella. Personal interview.
Eissler, K. R. (1978). *Sigmund Freud: His life in pictures and words*. New York: Helen & Kurt Wolff Books, Harcourt, Brace, Jovanovich.
Ferris, P. (1998). *Dr. Freud: A life*. Washington, DC: Counterpoint.
Freeman, L., & Strean, H. (1981). *Freud and women*. New York: Frederick Unger.
Freud, E. L. (1960). *The letters of Sigmund Freud*. New York: Basic Books.
Freud, M. (1982). *Sigmund Freud: Man and father*. New York: Jason Aronson.
Freud, S. (1988). *My three mothers and other passions*. New York: New York University Press.
Gay, P. (1988). *Freud: A life for our time*. New York: Norton.
Gay, P. (1990). *Reading Freud*. New Haven: Yale University Press.
Glicklhorn, R. (1979). The Freiberg period of the Freud family. *Journal of the History of Medicine, 24*, 37–43.
Jones, E. (1953, 1954, 1955). *The life and work of Sigmund Freud* (3 volumes). New York: Basic Books.
Kerr, J. (1993). *A most dangerous method: The story of Jung, Freud, and Sabina Spielrein*. New York: Knopf.
Krüll, M. (1986). *Freud and his father*. New York: Norton.
Margolis, D. P. (1996). *Freud and his mother*. Northvale, NJ: Jason Aronson.
Masson, J. (Ed.) (1985). *The complete letters of Sigmund Freud to Wilhelm Fliess: 1887–1904*. Cambridge, MA: The Belknap Press of Harvard University Press.
Masson, J. (1992). *The assault on truth*. New York: HarperCollins.
McGoldrick, M. (1998). History, genograms, and the family life cycle: Freud in context. In B. Carter & M. McGoldrick (Eds.), *The expanded family life cycle: Individual, family, and social perspectives* (3rd ed.). Boston: Allyn & Bacon.
Peters, U. H. (1985). *Anna Freud: A life dedicated to children*. New York: Shocken.
Roazen, P. (1993). *Meeting Freud's family*. Amherst, MA: University of Massachusetts Press.
Ruitenbeek, H. M. (1973). *Freud as we knew him*. Detroit: Wayne State University.
Swales, P. (1982). Freud, Minna Bernays, and the conquest of Rome: New light on the origins of psychoanalysis. *The New American Review, 1*, (2/3), 1–23.
Swales, P. (1986). *Freud, his origins and family history*. UMDNJ–Robert Wood Johnson Medical School, November 15.
Swales, P. (1987). *What Freud didn't say*. UMDNJ–Robert Wood Johnson Medical School. May 15.
Young-Bruehl, E. (1988). *Anna Freud: A biography*. New York: Summit Books.

Henry VIII

Fraser, A. (1994). *The wives of Henry VIII*. New York: Vintage.
Lindsey, K. (1995). *Divorced, beheaded, survived: A feminist reinterpretation of the wives of Henry VIII*. New York: Addison-Wesley.

Hepburn/Tracy Sources

Anderson, C. (1988). *Young Kate*. New York: Henry Holt.
Davidson, B. (1987). *Spencer Tracy: Tragic idol*. New York: Dutton.

Edwards, A. (1985). *A remarkable woman: A biography of Katherine Hepburn*. New York: Simon & Schuster.

Hepburn, K. (1991). *Me*. New York: Alfred A. Knopf.

Higham, C. (1981). *Kate: The life of Katharine Hepburn*. New York: Signet.

Kanin, G. (1988). *Tracy and Hepburn: An intimate memoir*. New York: Donald I. Fine.

Leaming, B. (1995). *Katherine Hepburn*. New York: Crown.

Morley, S. (1984). *Katherine Hepburn*. London: Pavilion Books Limited.

Jefferson Family

Binger, C. (1970). *Thomas Jefferson: A well-tempered mind*. New York: Norton.

Brodie, F. M. (1974). *Thomas Jefferson: An intimate history*. New York: Norton.

Fleming, T. J. (1969). *The man from Monticello*. New York: Morrow.

Gordon-Reed, A. (1997). *Thomas Jefferson and Sally Hemings*. Charlottesville, VA: University of Virginia Press.

Smith, D. (1998). The enigma of Jefferson: Mind and body in conflict. *New York Times*, B 7–8, November 7.

Jung Family

Broome, V (1981). *Jung: Man and myth*. New York: Atheneum.

Hannah, B. (1981). *Jung: His life and work; A biographical memoir*. New York: Perigee, Putnam Books.

Jung, C. G. (1961). *Memories, dreams, reflections* (Recorded and edited by Aniela Jaffe, translated by R. Winston & C. Winstons). New York: Vintage.

Stern, P. J. (1976). *C. G. Jung: The haunted prophet*. New York: Delta, Dell.

Kahlo/ Rivera Families

Herrera, H. (1983). *Frida: A biography of Frida Kahlo*. New York: Harper & Row.

Marnham, P. (1998). *Dreaming with his eyes open: A life of Diego Rivera*. New York: Knopf.

Rivera, D. (1991). *My art, my life*. New York: Dover.

Kennedy/Bouvier Family Sources

Collier, P., & Horowitz, D. (1984). *The Kennedys*. New York: Summit Books.

Davis, J. (1984). *The Kennedys: Dynasty and disaster*. New York: McGraw-Hill.

Davis, J. (1969). *The Bouviers: Portrait of an American family*. New York: Farrar, Straus, Giroux.

Davis, J. (1993). *The Bouviers: From Waterloo to the Kennedys and beyond*. Washington DC: National Press Books.

DuBois, D. (1995). *In her sister's shadow: The bitter legacy of Lee Radziwell*. New York: St. Martin's.

Hamilton, N. (1992). *JFK reckless youth*. New York: Random House.

Heymann, C. D. (1989). *A woman named Jackie*. New York: New American Library.

James, A. (1991). *The Kennedy scandals and tragedies*. Lincolnwood, IL: Publications International Limited.

Kearns Goodwin, D. (1987). *The Fitzgeralds and the Kennedys*. New York: Simon & Schuster.

Kelley, K. (1978). *Jackie Oh!* Secaucus, NJ: Lyle Stuart.

Kennedy, R. (1974). *Times to remember*. New York: Bantam Books.

Klein, E. (1998). *Just Jackie: Her private years*. New York: Ballantine.

Latham, C., & Sakol, J. (1989). *Kennedy encyclopedia*. New York: New American Library.

Leamer, L. (1994). *The Kennedy women*. New York: Villard Books.

McTaggart, L. (1983). *Kathleen Kennedy: Her life and times*. New York: Dial Press.

Moutsatos, K. F. (1998). *The Onassis women*. New York: Putnam's.

Rachlin, H. (1986). *The Kennedys: A chronological history 1823–present*. New York: World Almanac.

Rainie, H., & Quinn, J. (1983). *Growing up Kennedy: The third wave comes of age*. New York: Putnam.

King Family

King, M. L., Sr., with C. Riely (1980). *Daddy King, An autobiography*. New York: Morrow.

Oates, S. B. (1982). *Let the trumpet sound, the life of Martin Luther King, Jr.* New York: Harper & Row.

Nehru-Gandhi Family

Ali, T. (1985). *An Indian dynasty*. New York: Putnam.

Wolpert, S. (1996). *Nehru*. New York: Oxford University Press.

O'Neill Family

Bowen, C. (1959). *The curse of the misbegotten*. New York: McGraw-Hill.

Gelb, A., & Gelb, B. (1987). *O'Neill*. New York: Harper & Row.

Sheaffer, L. (1968). *O'Neill: Son and playwright*. Boston: Little, Brown.

Sheaffer, L. (1973). *O'Neill: Son and artist*. Boston: Little, Brown.

Reich Family

Mann, W. E., & Hoffman, E. (1980). *The man who dreamed of tomorrow: The life and thought of Wilhelm Reich*. Los Angeles: Tarcher.

Reich, L. O. (1969). *Wilhelm Reich: A personal biography*. New York: Avon.

Sharaf, M. (1983). *Fury on earth: A biography of Wilhelm Reich*. New York: St. Martins.

Wilson, C. (1981). *The quest for Wilhelm Reich: A critical biography*. Garden City, NY: Anchor Press/Doubleday.

Robeson Family Sources

Dean, P. H. (1989). Paul Robeson. In E. Hill (Ed.), *Black heroes: Seven plays*. New York: Applause Theatre Book Publishers.

Duberman, M. B. (1988). *Paul Robeson*. New York: Knopf.

Ehrlich, S. (1988). *Paul Robeson: Singer and actor*. New York: Chelsea House Publishers.

Larsen, R. (1989). *Paul Robeson: Hero before his time*. New York: Franklin Watts.

Ramdin, R. (1987). *Paul Robeson: The man and his mission*. London: Peter Owen.

Robeson, P. (1988). *Here I stand*. Boston: Beacon Press.

Robinson Family

Falkner, D. (1995). *Great time coming: The life of Jackie Robinson from baseball to Birmingham*. New York: Simon & Schuster.

Rampersad, A. (1997). *Jackie Robinson: A biography*. New York: Knopf.

Robinson, J. (1972). *I never had it made*. New York: Putnam.

Robinson, R. (1996). *Jackie Robinson: An intimate portrait*. New York: Abrams.

Robinson, S. (1996). *Stealing home*. New York: HarperCollins.

Tygiel, J. (1997). *Baseball's great experiment: Jackie Robinson and his legacy*. New York: Oxford University Press.

Roosevelt Family

Asbell, B. (Ed.). (1982). *Mother and daughter: The letters of Eleanor and Anna Roosevelt*. New York: Coward, McCann, & Geoghegan.

Collier, P., with D. Horowitz (1994). *The Roosevelts*. New York: Simon & Schuster.

Cook, B. W. (1992). *Eleanor Roosevelt 1884–1933: A Life: Mysteries of the heart, Vol. 1.* New York: Viking Penguin.

Felsenthal, C. (1988). *Alice Roosevelt Longworth.* New York: Putnam.

Kearns Goodwin, D. (1994). *No ordinary time. Franklin and Eleanor Roosevelt: The home front in World War II.* New York: Simon & Schuster.

Lash, J. P. (1971). *Eleanor and Franklin.* New York: Norton.

McCullough, D. (1981). *Mornings on horseback.* New York: Simon & Schuster.

Miller, N. (1979). *The Roosevelt chronicles.* Garden City, NY: Doubleday.

Miller, N. (1983). *FDR: An intimate biography.* Garden City, NY: Doubleday

Miller, N. (1992). *Theodore Roosevelt: A life.* New York: Morrow.

Morgan, T. (1985). *FDR: A biography.* New York: Simon & Schuster.

Roosevelt, E. (1984). *The autobiography of Eleanor Roosevelt.* Boston: G. K. Hall.

Roosevelt, E., & Brough, J. (1973). *The Roosevelts of Hyde Park: An untold story.* New York: Putnam.

Roosevelt, E., & Brough, J. (1975). *A rendezvous with destiny: The Roosevelts of the White House.* New York: Dell.

Roosevelt, J. (1976). *My parents: A differing view.* Chicago: The Playboy Press.

Roosevelt, T. (1925). *An autobiography.* New York: Charles Scribner's Sons.

Youngs, W. T. (1985). *Eleanor Roosevelt: A personal and public life.* Boston: Little, Brown.

Sullivan Family

Chapman, A. H. (1976). *Harry Stack Sullivan: The man and his work, his psychiatry and its relevance to current American dilemmas.* New York: Putnam.

Perry, H. S. (1982). *Psychiatrist of America: The life of Harry Stack Sullivan.* Cambridge, MA: The Belknap Press of Harvard University Press.

Turner Family

Bibb, P. (1997). *Ted Turner: It ain't as easy as it looks.* Boulder CO: Johnson Books.

Goldberg, R., & Goldberg G. J. (1995). *Citizen Turner.* New York: Harcourt, Brace.

Woolf Family

Bell, Q. (1972). *Virginia Woolf: A biography.* New York: Harcourt & Brace.

Gordon, L. (1984). *Virginia Woolf: A writer's life.* New York: Norton.

Heilbrun, C. G. (1988). *Writing a woman's life.* New York: Norton.

Leaska, M. (1998). *Granite and rainbow: The hidden life of Virginia Woolf.* New York: Farrar, Straus, Giroux.

Love, J. O. (1977). *Virginia Woolf: Sources of madness and art.* Berkeley, CA: University of California Press.

Rose, P. (1978). *Woman of letters: A life of Virginia Woolf.* New York: Harcourt, Brace, Jovanovich.

Index